Winfried Schmähl (Ed.)

Redefining the Process of Retirement
An International Perspective

With Contributions by
L. Bellmann, R. V. Burkhauser, B. Casey, M. Honig
K. Jacobs, A. Kruse, J. H. Petersen, J. F. Quinn
C. Reimers, W. Schmähl, L. Söderström, W. H. Staehle
H. Sundberg

With 16 Figures

Springer-Verlag Berlin Heidelberg New York
London Paris Tokyo Hong Kong

Univ. Prof. Dr. rer. pol. Winfried Schmähl
Zentrum für Sozialpolitik
– Wirtschaftswissenschaftliche Abteilung –
Universität Bremen
D-2800 Bremen 33
Federal Republic of Germany

ISBN 3-540-50826-0 Springer-Verlag Berlin Heidelberg New York Tokyo
ISBN 0-387-50826-0 Springer-Verlag New York Heidelberg Berlin Tokyo

Printing: Druckerei Schmidt u. Sohn, 6800 Mannheim 61
Bookbinding: T. Gansert GmbH, Weinheim-Sulzbach
2142/7130-543210

Foreword

Retirement has been and is the subject of considerable debate in many countries. In particular this debate has concentrated on the conflict between short and long term policy objectives, those of the labour market and those of the social security system. Earlier or later retirement, full or partial retirement are themes which continually appear.

This book contains revised versions of a series of papers presented at a conference organised by the editor and held in West Berlin in October 1987. The conference was attended by economists, lawyers, sociologists and administrators from universities and research institutes, ministries and social security authorities, trade unions and employers' organisations. I should like to thank the Commission of the European Communities (Directorate General V) and the State Minister for Health and Social Security of Berlin without whose financial support the conference would not have been possible, all others who helped with the arrangements and the contributors, whose papers can now be made available to a wider audience.

I hope the aquaintance with the experiences of the variety of countries considered here will stimulate further discussion and the search for economically and politically satisfactory solutions to a set of common problems whose importance can only increase as our societies begin to age.

Berlin, May 1989   Winfried Schmähl

Contents

V

VI

Authors

Lutz Bellmann is Research Officer at the Institute for Employment Research of the Federal Employment Institute (Institut für Arbeitsmarkt- und Berufsforschung der Bundesanstalt für Arbeit) in Nuremberg, F.R.G. and received his doctoral degree at the University of Hannover. His main research area is labour economics.

Richard V. Burkhauser is Professor of Economics and Senior Research Associate at the Institute of Public Policy Studies at Vanderbilt University (USA). He has published widely on the behavioral and income distribution effects of government policy toward aged and disabled persons. He is coauthor of *Disability and Work: The Economics of American Policy,* 1982, a critical analysis of the U.S. disability system, and of *Public Policy Toward Disabled Workers: A Cross-National Analysis of Economic Impacts,* which compares the U.S. disability system with those of seven industrial countries of Western Europe.

Bernard Casey studied at St. John's College Oxford and the London School of Economics. Between 1980 and 1985 he was a Research Fellow at the International Institute of Management/Labour Market Policy of the Science Centre Berlin; since 1986 he has been a Research Fellow at the Policy Studies Institute in London. As well as the situation of older persons on the labour market, he is interested in 'non-standard' employment forms and in the methodology of using labour force survey data. Currently he is working on a study of the changing labour market behaviour of older men in Britain over the 1980s and on the public-private mix of the costs of redundancy induced early retirement in Britain, Germany and the USA.

Marjorie Honig is Professor of Economics at Hunter College and the Graduate School of the City University of New York. She received M.A. and Ph. D. degrees from Columbia University, and is a member of the editorial board of the *Eastern Economic Journal.* Her research area is labor economics; specifically, the impact of government programs on labor supply and family structure. Her recent research has focused on retirement behavior.

Klaus Jacobs is working as an Economist at the Institute for Health and Social Research (IGES) in Berlin. His special research interest in the field of early retirement originates from his previous work at the Institute for Research on Social Policy at the Free University of Berlin and the Science Center Berlin (WZB). He is currently involved in an international project on the past and future role of the social policy of the firm with respect to early exit of older workers from the labor force.

Agneta Kruse is Senior Lecturer in Economics at the University of Lund, Sweden, and also the head of the Department of Economics. She received her Ph.D. in economics at the same university in 1979. Her current research interests include public sector economics, especially social insurance systems.

Jørn Henrik Petersen is currently Professor of Social Policy at Odense University, Denmark. He received his Ph.D. in economics from Arhus University, Denmark and his Dr.phil degree in history from Odense University. His current research interests include the history of old-age pensions, the economic theory of pensions and public choice. He is author of several books on social policy.

Joseph F. Quinn is Professor of Economics at Boston College. He has been a Visiting Professor at the University of Wisconsin at Madison and at the University of California at Berkeley. He has written on the impact of social security, pensions and mandatory retirement on the retirement decision, the economic status of the elderly and public sector – private sector pay differentials. He is currently writing a book with Richard Burkhauser on work and retirement in America.

Cordelia Reimers is Professor of Economics at Hunter College and the Graduate School of the City University of New York. She holds M.Phil. and Ph.D. degrees in Economics from Columbia University. Her research interests include the employment and earnings of minorities and immigrants in the United States as well as retirement behavior.

Winfried Schmähl is since March 1989 Professor of Economics and Head of the Department of Economics of the Centre for Social Policy Research, Bremen University (Fed. Rep. of Germany). From 1976 to February 1989 he was Professor of Economics at the Free University of Berlin (Institute for Research on Social Policy). He received his doctoral degree in Economics from the University of Frankfurt (Main) and was member of the Transfer-Enquête-Commission of the German Federal Government. Since 1984 he is a member, now chairman of the (permanent) Social Advisory Council on Pension Policy of the Federal Government. His research interests include economic problems of social policy, economic effects of demographic ageing, income distribution and redistribution (e.g. life cycle income analysis).

Lars Söderström is Professor of Economics at the University of Lund, Sweden. He received his licentiate in philosophy at the same university in 1969. His current research interest focus on the public sector.

Wolfgang H. Staehle is Professor of Business Administration, Institute of Management at the Free University of Berlin. He received his doctoral degree in Economics at the University of Munich; is Vice-Chairman of the German Industrial Relations Association, editor of 'Mensch und Organisation'. Recent major publications include e.g. "Management" 4th ed. 1989, "Management-Functions" 2nd ed. 1989, "Analysis of Work Situations" 1982 (with P. Karg).

Heimer Sundberg is a lawyer, LL.B. from the University of Helsinki. He is working as Government Counsellor at the Ministry of Social Affairs and Health, Helsinki, where he is head of the Social Insurance Bureau having as main tasks the preparation of new legislation concerning Social Insurance. He also keeps charge, at the ministerial level, of the international cooperation of the Finnish Social Insurance.

Retirement at the Cross-Roads

– Tasks and Problems Under Changing Economic and Demographic Conditions. Some Introductory Remarks –

W. Schmähl

Contents

1. Main Issues and Elements of an Analytical Framework

In the light of current labour market conditions and social security financing earlier or later retirement, full or gradual retirement are topics of political debate in most of the developed western countries. However, present problems and future objectives are often in conflict and this is a source of difficulty for political decision making. Experiences and expectations for the future often differ widely.

There are, therefore more than enough reasons for discussing this topic, both in the light of national policy and in an international perspective:

– What are the possibilities and conditions in different countries leading to the cessation of gainful employment for older workers?
– What are the effects of existing conditions and institutional arrangements especially those concerning pre-retirement and early retirement schemes (under social security schemes or under arrangements made by unions and employers' organizations)?
– What are the experiences in countries which have schemes of gradual, phased retirement? Are there for example enough part-time jobs for older persons?
– What are the possible effects of changing labour market conditions (influenced e.g. by demographic development), and in particular of changing institutional conditions (e.g. in social security schemes) which aim to postpone retirement?

These topics are of special interest for Western European countries and for the USA since all are confronted with an ageing population and an ageing labour force, baby-boomers reaching retirement ages and smaller cohorts

W. Schmähl (Ed.)
Redifining the Process of Retirement
© Springer-Verlag Berlin Heidelberg 1989

entering the labour market in the future (for an overview of the American discussion see Aaron and Burtless (1984)). Fertility rates below replacement level - as in some countries, for example the Federal Republic of Germany -, a higher hife expectancy and earlier leaving of the labour force are challenges for many areas of economic and social policy.

For the process of political decision making this implies difficult tasks. Adequate reaction to demographic changes - or even attempts to influence them - requires a long term perspective for political thinking and activities and an integrated approach which takes into account such different areas as labour market, social security, income distribution and the effects of such different instruments and factors as taxation, transfer payments, social security and occupational pensions, health and labour market conditions and how they influence retirement behaviour. Too often problems are dealt with in a more or less isolated manner, in politics as well as in research. Isolated analysis - or taking into account only the immediate political goal - tends to overestimate the effects of measures planned.

The title of the conference and of this book points to a special concern when dealing with problems of retirement. On the individual level retirement has to be looked upon as a process. This is obvious in cases of phased retirement. But retirement decisions - even when retiring fully at a certain point in time - depend on former events, in particular individual earnings development. The replacement level of the pension at retirement - influenced by social security and occupational pensions, income taxation before and after retirement - depends in many earnings related pension schemes on this. Thus in West Germany the complete earnings carreer determins the pension payment in the statutory pension scheme for wage and salary earners (Schmähl (1986)).

Not only the income aspects underline the process-character of retirement, so too do other aspects like type of previous work and future activities during the phase of retirement. Research shows that gainful employment just before retirement is only one, although the dominant pattern of life cycle events. Unemployment, disability or receipt of pre-retirement benefits are other ways in which the earnings phase may end and each of these has become more common in recent years. Moreover, receipt of an old age pension and no earnings from employment is now only one possibility after retirement. Other activities have to be taken into account too, as overview 1 shows.

A high degree of stability - especially of income development - is an important factor for sucessfull individual ageing. This is one of the main goals for (earnings related) social security schemes. This underlines the need of dynamic analysis, a life cycle view, and of longitudinal research.

In many countries steps have been taken or are expected to be taken to change the institutional regulations governing retirement age and the type of retirement within the social security system. Should there be

Overview 1. From Employment to Retirement – different types –

Full-time		Old-Age-Pension	
Part-time	(Flexible)	(Social Security)	(Full or Partial)

Employment (Earnings) → Retirement Age

+

Unemployment (no posibility to work) → Employment (officially) — Same job / Other job

Illness/Disability (no ability to work) → Full-time / Part-time

Pre-Retirement → Earnings from activity in the shadow-economy

Activity in own private household → Social work (no earnings)

- only one fixed retirement age – perhaps different for men and women –, or flexibility in retirement age (if so, within what ages – beginning at . . ., ending at . . .)?
- only the possibility of full (complete) retirement or of a phased retirement (perhaps in different combinations of partial pension and part-time employment)?
- a changing of the retirement age, increasing or lowering the legal age limits or changing the conditions for receipt of a pension to promote earlier or later retirement?

These are three fundamental questions to be answered when consideration is given to restructuring social security schemes and coping with the challenges coming from changing economic, social or demographic conditions.

The retirement age within a pension scheme (i.e. the age of eligibility for receipt of an old age pension) is one thing. Another is the effective age at which people do retire. This is the result of the behavioural responses by employees and employers, which themselves depend on many factors including existing alternatives for working or not working and the possibilities for receiving income.

One of the most interesting questions is how retirement behaviour can be influenced by political measures. And if behaviour has changed, what will be the effects, on the labour market (who retires earlier or later?), on financing different branches of social insurance (retirement, unemployment, health) and on income distribution? The distributive effects alone are highly complex. Some of the dimensions relevant for individual as well as political decisions can be seen from overview 2.

Overview 2. Goal Area: Income and Income Distribution
Main aspects concerning (political and individual) retirement decisions

---

Individual perspective

1. Changes of the absolute amount of disposable income at retirement

    social security pension / earnings
    income tax
    occupational pensions
    transfers in cash
    income from activities during retirement
    – in the official sector of the economy
    – in the shadow economy
2. Stability of income development over the life cyle, replacement rate

3. "Internal rate of interest" of own contribution payments when retiring earlier or later (incentives depending on pension furmula etc.).

Macroeconomic perspective

4. Income distribution between pensioners and workers (pension level)

5. Income distribution between cohorts

To sum up: thinking about a redifinition of the process of retirement requires an analysis which integrates different phases and elements of the individual life cycle, different areas of political goals, and different institutions and decision units. This is summarised in overview 3.

Overview 3

Three Levels of Analysis		
Individual lifecycle	Area of political goals	Institutions and decision units
Beginning of gainful employment Development of individual ability to work (health, retraining, age specific productivity)	Schooling Training Economic performance (growth, business cycle employment/unemployment)	Private households Firms Social security old age and invalidity health unemployment
Possibilities for gainful employment (age- and sex specific probability of unemployment and re-integration) Income (household structure – familiy life-cycle; working time)	Income Health Financing status of social security Feeling of security of the insured Demographic development	Public authorities, government Labour unions/employer organizations
Retirement Replacement rate Activities during retirement phase		

2. Experience from the Past

Labour market problems have above all increased the incidence of early retirement in most OECD countries during the seventies. This was the result of activities of firms, often in accordance with preferences of workers and interests of unions and often promoted or even accelerated by political decisions giving incentives within social security systems or outside then for early retirement of the older workers in favour of better employment opportunites for younger workers. Often different ways exist for early retirement. Stoping the entry into one of these ways may increase demand and utilization of other ways (see overview 1) – often with the consequence of cost-shifting between public and private households or between different public budgets. This is pointed out in detail in the contribution of Bernard Casey, based on an international comparison. Such responses have to be taken into account when attempts are made to stop the trend or even to change its direction. It is obvious – as mentioned before – that old age pension policy cannot be dealt with separately from labour market conditions. Firms decisions on labour input as well as on occupational pension schemes are of strategic importance, a lesson not to be forgotten while thinking on choosing instruments of public policy.

The experiences of a number of countries are discussed in several contributions to this book, which explain the background to developments and decisions. Klaus Jacobs and Winfried Schmähl analyse past trends for early retirement in West Germany. Flexibility of retirement age, especially for men, was introduced in there 1972. The authors discuss also the different goals and preferences of those playing an active part in this development. These goals are, of course, also important when considering political measures to cope with future problems aimed at later retirement, combined with possibilites for phased retirement. Steps have now been taken in Germany to implement such a combined strategy in the statutory pension insurance scheme (see below).

For this reason the approaches and experiences especially of the Scandinavian countries which already have systems of gradual retirement are of great interest. Agneta Kruse and lars Söderström give an overview of the possibilities in Sweden to retire early and to retire on a gradual basis. They show very clearly that it depends very much on individual factors which of the possibilities are used and that they are of different attractiveness for workers with higher or lower earnings. Only a careful systematic analysis of the institutional regulations of existing alternatives can give a comprehensive basis for research on behavioural responses to political measures – a fact often neglected in decision making and in research.

Partial pensions (in existence since 1976) have become the mostly prefered means of early retirement in Sweden. What is important – also in international comparision – is the large number of part-time jobs for older persons in Sweden, a situation quite different to that in Germany, for example. In West Germany the lack of part-time work opportunities is one decisive factor contributing to the unemployment of older women – who are often seeking part-time jobs – and of people not fully able to work full-time. The large number of invalidity pensions in Germany is to a great part caused by such unfavourable labour market conditions.

Denmark introduced a system of early retirement in 1979 and a partial pension scheme in 1987. Jørn Henrik Petersen points out the main characteristics of these schemes and the attitude of important groups of the society concerning these opportunities. Unions e.g. fear that the partial pension system gives too much influence to employers to introduce flexible working times systems which are advantageous mainly to the firms rather than their workers. This seems to be an issue in many countries where unions are resisting the spread of part-time work and more flexibility in working time.

In Finland different possibilities for flexibility of the retirement age and for gradual retirement were introduced in 1986 and 1987, as explained in the contribution of Heimer Sundberg. It is too early to obtain reliable information on the effect of these schemes, in particular for partial pension schemes, and this holds too for Denmark. – Overview 4 gives information concerning the main features of the partial pension schemes, in Sweden, Denmark and Finland.

Overview 4. Partial pension schemes in scandinavian countries

	Sweden	Denmark	Finland
Introduced in	1976	1987	1987
"Normal" retirement age	65	67	65
Partial retirement phase from . . . to (age)	60 – 65	60 – 67	60 – 65
Reduction of gainful employment per week	At least 5 hours, working hours on average at least 17 hours and no more than 35 hours	Working hours on average between 15 and 30 hours	to 16-28 hours
Conditions for eligibility (not complete)	Employees and self-employed must have been insured in system for supplementary pension (ATP) for at least 10 years after age of 45; gainful employment for at least 5 within the previous 12 months	Employees: at least 9 months employed during last 12 months before claiming for partial pension; insured in scheme for supplementary Labour Market Pension for at least 10 years during last 20 years	Employed in private sector
Amount of partial pension payment	65 % of income reduction because of working part-time	Fixed amount per hour of reduced working time; reduced after 2½ years of payment to 80 %	Between 44 % and 60 % of earnings reduction (depending on age at retirement), maximum 75 % of full pension
Alternatives for early retirement	Invalidity pension (can be combined with part-time employment), old age pension with deductions	Complete retirement at 60 by voluntary early retirement	Complete retirement at 55 (individual early retirement, a type of invalidity pension), introduced in 1986
Acceptability of partial pension up to now	10-30 % of all employed between 60 and 64 years of age	Too early to tell	Too early to tell

Source: Kruse and Söderström, Petersen, Sundberg (all in this volume). Jacobs (1988), p.3. Swedish Employer's Confederation (1986).

However, some general lessons can be learned from the past concerning early retirement provisions. They were mainly introduced to relieve labour markets and not – as was the initial intention – as an instrument of humanization of working life. Firms obviously prefered those opportunities for retiring workers early where they could make the decision on when and who retires by themselves. It seems plausible that the lowering of the retirement age influences the expectations for the "normal" age of retirement (e.g. Blau (1985), or Achenbaum (1986), chapter 5 for the USA). This will fall, too. And the age limit for looking upon a worker as an older worker will also be reduced by this development. That means that problems for reintegration of workers – either after unemployment or (concerning women) after the "family phase" – begin at a lower age. The acceptance of possibilites for phased retirement offered in some countries depends to a high degree on the availability of adequate part time jobs for older persons as well as on the effects of alternatives – above all of possibilites for full early retirement – on income. The Scandinavian schemes of phased retirement are simultaneously systems for earlier retirement up to now. Integration into and coordination with "normal" retirement schemes seems not to have been fully satisfactory. In Germany e.g. the introduction of gradual retirement is discussed concerning its effects on working conditions for older persons and as an instrument for lengthenig working life.

3. Expectations and Problems for Future Development

In the light of European – and in particular German – discussion on strategies to extend the working life and postpone retirement, research done in the United States is of special interest. Here also a trend to earlier retirement can be found. What is special is the important role of occupational pension schemes in influencing the retirement age. Occupational pension plans can, for example, penalize "later" retirement. Richard Burkhauser and Joseph Quinn give an interesting overview of this as well as of American experience and research done in the field of retirement behaviour. Another aspect – as pointed out also in the contribution of Cordelia Reimers and Marjorie Honig – is the incidence of work after retirement from a main job, often on a part-time basis. This is a special form of retirement, that is not very common in Germany. Income in retirement seems to be an important factor for such a decision. The evaluation of this in the light of distributive considerations needs a careful micro-analytical analysis of the factors behind it.

In 1983 U.S. parliament decided on measures to postpone via several steps the retirement age (details can be found in the appendix of the contribution of Reimers and Honig). How much this will affect the effective retirement age will also depend on the reaction of firms concerning the incentives given in there occupational schemes for retiring. Burkhauser and Quinn point out that the effect on labour supply can be remarkable.

These issues have become of special importance foro the German discussion. One of the measures to reform the German statutory pension
scheme and adjust it to changing demographic and economic conditions will
have to be a redifinition of the rules for receiving an old age pension. It is to
be expected – although *final* political decision will not be made before the
end of the year 1989 – that beginning in 2001 the normal retirement ages for
men and women (i.e. the age of eligibility for a full, or non-reduced pension)
will be increased stepwise to 65 reaching this level by 2006 for men and by
2012 for women. It will be possible in the future, too, to retire up to 3 years
earlier – however with an actuarial reduction of the pension. Such reductions
do not exist in the German pension scheme up to now. Exceptions to the
raising of the retirement ages will be made for those eligible for invalidity
pensions and for the handicapped. They will be able to retire at 60. The impact of raising the (early) retirement ages will be influenced in an important
way by the extent to which people can and will choose the possibility to get
an invalidity pension. A further proposed reform is the introduction of the
possibility to receive a partial pension – combined with reduced working
hours – into the statutory scheme. A summary of the German discussion on
these matters is to be found in the paper of Jacobs and Schmähl. It is not surprising that unions will not negotiate over a longer wowrking life (see also
Johnson 1988, p. 19); what is, however, open to question is how intensively
they are against any redefinition of social security rules.

It has become obvious in discussion on pension reform that decisions on
central elements of a pension scheme – such as those concerning retirement
ages – must be announced and made early enough. Only in this way can
people – as well as firms – adjust their planning to the new conditions. If decisions are required to be made some years before they become effective, future circumstances and economic conditions have to be anticipated. If an increase in the average retirement age is seen as necessary to sustain the financial viability of the social security system, it should be ensured that this does
not have a negative impact on economic development, in particular on the
labour market. This points to a dilemma: the rules of an retirement system
should be as stable as possible for as long as possible, and – as mentioned
above – changes should be announced early enough. In other words, the
central rules of the retirement system should not change abruptly or often
simply because of changing economic conditions. People need some feeling
of security concerning their old age provisions. This is important in determining their willingness to finance pension payments, to bear the burden,
and not seek to avoid it. On the other hand the retirement system should not
exercise a negative influence on economic development. Societies will be
better able to cope with income redistribution in an ageing population the
higher income growth is. Raising the retirement age in a period of high
unemployment, will only redistribute the burden of unemployment and will
not reduce demographically induced public expenditure – the main objective of policy makers (see Schmähl (1987)). Therefore the starting year for
raising the retirement age in West Germany was the most controversial ele-

ment in this package of proposals the government and the biggest opposition party in parliament agreed upon in February 1989.

Labour market conditions and decisions by the firms will be of central importance for realizing a concept of postponing retirement combined with a model of partial retirement. Especially a sufficient supply of part-time jobs is needed. A partial retirement scheme can prevent people with reduced working capacity having to leave the labour force totally. This requires, however, that the jobs offered are attractive and adequate for those workers (see e.g. Haveman et al. (1984), Haveman and Wolfe (1985), Newey (1987)). Demographic development – at least in Germany – might lead to a shortage of higher qualified native-born workers. Technological development and structural changes in the economy – a trend towards service acitivities – could improve employment chances for the elderly: In the future more highly-qualified workers will be demanded by the firms. But the qualifications requried will change, too. Planning activities and experience will become more important. The experience of older workers may become more interesting for firms if more team work is necessary, demanding social competence as well as specific "technical" knowledge. It seems as if in some firms a re-thinking of the strategy of simply rejuvenating the human resources of the firm has already started, as Wolfgang Staehle points out in his contribution.

In the future retraining will more and more become a central issue. Ability and willingness to learn will become of increasing importance, also – or even particularly – for the elderly. It is necessary to integrate older workers as well as part-time employees in retraining activities. If working life is expanded then the retraining of older persons will become more attractive both for firms and for workers themselves, because investment in human capital can be amortized over a longer period.

The possession of (higher) qualifications by older workers is also an important factor not to become unemployed. Highly-qualified labour seems to be substituted by capital much less than low or unqualified labour (for West Germany see Kugler et al. (1988), p. 498). Higher complexitiy as well as flexibility of production-technology is likely to increase the demand for highly-qualified manpower (see for the U.S. Bartel and Lichtenberg (1987), for West Germany Schmidt and Gundlach (1988), pp. 120-125).

It should, however, not be forgotten, that labour force participation, at least in part, is influenced by environmental conditions at the work place and by the dominating "work ethics" affecting the preferences for work or "leisure". To what extent the value orientation towards work has changed – as is often assumed (for Germany e.g. Strümpel (1988)) – needs careful consideration, based on longitudinal data, disentangling period, age and cohort effects.

The experiences of the last years cannot be assumed to be valid in the future. This – in my view – holds for preferences as well as for employment opportunites, chances for older persons on the labour market or the nature of skills required. On the other hand, even the most able researcher is by far from being a "prophet". Taking into account that research *can* play an important role in public decision making, the need for more scientific work in this important field is underlined.

A model of partial pension – which needs an adequate supply of part-time jobs for older workers – could improve the acceptance of part-time work for all (and not just for older) men in those countries where part-time employment has up to now been almost exclusively a female phenomenon. To reach this situation means, amongst other things, that part-time employment should imply no higher risk of dequalification or reduction in opportunities for promotion than full-time employment. The spreading of part-time employment for men might also improve the possibilities for women to better arrange family life and working life, especially in the early years of family formation, better enabling men to take over part of family duties even for a period in their working life.

Chances of older workers on the labour market will be, however, determined by costs for the firms and "productivity". Wage systems and occupational pension contracts too have an influence on effective retirement (see for an overview e.g. Ippolito (1987)). Lutz Bellmann discusses in his contribution some of the problems caused by wage systems based on seniority. To date we know too little on the development of productivity over the life cycle for different occupations, different groups of workers, different cohorts etc. This is also a field for further research.

All this further illustrates the high complexity of the topic and the need for an integrative approach to deal adequately with these important problems. No quick answers or general solutions can be given. But for the future these topics seem to be of greater relevance not only in relation to reforms in social security but also in relation to living conditions of the people than many other topics economists now are considering (for example, the possible effects of social security on savings and capital formation).

We hope the contributions published here help to broaden knowledge of the process of retirement, provide additional information and stimulate further thinking and research on this central aspect of life and of social and economic policy.

References

Aaron, H. J. and G. Burtless (1984) (Eds.) Retirement and Economic Behavior. Washington, D.C.

Achenbaum, W. A. (1986) Social Security: Visions and Revisions. Cambridge, Mass.

Bartel, A. M. and F. R. Lichtenberg (1987) The Comparative Advantage of Educated Workers in Implementing New Technology. In: Review of Economics and Statistics. Vol. 49, pp. 1-11

Blau, Z. S. (1985) (Ed.) Work Retirement and Social Policy, Current Perspectives on Aging and the Life Cycle

Haveman, R. H., B. Wolfe and J. L. Warlick (1984) Disability Transfers, Early Retirement., and Retrenchment. In: Aaron and Burtless (1984), pp. 65-93

Haveman, R. H. and B. L. Wolfe (1985) The Effect of Disability Transfers on Work Effort: Research Results and Their Use in Policy Decisions. In: H. Hanusch, K. W. Roskamp, J. Wiseman (Eds.) Staat und Politische Ökonomie heute. Stuttgart and New York 1985, pp. 261-278

Ippolito, R. A. (1987) The Implicit Pension Contract – Developments and New Directions. In: Journal of Human Resources. Vol. 22, pp. 441-467

Jacobs, K. (1988) Teilrentenmodelle: Erfolge im In- und Ausland. In: Wissenschaftszentrum Berlin, Internationale Chronik zur Arbeitsmarktpolitik. No. 32, pp. 1-4, 9

Johnson, P. (1988) The Labour Force Participation of Older Men in Britain, 1951-81 (Centre for Economic Policy Research, London, Discussion Paper No. 284)

Kugler, P., U. Müller and G. Sheldon (1988) Struktur der Arbeitsnachfrage im technologischen Wandel – Eine empirische Analyse für die Bundesrepublik Deutschland. In: Weltwirtschaftliches Archiv. Vol. 124, pp. 490-500

Newey, M. (1987) An Examination of Invalid Pensioners in Transition to the Labour Force (The Social Security Review, Background/Discussionpaper No. 15). Department of Social Security, Australia, Woden Act

Schmähl, W. (1986) Economic Problems of Social Retirement – General Aspects in Western Europe and Possible Solutions in the Case of the Federal Republic of Germany. Maastricht

Schmähl, W. (1987) Social Policies for Reducing Demographically-Induced Costs in Social Security. In: European Journal of Population. Vol. 3 (1987), pp. 439-457

Schmidt, K. D. and E. Gundlach (1988) Investitionen, Produktivität und Beschäftigung, Tübingen

Strümpel, B. (1988) Work Ethics in Transition. In: G. Dlugos et al. (Eds.) Management under Differing Labour Market and Employment Systems. Berlin, New York, pp. 121-132

Swedish Employer's Confederation (1986) Insurance Schemes on the Swedish Labour Market, 7th Ed., Stockholm

The Process of Retirement in Germany: Trends, Public Discussion and Options for its Redefinition

K. Jacobs and W. Schmähl

Contents

1. Developments in the Transition to Retirement in the Federal Republic of Germany

The transition from employment to retirement has changed significantly in the Federal Republic of Germany since the early 1970's. This is valid not only with respect to retirement age, which, for an increasing number of the employed[1], now lies far below the once "standard" retirement age of 65, but also with respect to the types of transition. Exit from gainful employment is in many cases no longer equivalent to receiving a pension from the statutory pension system. Not only can an *old-age pension* be received beginning at age 60, but an age-free *general disability pension* allows those with health problems to draw pension money even prior to this retirement age. In addition, we notice growing importance of transition routes with "interim periods" between exit from employment and the start of retirement benefits. That is, we see *unemployment* among older workers with little or no prospect of ever returning to work as well as *pre-retirement* labor agreements for workers of numerous branches, based on the Pre-retirement Act of May, 1984.[2]

---

[1] We shall restrict ourselves here to wage-earners and salaried employees and exclude lifetime civil servants ("Beamte"). In 1986, around 90% of all employees were either wage-earn-

[2] Beyond these, in many branches, for example in the cigarette industry (cf. Schwahn (1988)), as well as in individual firms (cf. Schusser (1988)), there exist other possibilities for premature transition to retirement.

W. Schmähl (Ed.)
Redifining the Process of Retirement
© Springer-Verlag Berlin Heidelberg 1989

In contrast to other countries, especially to the USA, private (occupational) pensions do not play a very important role in Germany. Althoug almost 50% of workers in the private sector are covered by private schemes, these programs are insufficient to serve as the primary source of income.[3] By themselves, they are not an important route into retirement.[4]

Because of the possibilities of early exit from employment which lie in part outside of the pension system, the use of pension recipient data to measure annual entry to retirement and its change over time (cf. Conradi et al. (1987)) understates the actual extent of this process. Nonetheless, the entry figures for single birth cohorts (figs. 1 and 2) illustrate a remarkable contrast. While 23% of the male and 39% of the female recipients born in 1913 were drawing pension from the statutory pension system by age 60, those respective percentages for age-60 recipients born in 1923 rose to 50% and 63%. Accurate figures concerning the number of older workers who have already left work but are not drawing pension are not easy to obtain. Depending on the source and the definition, the number of older unemployed fluctuates

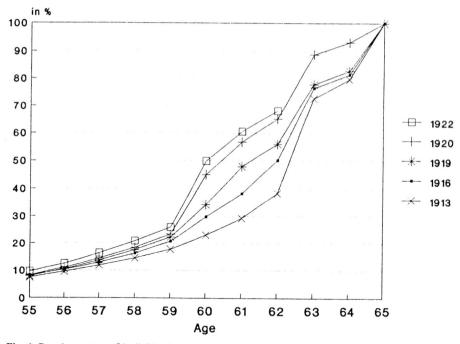

Fig. 1. Pension entry of individual male birth cohorts by age.

Source of data: Reimann 1985

---

[3] However, for employees in a leading position with high earnings occupational pensions can be higher than social security pensions.

[4] Schmähl (1987).

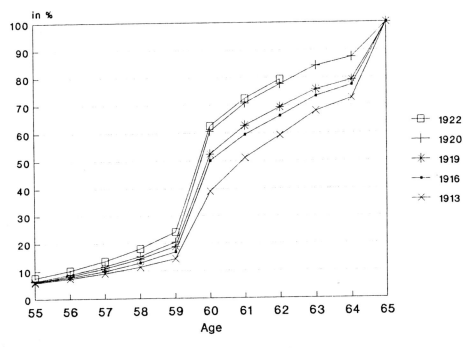

Fig. 2. Pension entry of individual female birth cohorts by age.

Source of data: Reimann (1985)

considerably.[5] This applies equally to data concerning the total number of recipients of pre-retirement benefits, which also are not even listed according to age.[6]

The trend to ever earlier exit from employment is often documented in age-specific labor force participation rates. Here, with regard to certain age groups or individual age cohorts, the total labor force is seen in relation to total population. Because the unemployed are considered to be actively participating in the labor force, we believe the actual extent of early retirement is

---

[5] Thus, by the end of September 1985, registration figures at the official unemployment offices listed 37 067 males aged 59 as being out of work ("arbeitslos"). The microcensus taken in June 1985, contrasted with a "mere" 23 000 unemployed (here: "erwerbslos"; differentiation between the two concepts is made particularly in Brinkmann (1980) as well as Mayer (1987)). Starting with 1986, unemployed persons need not make themselves available to employment offices once they have reached their 58th birthday. These persons still have rights to unemployment compensation, but are no longer included in the figures for unemployment released by the Federal Agency for Employment. For this reason, the 21 886 unemployed 59-year-old males registered by the end of September 1986, proved 40% lower than the number from the previous year.

[6] Compare IAB (1986) on the empirical registration of the Pre-retirement program.

also underestimated by this measure.[7] Nonetheless the drop in these rates is
also dramatic since the early 1970's. For example, while the participation rate
for 64-year-old males was still nearly 60% in 1972, it was only 51% for 60-year-
olds in 1986 and just 18% for 64-year-olds.[8] The decline in labor force participation is particularly vivid when seen via cohort analysis of individual years
of birth. The male participation rate for 55-year-olds in all of the cohorts exa-
mined was 90% (fig. 3). But, thereafter the younger the cohort, the earlier
and the larger was the decline in labor force participation.

The cohort data for women (fig. 4) show two opposing trends: an increase in labor force participation up to the age of 59 by younger cohorts reflecting the general increase in female labor force participation (cf. DIW
(1987)). After this age, the picture is reversed and labor force participation of
younger cohorts is lower than that of older. This is due mainly to the fact that
– since 1957 – women have had the possibility to receive pension benefits at
age 60. Because of the general rise in their labor force participation, ever

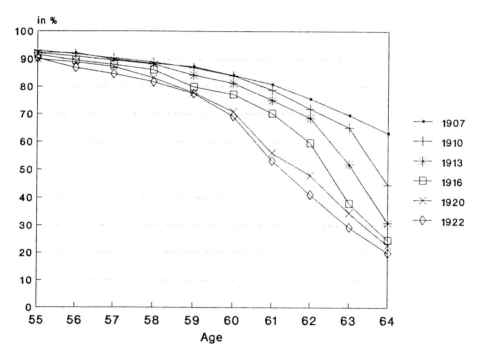

Fig. 3. Labor force participation rates of male birth cohorts by age.

Source: Jacobs et al. (1988)

---

[7] Little is known concerning the volume of "shadow" activities, and particularly, whether
these activities increase with a premature exit from regular employment. However survey
results indicate that the supplementary-income activity rate among retirees is quite low: in
1984/85 is was only 3.8% (cf. Helberger and Schwarze (1986), p. 279).

[8] Calculated on the basis of the microcensus.

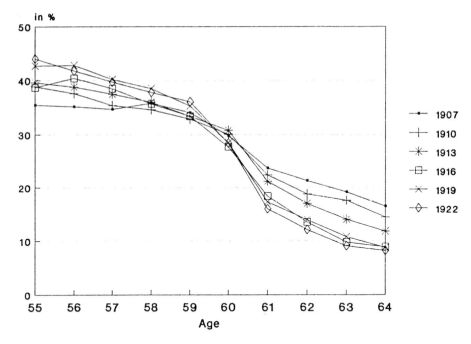

Fig. 4. Labor force participation rates of female birth cohorts by age.

Source: Jacobs et al. (1988)

more women are fulfilling the necessary pre-conditions for pension[9] and therefore are able to make use of the possiblity of drawing pension.

The considerable decline in labor force participation by older persons – male as well as female – cannot be viewed separately from the development in the labor market from 1970 onward. The rise in unemployment since that time does not effect the older workers more severely than the younger, however it is usually equivalent to a termination of employment. Most of the changes in the legislative and judicial decisions – particularly those in the area of the statutory pension system – are to be seen in this light. They have contributed to the outlined trend toward early exit from work. In total, four different phases of progressive change may be differentiated (cf. Orsinger and Clausing (1982), Kohli and von Kondratowitz (1987)), some of which overlap. Nonetheless, they are reproduced clearly by the participation rates of male cohorts in particular.

The first phase started in 1973 with the introduction of a "flexible" old-age pension at age 63 which was immediately accepted by many workers. This becomes quite vivid when comparing the two birth cohorts 1907 and 1910 in Fig. 3: those born in 1910 could make use of this regulation not yet a-vailable to earlier cohorts.

---

[9] Required is – aside from a minimum time period of 15 contribution years – an employment history for most of the last 20 years before age 60.

The second phase is characterized by the gradual lowering of the age limit for pension benefits to severely handicapped persons. With the introduction of this pension category in 1973, the age limit was 62 – then lowered in 1979 to 61 and in 1980 to 60. The effects of such institutional changes are also reflected in Fig. 3: those persons born in 1916 were first able to qualify at age 62; those born in 1920 however at age 60. This will explain the "bulges" in the participation rates of both cohorts at this age. So, too, can the significance of the change in age limit be seen in the behavior of pension entries of single birth cohorts (fig. 1): 12% of all males born in 1919 retired at age 60, as opposed to 22% of those born in 1920.

The third phase is related to a change in judicial decision concerning occupational and general disability pensions (cf. Kaltenbach (1986)). According to the so-called "concrete method of interpretation", the receipt of these pension benefits is no longer strictly dependent on medical criteria; these would allow at least part-time employment in certain instances of disability. Now a decision of the Federal Court of Social Affairs stipulates in addition that a part-time job must be first proven available for each concrete case of partial disability. But because the labor market remains practically closed to part-time-work seekers, particularly to older persons, any partial disability gives reason for claiming general disability pension rights, and thus a complete exit from gainful employment. This led, particularly in the group of 55 to 59-year-olds, to a general rise in the number of pension entries via general disability claims.[10]

The fourth phase is coupled directly to the labor market; it includes mainly the so-called "59er rule", but also the Pre-retirement program. The "59er rule" is a good example of how a change in the labor market led to greater use of a long-standing possibility for early exit from employment. Ever since 1957, a statutory pension insured person had the privilege of drawing pension benefits at age 60, provided that during the previous one and a half years the recipient had been unemployed for at least one year. By no later than the end of the '70s, many firms were using this regulation to "rejuvenate" their staff at the cost of the unemployment and pension insurance systems. Otherwise hard-to-release workers were offered severance pay as well as a topping-up of unemployment compensation benefits to equal their former net wages while they "waited" till age 60 to qualify for unemployment pension benefits. The reimbursement obligation imposed in 1982 – and more severe in 1984 – did not serve to diminish the significance of this form of exit from gainful employment, as the age-specific numbers of unemployed prove (figs. 5 and 6).[11] Quite to the contrary, multiple renewal of the

---

[10] The percentage of male general disability pensions to the yearly total of retirement entries increased between 1976 and 1980 by more than 10% points to 42.2%. Primarily responsible was a disproportionate rise in the number of 55 to 59-year-olds which cannot be put down entirely to demographic causes.

[11] Reimbursement by the firms for benefit money paid out as a result of the "59er rule" became obligatory. From the very beginning, certain firms were made exempt from this ruling. This constitutes a violation of the Equal-Treatment Amendment to the Constitution, according to the Federal Court for Social Affairs. Until final ruling by the Federal Court for Constitutional Affairs, the reimbursement clause has been suspended.

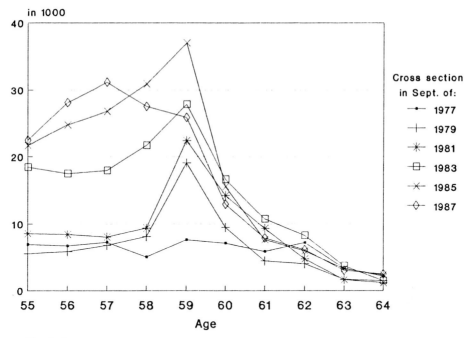

Fig. 5. Registered unemployed men by age.

Source: Federal Office for employment

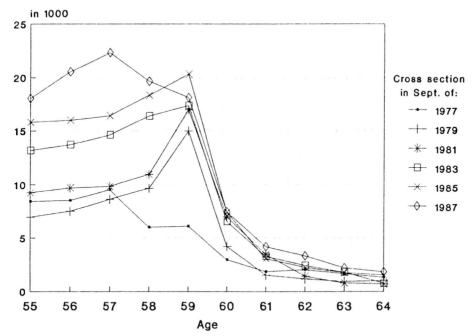

Fig. 6. Registered unemployed women by age.

Source: Federal Office for employment

maximum time period for receiving unemployment compensation makes it possible for older unemployed persons to lower the exit point ever lower.[12]

In addition – in some way even in contrast – to these four phases a fifth phases can be mentioned, related to changes in the eligibility rules for invalidity pensions and the minimum requirement concerning years of insurance (waiting period) for receiving an old age pension at age 65 in 1984 and the introduction of a credit for child rearing in 1986. Invalidity pensions now only can be received of within the last 5 years at least 3 years are covered by obligatory insurance. That means that voluntary insured persons cannot receive an invalidity pension if their covered employment dates back more than two years. Invalidity pensions dropped from 1984 to 1985 by about 33 %. This new condition was especially relevant for women. On the other hand the "waiting period" for receiving an old age pension at age 65 was reduced from 15 to 5 years of coverage. In 1986 all women who have born children are credited an extra year of insurance per child. All together this increased remarkably the number of persons (here as well especially women) retiring at the "normal" retirement age and stopped the trend even earlier retirement for women.

The Pre-retirement Act became effective in May of 1984 and will be discontinued till the end of 1988. This Act has served as a standard in many industrial branches for labor/management agreements for the transitional period to retirement.[13] Pre-retirement as a rule begins at age 58 and continues until the earliest possible age for drawing pension benefits, i.e. for women and handicapped until age 60, otherwise age 63. During this phase, the employer pays a pre-retirement sum amounting to 65 % of the previous gross income[14]; if the position vacated is filled by an unemployed person, then the Federal Agency for Employment takes over a share of 35 %. At the end of 1987, there were roughly 140000 cases of pre-retirement since the program began (cf. DIW (1988)).[15] This figure lies considerably beneath the original expectation. Reasons given for this include start-up difficulties and competition from the "59er rule". In addition, the metal industry – by far the largest industrial branch has come to an only remotely attractive agreement on pre-retirement; for civil servants, there exists no pre-retirement agreement at all (cf. Kühlewind (1986), p. 214).

By the end of January 1988, the Federal government decided not to extent the Pre-retirement Act beyond 1988. The employers had always seen this regulation as being too costly for them while the unions – after some ini-

---

[12] Starting with July, 1987, unemployed 54-year-olds and older qualify for up to 32 months of compensation. Beyond this fact, after age 58, they are no longer required to be at the disposal of the employment offices; see also 4.

[13] For a detailed overview of all contract implementations of the Pre-retirement Act, see Naegele (1987).

[14] Most agreements contain however a higher pre-retirement benefit of 75 %.

[15] The average rate of positions re-occupied equals 53 %. The total "effective employment balance" is estimated at nearer 70-80 % due to the otherwise necessary layoffs/redundancies (cf. (IAB 1987).

tial disagreements on the respective importance of shortening the work life or reducing the number of working hours per week – are demanding a prolongation of the Pre-retirement Act under improved conditions, e.g., with increased funding from the Federal Agency for Employment (cf. Naegele and Neumann (1987)). For the employer, such company settlements as the "59er rule" are far more attractive, aside from being less costly. It also gives management the sole deciding power as to who should receive an offer to take leave and when this may occur. The pre-retirement regulation, in contrast, allows an employee to make such a request (cf. Wolf and Kohli (1988)).

2. Public Discussion at Present: Differing Approaches and Interests

The decision against the prolongation of the Pre-retirement Act has revitalized the public debate on shaping the pathways to retirement. There has been a stormy controversy in the past years. This is due primarily to the fact that within the two areas concerned – labor market and social security – a multiplicity of varying interests plays a role. Important sectors of economic and social policies are affected, but what is special in this debate is that the action in one sector influences the action in the other sector. Added to this are the differences in time perspectives fundamental to certain suggestions.

With respect to these two areas, the following conflicts of purposes should be underscored:

The case for continuing a policy of early retirement is clear. Due to the still very high rate of unemployment, much stands in favor of retaining or further improving the possibilities for early departure from work. This becomes especially valid whenever such measures prove effective in providing greater total employment, i.e. when they contribute better than all other possible measures to incorporating younger members of the work force into the working world, or preserving these from unemployment. The case against early retirement is also clear. In the long run the financial problems for the social security system, especially in light of the demographic development, will considerably heighten the need for reform.

To better understand the issue we examine the positions held by different actors in the retirement process. Conflicts of interests and purposes arise out of the differing preferences of key actors: *Managements* who – for whatever reason – are interested in reducing or rejuvenating the number of their employees will favor solutions which are cost-efficient for themselves and which do not limit their own decision freedom in personnel policy-making. In contrast are those interests of *employees,* apart from a good financial backup, being able to decide alone whether and when to leave work for retirement. *Trade unions,* as the representative of all actively employed and former employed (i.e., retirees), are interested in solutions which neither cause extra premium burden for contributors nor reductions in pension benefits. Beyond this, there is also a desire on the part of trade unions for reasons of organizational policy to prefer uniform solutions.

The respective *social insurance institutions* are interested in policies which will not increase the burden on their own budgets. In particular, the assignment of various "risks", such as unemployment or demographic changes, is hotly disputed among the various federal agencies and organizations. Yet also the various *public entities* (federal, state, and community), which are responsible for financing the social security system, have an interest in keeping their respective budgets free form extra burden and rebuffing these to the budgets of social insurance institutions or the contributors themselves or other groups. The legislative branch sees itself confronted with the task of developing solutions which are considerate of the diverging interests in a manner satisfactory to all concerned parties. Within this task, the danger exists that the more pressing short-term tasks receive first attention in the political process – particularly when a politically visible (showworthy) result has to be produced in relatively short time – and that other tasks which lie further ahead, having long-term results, will be put off or pushed aside. Above all, it is essential that no decision be made which – in light of the demographic structural changes – will further increase the already rising financial needs in the social security system, particularly within the pension insurance system, since such alterations can only with great difficulty be undone again.

Employee preferences and behavior are of particular significance. In this regard, (empirically founded) knowledge is quite limited. Research in economics has restricted itself to developing normative statements of fact concerning optimum behavior under set conditions, rather than to seeking explanation of certain behaviors. One difficulty in the research of employee behavior and the indicators of possible reactions to change in conditions lies in the fact that the group of persons being researched is very heterogeneous. This fact applies in particular to three very important factors of influence:

—   condition of health
—   the type of work performed
—   level of income.

Also of significance is the manner in which employee preferences and behavior change over the life course. Because of the ever-earlier threshold to retirement, also expectations in favor of retiring early are influenced. Conceptions of a "normal age" at which the transition to retirement is begun, are influenced by the socio-legislative regulations affecting the conditions under which pensions may be drawn or claimed. The longer that possibilities exist for early exit from gainful employment, the greater will be the influence upon such conceptions of a point in time when the exit should take place. Another effect ist, that the phase in which a worker is looked upon as "older" begins ever sooner.[16] At the same time, life expectancy continues to

---

[16] For example, the extension of the maximum legal period for receiving unemployment compensation on and beyond the "normal" period of one year – now possible starting at age 42 and older – is explained by the special employment problems afflicting "older employees" (cf. Sozialbericht (1986), sect. 25).

rise. We now consider those employees as being "older" who still have almost half of their lives ahead.

The individual assessment of the possibilities for an earliest-possible retirement will be chiefly defined by the above-mentioned factors of influence. Where there is a health handicap, whenever work becomes a necessary evil, wherever a prospect of useful activity during the retirement phase is deemed possible, the desire to exit gainful employment at the earliest moment is understandable and will probably be realized if financial security is assured. Demands which are directed toward removal of possibilities for early retirement, or toward making related conditions less favorable, are seen from this angle as destructive of those social achievements brought about by other administrations.

To just what extent such description of the combination of influential factors agrees with reality will require further investigation. Some writings in Psychology/Gerontology have – for a long time – argued that the performance rate does not decline during the older years of working life.[17] It must also not be generally assumed that gainful employment no longer plays a role in the personal fulfillment and social recognition of older employees. If this should play a role, then a lowering of the retirement age would go against this – regardless of any regulation or social process which might be at the source of such lowering.

An additional difficulty in determining which factors are influential for preferences and behavior by (older) employees lies in the fact that information concerning current phenomena may not necessarily be applied to future conditions. In particular, the difficult question of preference changes arises. When we visualize, for example, the fact that in the year 2020 those cohorts who are now just at the beginning or the middle of their working lives will be entering retirement age, we can easily imagine how, in comparison to the present-day "pensioner generation", other experiences and expectations will come into play.

Decisive in answering the question of whether existing socio-legislative regulations will be used by the older worker, are the consequences for their income. No regulation should be regarded in isolation, but always in contrast to the possible alternative actions. At the same time, conditions within the larger framework must be taken into account (for example, expectations of society or of other employees toward older employees as to the point in time when exit from gainful employment should be taken, i.e. their position vacated). If the sole alternative to early retirement is unemployment, then the decision should be relatively easy for the employee to make. The decision-making situation is changed, however, when not only attractive alternatives for full retirement can be presented to older employees, but also attractive plans for a gradual switch-over to the retirement phase.

---

[17] See also particularly the works by Thomae and Lehr, e.g. Lehr (1979), on changes in retirement age, to which Bäcker (1982), (among others) takes a critical viewpoint.

Also with regard to acceptance of possibilities for a gradual exit from working life, we cannot assume that previous experiences will prove directly valid. One example: in the German cigarette industry, shows complete retirement as preferred over a combination of part-time employment together with a partial pension, in spite of reduced personal income (cf. Schwahn (1988)). Yet, as long as firms continue to show little interest in making suitable part-time positions available (e.g. for organizational reasons), such possibilities for further employment on a reduced scale will hardly be made particularly attractive. In this manner, the incentives to make a complete exit become increased. By the employee's view, the attractivness of a gradual exit depends to a great extent on whether one may continue one's work in the previous position or whether part-time employment will only be possible in a different job or assignment. This will be an important factor in assessing the respective employment and income (or loss of income) which may be expected. Total or partial departure from gainful employment also offers additional opportunities: for example, are there employment possibilities in the "shadow" sector, or are there satisfying possibilities in social/community work? A reminder here of the increase in the number of "young seniors" due to simultaneous increases in life expectancy and early exit from gainful employment.

All of these aspects show clearly the importance of considering observed tendencies as well as forecasts concerning future conditions whenever decisions are to be prepared or made with respect to changes in the conditions for point in time and type of exit from gainful employment.

3. Changes in the Structural Framework

The current discussion on employment of older workers or the point in time for retirement is strongly influenced by the present conditions on the labor market. Because new institutional regulations in this area must have – as mentioned earlier – more long-term character and be able to withstand even the most fundamental changes in surrounding structural framework[18], it becomes most essential that those changes in structure beginning to show themselves today be included in the discussion and considered in the making of new legislative regulations. Not only do we mean here changes in the age structure of the population, but also changes in production and economic structures as well as the resulting changes in employment conditions for older employees and general changes in employment. However much more is known about demographic changes than about changes in the conditions of work. Our comments on the latter is more speculation.

---

[18] Among other reasons, inthe interest of having valid long-term framework conditions as an orientation point for decisions by firms and employees, as well as building up trust in the old-age insurance system, which requires in itself considerable continuity.

The strong decline in birth rate in the Federal Republiic of Germany since the mid 60's in congruence with steadily increasing life expectancy is leading toward a considerable *shift in age structure.* Even if the long-term assumptions concerning future fertility rates as well as the development in size and age structure of the foreign members of the population are clouded by many hardly determinable factors, the number of seniors will definitely climb significantly both in absolute and in relative terms over the next forty years, relative not only to total population but also to the labor force (see overview 1). Whereas from 1985 to the year 2030, according to the middle variant of the (official) population projection (assuming a constant net reproduction rate of 0.6), the population number (German nationals only) will decline by 14 million, while the number of people aged 60 and above shall rise by 4 million. In 1985 there were nearly 39 persons age 60 or over for every 100 in the activity phase (i.e. between ages 20 and 60). By the year 2030, this age (depency) ratio will have reached 81 per hundred.[19] As for the financement of social security – in particular of old-age pensions – grave consequences for contribution rates may be expected under unchanged conditions (most importantly, should benefit levels remain the same). The present constribution rate of 18.7% (1988) would have to be roughly doubled (cf. Schmähl (1983 a)).

Particularly because the effects of demographic aging can be foreseen fairly well at this time, they should receive a central place within each long-

Overview 1. Development of population and dependency ratios from 1985 to 2030
– german nationals –[a]

Year	Number of persons (in millions) aged				Youth dependency ratio col. 1/ col. 2	Age dependency ratio col. 3/ col. 2	Total dependency ratio col. 1+3/ col. 2
	< 20	20–<60	60+	Total			
1985	12.9	31.6	12.1	56.6	40.8	38.5	79.3
1990	11.1	32.5	12.6	56.2	34.0	38.9	72.9
2000	10.7	30.1	14.1	54.9	35.4	46.9	82.3
2010	8.9	28.2	14.4	51.5	31.5	51.1	82.6
2020	7.2	25.4	14.8	47.3	28.2	58.2	86.3
2030	6.5	19.9	16.2	42.6	32.5	81.2	113.7

a) 1985 statistical results. From 1990 onwards projection figure based on assumptions made 1987 in Bundesminister des Inneren (e.g. net reproduction rate 0.6 constant, increase of Life expectancy up to 1995 by 2.3 years (male), 2.0 years (female) of newborn people and of people at age of 60 by 1.4 years.

Source: Bundesminister des Inneren (1987).

[19] If we include foreign population members, the age dependency ratio will increase – according to the assumptions of the demographic projection – nearly to the same level. Variant C (Bundesminister des Inneren (1987)) is based on a net immigration flow up to the year 2009, while for the year 2010 and the following period a net flow of zero is assumed. Therefore the ratios for German nationals and the total population are close together.

term oriented socio-economic policy. As concerns the financing of old-age pension schemes, the "pensioner ratio" (= the ratio of the number of pension beneficiaries to the number of contributors) is a far better index than the old-age dependency ratio. The former is not only determined by age structure but also by the frequency by which paying members and pensioners are represented in the various age groups, i.e. determined by employment behavior and socio-legislative regulations. German social insurance institutions even calculate the pensioner rate in the year 2030 to be equal to or in excess of 100 (under unchanged conditions). By using pensioner ratios, it may be plainly seen that a longer stay in working life would ease twofold the load imposed by demographic aging: the number of pensioners would be lowered and the number of gainfully employed persons would rise. This will explain why a measurable relaxing of pressure is expected from the reform suggestion to prolong the *average* age of retirement entry – not to be confused with a change to the statutory retirement age – in order to adjust social security to demographic structural changes (cf. Schmähl (1986), and Sozialbeirat (1986)). Nonetheless, this will only be realistic if fundamental improvements in the labor market situation occur; a continued high rate of unemployment under older workers would make the effect of a rise in retirement age equivalent to a mere shifting of the burden from social security to other social budgets (such as to unemployment insurance or social assistance).

Whereas, on the one hand, the demographic development is leading to financing difficulties in this area of social security, on the other, it is hoped that a long-term easing of the tension on the labor market will also be a result, since the number of persons in working age will probably decline faster than will, for example, the demand for labor. If, in addition, the demographically-caused reduction in working person potential should lead to improvement in the job possibilities for older workers, then this could raise the average retirement age without having to impose statutory changes. A falling supply of labor could also lead to a rise in the female participation rate, which in turn would also help ease the financial situation for the pension system (cf. Thiede (1986)), albeit only for an interim period.[20] In particular the trade unions point out, however, that in light of new labor-market forecasts extending beyond the year 2000, which have high unemployment figures appearing as probable, there must be active new policies for employment and working hours in order to create the prerequisites for prolonged employment of older workers as well as greater female employment (cf. Bäcker (1987)).

Apart from the developments in age structure and general labor market conditions, *changes in economic and employment structures* will probably have a future effect on the age and type of transition to retirement. Initial investigations on the level of individual branches of the economy (Jacobs et al. (1987)) have shown that early exit by older workers from gainful employment is not just restricted to those branches which, due to economic problems,

---

[20] For a more elaborated analysis see Schmähl (1989).

have demonstrated a general decline in employment. Expanding branches, too, e.g. in the service sector, show a significant decline in the employment of older workers. This may be interpreted as the difficult labor market situation being responsible for early exit of older employees in many branches, since, once created, the possibility for early exit apparently has also been used where direct labor-market political pressure did not exist or only to a lesser degree. Even though in the Federal Republic of Germany a decline in the employment of older workers can be observed in all branches of the economy, it does go, however, much lower within many areas of the service sector when these are compared to construction or manufacturing industries on the whole. By means of a further expansion of the tertiary sector, for which in the Federal Republic a need to catch up is often acknowledged in international comparison (cf. Krupp (1986)), not only new employment potentials could be created in general, but also employment possibilities for older workers could be improved. This is all the more true because the chances for creating part-time jobs in the service sector are judged to be particularly favorable (cf. DIW (1986), p. 208). If we should succeed in creating more suitable part-time jobs, especially for older employees (above all male), then this could reduce, on the one hand, the frequency of general disability pensions (since – as mentioned – due to the "concrete method of interpretation" a lack of part-time jobs is often decisive), on the other hand, provide a realistic background for concepts dealing with partial or gradual transitions to retirement. It must also be considered that among older workers widespread wishes for part-time employment exit (cf. Landenberger (1983)), which would have to be answered with respective job offers by employers whenever a change in the labor market situation permits. Essential in assessing future employment opportunities of older workers are also the *demands* placed upon them by the employers, concerning e.g. qualifications. The introduction of new technologies has surely increased the trend to earlier exit because the older workers were not able in many cases to adjust to new conditions, or did not desire to, or employers purport this as being so, but also because qualifying measures did not appear – in the viewpoint of the employers – to be worthwhile for these employees who would not be with the firm so long. This was all the more true as long as, on the one hand, a large labor supply of well-trained younger employees was available, and on the other hand, attractive forms of retiring older employees completely existed or were created. In light of the demographically caused decline in the labor suply, but also because of *new qualification structures of older employees,* this could change in future. The older employees of years to come will not only be considerably better trained than those of today; for them, retraining and further education will become accepted elements of their professional lives. Not only working with new technologies but also adjusting to new demands will be common practice for those employees who today are just at the beginning or in the middle of their working lives. At the same time, the question is posed whether as a result of technological changes perhaps other factors of performance in older workers might be of significance, where today the concept of performance development within the life cycle is often characterized by a decline in physical ability during the latter phases of working life. The interest of firms in qualifying older workers may also increase when the number of working years in a firm rises because of a tendency for prolonging the employment phase, improving the chances for using this investment more completely.

On the whole, the apparent structural transitions signify that decisions concerning the setting up of conditions for transition from work to retirement cannot merely build upon previous experience but must evolve out of regard for possible new conditions arising.

4. Possibilities for Changing the Transition to Retirement and Questions to be Decided

With regard to the further development in transition to retirement, several questions must be answered. Should the process to ever earlier exit, as described in the first section, be supported and promoted by continued staturory measures? Or should not other incentives be created, in light of the other structural changes described in section three, which would promote a later transition? Just how effective such incentives would be depends for the most part on the reactions of the actors involved. Thus, these questions are of normative and positive nature. The apparent changes in the age structure of the population, with their long-term consequences, but also the fact that the design of the social security system requires a considerable measure of continuity, both serve to underscore the necessity of making political decisions which are long-term oriented. The task of social science will be, in particular, to improve the prerequisites for this by uncovering long-term tendencies and shedding light on various connections.

4.1 Several Fundamental Questions

Concerning the point in time of transition from work to retirement, the essential question is whether this should occur earlier than it has up to now, later, or unchanged. With regard to the type of transition, it must be clarified,

— whether the exit is complete or only partial and
— whether the exit is simultaneously connected with receiving an old age pension from the statutory pension system or whether certain interim phases are built in before actual pension receipt.

This also effects the question of the respective institutions involved (e.g. pension system or unemployment insurance) and the roll of lawmakers on the one side as well as of unions and employers' associations on the other. Furthermore, investigations are necessary into how the various measures will affect the income situations of the (previous) employees.

A high degree of flexibility will most likely be desirable during further considerations, and a return to the strict limitations of transition no longer seems worth striving for – at least from the standpoint of the employee. Here the question arises of whether this flexiblity should be guaranteed within the framework of the pension system or whether the system should provide relatively uniform regulations which may be complemented by flexible regulations decided on by employers and employees or their respective organizations.

In coming to a decision on such fundamental "strategy", the expectations concerning adaptability of systems and regulations will play an important role. If statutory systems can only be changed with relative difficulty (and should only seldom be changed), then it would follow that the more flexible regulations suited to the respective conditions ought to be left over for employers and employees to agree upon. It should be noted, however, that such intitial pre-retirement regulations have different financial implications. From the viewpoint of the statutory pension system, such pre-retirement agreements on the level of individual firms or entire branches which are directed toward retirement at age 63 are to be preferred over those regulations which foresee pension payments starting at age 60 (especially by receipt of old age pensions after long-term unemployment). This is the case in such types as the "59er rule", which allows firms to reduce or restructure their staff at the cost of the pension and/or unemployment insurance system. If the attractivness of this regulation for firms is to be lessened, it will be necessary to make effective again the no longer practiced reimbursement obligation by the firms. This must be done soon in a manner which will not pose any doubts as to its constitutionality.

Decisions which are made concerning the point in time and type of exit from work life are closely connected to strategies of distribution of the individual volume of working time over the life course and the resulting consequences for the work volume of the economy in single calendar years. The whole volume of labor input (per hours) of the economy (measured in working hours) in the Federal Republic of Germany has declined from 1960 to 1985 by over 20% (1970-1985, roughly 16%). This is mainly due to the annual average working time achieved by employees and only partially to a reduction in the number of employees (cf. Reyher and Kohler (1986), p. 31). A further reduction in the weekly or yearly working time could be connected to a prolongation of individual working life and thus contribute to a redistribution of individual working time within a life course. This could also bring about positive effects for individual health, in so far as health restrictions may be a result of work stress. A reduction of working time in the early phases of working life could (as long as it is not connected with an intensification of work) lead to greater performance at an older age and improve the possibility of remaining active longer.

In the discussion concerning the various forms for shortening working time – shortening of weekly, yearly, or life working times – all the connected consequences must be considered, even if these should only occur in the long term. Of prime importance is the effectivity of the various alternatives concerning employment policy. Great doubts were raised at the introduction of the Pre-retirement Act, one form of shortening life working time, as to its employment-political suitability (cf. Schmähl (1983 b), Schmähl and Conradi (1984)); its effects upon employment have lagged considerably behind the expectations (cf. Kühlewind (1988)). Yet even when a positive effect upon employment is to be expected, and this effect is even higher than with other forms of working time reduction, global political assessment becomes necessary in consideration of all additional effects which could occur (e.g. upon the financial situation of public, in particular pension insurance).

4.2 Questions in Connection with the Design of the Statutory Pension Insurance

The following examples will show clearly what type of decisions must be made when changes in point in time and/or type of exit from employment is intended via redesign of the statutory pension system. In the first instance, we shall consider how a prolongation of the employment phase may be obtained. Following this, we shall briefly discuss possibilities *within* the pension insurance system for structuring a combination of part-time work and partial pension.

In striving for a *prolongation of the employment phase by making the point in time for exiting more flexible* (assuming unchanged complete exit from working life), we must first clarify how the choice of a particular point in time will effect the amount of pension and hence the employee's income. As already mentioned, decisions concerning pension level stand in close connection with the financial solvency of the insurance institutions. In the present-day system, there are financial incentives for an early exit because this will not lead to actuarially calculated pension reductions. Only relatively small reductions in pension occur due to the shorter insurance period, but the longer pension period remains unconsidered. By removing these incentives through the introduction of actuarial deductions for early exits (and respective additions for longer employment), a first step for prolonging the employment phase might be taken.[21] The first question to be answered here would be which age would serve as an index age limit. For the German situation, this would be, for example, age 65 or age 63, or even – in considering the frequency of pension entry for women, and now also increasingly for men – age 60. If we choose age 65 as the reference retirement age, then the introduction of actuarial deductions would indeed mean a substantial worsening in comparison to present-day regulations for those exiting early. Yet this system by itself would not produce any incentive for prolonging the employment phase. In order to achieve this, we would have to increase, for example, the deductions and additions.

---

[21] There is, however, the opinion that the transfer of the principle of individual equivalence is basically incompatible with the aims of a social insurance scheme (cf. e.g. Bäcker (1987), p. 302).

Apart from defining the reference retirement age and the level of deductions and additions relative to year of age and/or insurance period, we
must also decide upon the earliest age for receiving a pension (with deductions) and until what age pension-increasing additions shall be paid. With regard to income distribution, we must decide which pension level (pension
payment to previous work income) under which conditions (e.g. length of insurance period) and to which point in time (age) should be achieved, whereby this must also be capable of financing in longer terms. The level of actuarial deductions depends, for the most part, on the respective reference age
limit selected.[22] When one considers the pension level in the Federal Republic of Germany, it will become clear that the possibilites for reductions
are not very abundant if we are to avoid the danger of having pensioners become welfare recipients despite even a longer insurance period (cf. Schmähl
(1984)).

In November 1988 a first draft of a law on pension reform was published
proposing a constinction of different measures to copie with the challenges
of structural changes for pension financing. One of the central measures proposed is a step by step increase of all (early) retirement ages to have in the
future main by only one retirement age at 65 (see also the introduction for
this volume).

Positive effects for the financial situation of pension insurance occur
when the average pension age increases. The simple setting of an age limit is
not sufficient to assure this increase; it will depend decisively on the reaction
of the workers involved, whose decision will be based upon the existing alternatives as well as upon their own condition of health and the labor market
situation. If the result of the regulation should lead to a rise in the average retirement age, then we may expect under unchanged conditions a favorable
effect upon pension insurance funds. At a constant pension level, the reduced number of pension recipients and the higher number of contributors
would make a contribution rate possible which, at its peak (around the year
2030), could lie at roughly three percentage points lower for every year by
which the average pension entry age was raised.

It must be considered, however, that the fiscal effect of individual measures might be reduced if other measures for structuring the future financial
situation of pension insurance are also undertaken. The more the rise in
pension spending can be held back by other measures, the less will be the effect of a rise in the average retirement age on pension financing. This would
also be the case if a change in the pension formula (for the calculation of pensions) would lead to a certain pension level only after a longer period of insurance. One has, however, to make a clear distinction between the point of
time when there are political decisions e.g. on changes the retirement ages,
the date when these new conditions shall start to be effective and the effects

---

[22] According to calculations by Müller, deductions equalling 10.93% occur to pensions received from age 60 onward, where a reference age limit of age 63 is assumed. Deductions
equalling 17.24% are figured for a reference age limit of 65 years (cf. Müller (1987), p. 48).

itself, influenced e.g. by the conditions of the labor market and the behavioral reactions of employees and firms.

The *integration of a partial pension concept into the present-day pension insurance system* also leads to a series of questions in need of answers. If the possibility of a reduction of annual or weekly working time in contrast to full-time work is to be fundamentally incorporated into the latter phase of working life, then we must clarify at what starting point such a reduction will be possible and how long the phase of part-time employment should last. The above mentioned aspects – particularly with regard to the actuarial deductions and additions – must also be regarded here. We must also decide to which pre-conditions a claim to such a regulation should be coupled (e.g. a minimum number of insurance years), which will determine the group of people who may claim. The structuring of any respective regulation in this case, that of partial pension shall determine the attainable pension level and in turn, dependent upon the number of claims made, the development of expenditure within the pension system.

There are different forms for structuring the partial pension phase, which may be differentiated according to whether this phase

— starts prior to the earliest possible point in time for receiving an old age pension
— or afterward
— or in accordance with the age of retiring completely
— or is overlaid in a period which begins prior to and ends after today's retirement age.

Another question to be answered is whether during the phase of partial pension receipt, an unchanged volume of part-time work occurs or whether various stages in reducing working time will be possible (cf. Overview 2).

Model calculations carried out by members of pension insurance institutions provide initial reference points concerning the effects upon the individual pension level (cf. Overview 3). The calculations are based on very simplified assumptions. The situation of one employee is analyzed who exits from employment at age 63, having achieved an average relative wage position of 100% during his 45 years of insurance contribution time (for an "average earner") and who at the point in time of his exit is just making the average gross earning level. His net earnings are calculated under consideration of the average income tax payment and the employee's contributions to social security. When the net pension (after deducting contributions to health insurance) is figured in relation to this income, the net pension level equals 67.2%.

If we now introduce a partial pension phase beginning at age 60 and ending at age 65, reducing the working time by half, then we have a net pension level of 84.5% (without actuarial deductions and additions, i.e. if only the adjusted insurance period is considered), which will fall to roughly 67% at the time of full pension receipt (age 65). It is assumed that further pension claims are acquired through part-time work, but not through partial pension receipt.

Overview 2. Types of transition from working life to retirement

Working time
(e.g. per week)

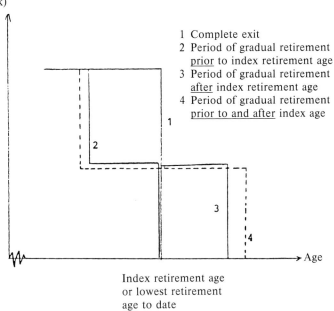

1 Complete exit
2 Period of gradual retirement
   prior to index retirement age
3 Period of gradual retirement
   after index retirement age
4 Period of gradual retirement
   prior to and after index age

Index retirement age
or lowest retirement
age to date

Working time
(e.g. per week)

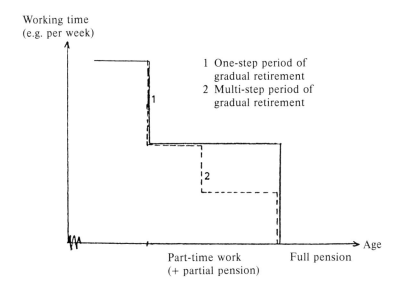

1 One-step period of
   gradual retirement
2 Multi-step period of
   gradual retirement

Part-time work   Full pension
(+ partial pension)

Overview 3. Models showing consequences of a partial pension within the statutory
                pension system

Case 1   Full-time work   Full pension
——————   —————————————>   ——————————————>
(without partial pension)   Age 63
                                                            (index age)

Case 2   Full-time work   Full pension
——————   —————————>   ——————————————> —————————>
(with partial pension)   Part-time work
                                                          + partial pension

(a) without deductions and additions
    (i. e. regarding only the adjusted number of insurance years)

(b) with deductions and additions
    based on actuarial calculations

	Case 1			Case 2				
DM per month	Full-time work before age 63	Pension after age 63	Full-time work before age 60	Part-time work + partial pension between age 60 and 65		Pension after age 65		
				(a) without	(b) with	(a) without	(b) with
Gross	3156,–	1598,–	3156,–	2324,–	2243,–	1580,–	1587,–
Net	2236,–	1503,–	2236,–	1889,–	1817,–	1487,–	1494,–
Net replacement rate [a]	(100%)	67,2%	(100%)	84,5%	81,3%	66,5%	66,8%

a) Net pension + net part-time income in relation to net full-time income.
   Numbers taken from Clausing (1988).

   Possibilities for refining such calculations will not be expounded upon
here. It seems important, however, that the different taxation of earnings
and pensions is decisive for achieving a significantly higher net pension level
during the partial pension phase than with a complete exit. This underscores
the necessity for considering the resulting total effect upon available income
when comparing alternative possible regulations. Other transfer payments
(e.g. "Wohngeld" – rent rebate) should also be considered when assessing
the available income.
   Relaxation for pension insurance always occurs whenever a partial pension (simultaneous to part-time work) is claimed instead of complete exit at
this point in time. Of course a partial pension program can also further increase the financial problems of the pension system if it recruits those who
would have remained in full-time employment without such a program. This
will be especially true if no actuarial deductions or additions are planned,
which, in a longitudinal perspective, would avoid a shifting in the burden
with reference to the index retirement age. The introduction of new condi-

tions, e.g. premature pension receipt, would lead to a phase of greater financial burden in cross-sectional perspective, i.e. within single calendar years. If the possibility of a partial pension is to be created within the pension insurance system, then we must ascertain at which age the partial pension phase may begin without causing a further reduction in the employment phase on the whole. To reduce the possibility of additional pension expenditure it will be necessary not to start the phase of partial retirement earlier than the lowest age for complete retirement. At the same time, incentives must be created which go in the direction of prolonging the partial pension phase, and thus the total employment phase.

Deeper-reaching simulation studies are needed to supply clues for determining which structures of partial pension models, using realistic assumptions concerning the behavior of workers and employers, can contribute to reduce the financial pressure upon pension insurance funds. Yet even if partial pensions should prove to be financially neutral, such a model might be seen from a gerontological view as being positive with respect to the preferences of older employees, because fewer disability-conditioned complete exits occur, for example, but also more healthy employees take advantage of this opportunity for reducing their working time.

The prerequisites for and effects of changed conditions for the transition from employment to retirement require in many instances still closer analysis. This should consider the multi-facet relations between the various problem areas (such as labor market, pension finances, demographic development, income distribution) just as much as the interplay of various institutions and respectively employed instruments. Nevertheless, neither the complexity of this question, nor the present-day unfavorable employment situation should become arguments for putting off action on the above questions. Particularly with regard to the future development of the pension system, long-term oriented decisions are needed. Short-term changes in the conditions for the transition from work to retirement should be avoided – particularly where attempts at prolonging the employment phase are concerned. Employees as well as firms must receive sufficient time to adjust their behavior to changed conditions.

In laying the groundwork for careful decision making, we must clarify our aims as well as take stock of experiences in other countries.[23] Important clues might be gained concerning problems of execution as well as the effects of various regulations for structuring the transition between these two so important phases of life. At the same time, these may provide valuable new ideas for theoretical and empirical analyses of political instruments as well as for restructuring political regulations.

---

[23] This is particularly the case with respect to partial pension schemes which already exist in a number of countries. So far all of these programs have failed for a variety of reasons, with the only exception of Sweden. For a comparison of partial pension systems in Denmark, Finland, France, Sweden and the United Kingdom, cf. Jacobs (1988) and Laczko (1988).

References

Bäcker, G. (1982) Ältere Arbeitnehmer – Probleme einer fehlgeleiteten Sozialpolitik?. In: K. Dohse, U. Jürgens und H. Russig (Hrsg.). Ältere Arbeitnehmer zwischen Unternehmensinteressen und Sozialpolitik. Frankfurt/New York: Campus, pp. 61-86

Bäcker, G. (1987) Wieder länger arbeiten? Quantität und Qualität der Arbeitsplätze sind entscheidend! – Anmerkungen zur Diskussion um die Heraufsetzung der Altersgrenzen in der Rentenversicherung. In: WSI-Mitteilungen, Vol. 40, pp. 295-304

Brinkmann, C. (1980) Zum Unterschied in der Erfassung von Arbeitslosen durch die Bundesanstalt für Arbeit und von Erwerbslosen im Mikrozensus In: D. Mertens, W. Klauder (Hrsg.). Probleme der Messung und Vorausschätzung des Erwerbspersonenpotentials. Beiträge zur Arbeitsmarkt- und Berufsforschung (Beiträge aus der Arbeitsmarkt- und Berufsforschung) 44, Nürnberg. pp. 172-180

Bundesminister des Inneren (1987) Modellberechnungen zur Bevölkerungsentwicklung in der Bundesrepublik Deutschland. Bonn, mimeo

Clausing, P. (1988) Stufenweiser Übergang in den Ruhestand und Veränderungen der Erwerbsphase – Probleme der Realisierung aus Sicht der gesetzlichen Rentenversicherung. In: W. Schmähl (Hrsg.). Verkürzung oder Verlängerung der Erwerbsphase?. Tübingen: Mohr, pp. 178-190

Conradi, H., K. Jacobs and W. Schmähl (1987) Vorzeitiger Rentenbezug in der Bundesrepublik Deutschland. In: Sozialer Fortschritt, Vol. 36, pp. 182-189

DIW (Deutsches Institut für Wirtschaftsforschung) (1986) Strukturverschiebungen zwischen sekundärem und tertiärem Sektor. Gutachten im Auftrage des Bundesministers für Wirtschaft. Berlin

DIW (Deutsches Institut für Wirtschaftsforschung) (1987) Immer mehr Frauen im Beruf. Zur längerfristigen Entwicklung des Erwerbsverhaltens von Frauen. DIW-Wochenbericht 29/87 (bearb. von S. Jäkel und E. Kirner)

DIW (Deutsches Institut für Wirtschaftsforschung) (1988) Vorruhestandsregelung sollte verlängert werden. DIW-Wochenbericht 4/88 (bearb. von V. Meinhardt und R. Zwiener)

Helberger, C. and J. Schwarze (1986) Umfang und Struktur der Nebenerwerbstätigkeit in der Bundesrepublik Deutschland. In: Mitteilungen aus der Arbeitsmarkt- und Berufsforschung 2/1986, pp. 271-286

IAB (Institut für Arbeitsmarkt- und Berufsforschung) (1986) Zur statistischen Erfassung des Vorruhestands. Überblick über die vier wichtigsten Statistiken und die neuesten Ergebnisse. IAB-Kurzbericht vom 23.12.1986 (VII/1-Kw). In: Beiträge aus der Arbeitsmarkt- und Berufsforschung 42.8

IAB (Institut für Arbeitsmarkt- und Berufsforschung) (1987) Vorruhestand: Wiederbesetzung nach Wirtschaftszweigen. IAB-Kurzbericht vom 18.5.1987. In: Beiträge aus der Arbeitsmarkt- und Berufsforschung 42.9

Jacobs, K. (1988) Teilrentenmodelle: Erfahrungen im In- und Ausland. In: Internationale Chronik zur Arbeitsmarktpolitik, Vol. 32, Wissenschaftszentrum Berlin

Jacobs, K., M. Kohli, and M. Rein (1987) Testing the Industry-mix Hypothesis of Early Exit. Discussion paper IIVG/dp87 – 229. Wissenschaftszentrum Berlin

Jacobs, K., M. Kohli, and M. Rein (1988) Evolution of Early Exit: A Comparative Analysis of the Labor Force Participation of the Elderly. Erscheint in: M. Kohli et al. (Hrsg.). Time for Retirement. Comparative Studies of the Decreasing Age of Exit from the Labor Force, London and New York: Cambridge University Press

Kaltenbach, H. (1986) Probleme der Rentenversicherung bei den BU-EU-Renten einschließlich der Zukunftsperspektiven. In: Die Angestelltenversicherung, Vol. 33, pp. 357-361

Kohli, M. and H.-J. von Kondratowitz (1987) Retirement in Germany: Towards the Construction of the "Citizen of the Work Society". In: K.S. Markides and C.L. Cooper (Ed.). Retirement in Industrialized Societies. London: John Wiley & Sons, pp. 131-166

Krupp, H.-J. (1986) Der Strukturwandel zu den Dienstleistungen und Perspektiven der Beschäftigungsstruktur. In: Mitteilungen aus der Arbeitsmarkt- und Berufsforschung 1/1986, pp. 145-158

Kühlewind, G. (1986) Beschäftigung und Ausgliederung älterer Arbeitnehmer. Empirische Befunde zu Erwerbsbeteiligung, Rentenübergang, Vorruhestandsregelung und Arbeitslosigkeit. In: Mitteilungen aus der Arbeitsmarkt- und Berufsforschung 2/1986, pp. 209-232

Kühlewind, G. (1988) Erfahrungen mit dem Vorruhestand aus beschäftigungspolitischer Sicht. In: W. Schmähl (Hrsg.). Verkürzung oder Verlängerung der Erwerbsphase?. Tübingen: Mohr, pp. 54-63

Laczko, F. (1988) Partial Retirement: An Alternative to Early Retirement. In: International Social Security Review, pp. 149-170

Landenberger, M. (1983) Arbeitszeitwünsche. Vergleichende Analyse vorliegender Befragungsergebnisse. Discussion paper IIM/LMP 83-17. Wissenschaftszentrum Berlin

Lehr, U. (1979) Flexibilität der Altersgrenze oder Herabsetzung des Pensionierungsalters? Psychologische Aspekte. In: Zeitschrift für Betriebswirtschaft, pp. 137-144

Mayer, H.-L. (1987) Definition und Struktur der Erwerbslosigkeit. Ergebnisse des Mikrozensus 1985. In: Wirtschaft und Statistik, pp. 453-466

Müller, H.-W. (1987) Zur Verkürzung der Rentenlaufzeiten – Möglichkeiten und finanzielle Konsequenzen. In: Deutsche Rentenversicherung, pp. 30-55

Naegele (1987) (Hrsg.) Theorie und Praxis des Vorruhestandsgesetzes. Ergebnisse einer Wirkungsstudie. Augsburg: Maro

Naegele, G. and K.-H. Neumann (1987) Sicherung und Ausbau des Vorruhestandsgesetzes. Integrierter Schlußbericht auf der Grundlage der Betriebsfallstudien, der Ergebnisse der Expertenbefragung und der Sekundäranalysen. Köln und München

Orsinger, C. and P. Clausing (1982) Verkürzung der Lebensarbeitszeit im Spiegel der Rentenversicherung. In: Die Angestelltenversicherung, Vol. 29, pp. 261-268

Reimann, A. (1985) Trend zur Frühverrentung noch ungebrochen. In: Die Angestelltenversicherung, Vol. 32, pp. 406-413

Reyher, L. and H. Kohler (1986) Arbeitszeit und Arbeitsvolumen: Die empirische Basis der Arbeitszeit-Politik. In: Arbeitszeit und flexible Altersgrenze, Beiträge aus der Arbeitsmarkt- und Berufsforschung 75, 2. Aufl., Nürnberg. pp. 29-55

Schmähl, W. (1983 a) Geburtenentwicklung, Altersgrenze und Beitragssätze in der Rentenversicherung. Einige quantitative Zusammenhänge für die Bundesrepublik Deutschland. In: Sozialer Fortschritt, Vol. 32, pp. 217-220. Reprinted in Schmähl (1988)

Schmähl, W. (1983 b) Bekämpfung der Arbeitslosigkeit durch Verkürzung der Lebensarbeitszeit?. In: Wirtschaftsdienst, Vol. 63, pp. 337-341

Schmähl, W. (1984) Rentenniveau, Rentenhöhe und Sozialhilfezahlungen – Einkommensmäßige "Über- und Unterversorgung". Zur Präzisierung verteilungspolitischer Ziele für die gesetzliche Rentenversicherung. In: Deutsche Rentenversicherung, pp. 563-577. Reprinted in Schmähl (1988)

Schmähl, W. (1986) Strukturreform der Rentenversicherung – Konzept und Wirkungen. Versuch einer Zwischenbilanz. In: Die Angestelltenversicherung, Vol. 33, pp. 162-171. Reprinted in Schmähl (1988)

Schmähl, W. (1987) Public and Private Pensions for Various Groups in the Federal Republic of Germany: Past Experience and Tasks for the Future. In: International Social Security Association (Ed.). Conjugating Public and Private: The Case of Pensions. Geneva 1987, pp. 57-79, also in: International Social Security Review 3/86, pp. 258-276

Schmähl, W. (1988) Beiträge zur Reform der Rentenversicherung. Tübingen: Mohr

Schmähl, W. (1989) Labour Force Participation and Social Pension Systems. In: C. Conrad et al. (Eds.). Worte, Retirement and Intergenerational Equity (in print).

Schmähl, W. and H. Conradi (1984) Der Kosten- und Beschäftigungseffekt von Vorruhestandsregelungen. In: Wirtschaftsdienst, Vol. 64, pp. 126-131

Schusser, W. H. (1988) Stufenweiser Übergang in den Ruhestand aus der Sicht der betrieblichen Praxis. In: W. Schmähl (Hrsg.). Verkürzung oder Verlängerung der Erwerbsphase? Tübingen: Mohr, pp. 213-224

Schwahn, J. (1988) Erfahrungen mit dem Vorruhestand und betrieblichen Modellen des Übergangs in den Ruhestand aus Arbeitgebersicht: Das Beispiel der Zigarettenindustrie. In: W. Schmähl (Hrsg.). Verkürzung oder Verlängerung der Erwerbsphase?. Tübingen:Mohr, pp. 88-95

Sozialbericht (1986) Bundesminister für Arbeit und Sozialordnung (Hrsg.). Sozialbericht 1986, Bonn

Thiede, R. (1986) Die Erhöhung der Frauenerwerbsquote zur Entlastung der sozialen Sicherung im demographischen Wandel. In: Sozialer Fortschritt, Vol.. 35, pp. 251-254

Wolf, J. and M. Kohli (1988) Neue Altersgrenzen des Arbeitslebens. Betriebliche Interessen und biographische Perspektiven. In: L. Rosenmayr and F. Kolland (Hrsg.). Arbeit – Freizeit – Lebenszeit. Opladen: Westdeutscher Verlag, pp. 183-206

Early Retirement in Sweden

A. Kruse and L. Söderström

Contents

1. Introduction

In this paper we report and to some extent discuss how the Swedish social security system has been organized with respect to early retirements. We look in particular at the so called partial (or part-time) pension which was introduced in 1976. By this pension individuals in the ages 60 to 64 years are compensated for their income loss due to early retirement, provided that they do not leave the labor market.

Other provisions in the Swedish social security system for an early retirement are given by the opportunity to get advanced withdrawals of one's old age pension rights and the opportunity to apply for a disability pension in case one cannot find a suitable full-time employment. Also these provisions

W. Schmähl (Ed.)
Redifining the Process of Retirement
© Springer-Verlag Berlin Heidelberg 1989

are restricted to individuals in the ages 60 to 64. About 35 percent of all individuals in this age group are now getting a public pension benefit.[1]

These provisions for an early retirement were introduced in the 1970s, at the same time as the statuary pensionable age was lowered from 67 to 65 years, and the basic level for the old age pension benefit and the disability pension benefit was adjusted upwards. This contributed to a rapid increase in public expenditures for pension benefits. Between 1970 and 1986, these expenditures increased by 187 percent, to be compared with a modest increase in GNP by 35 percent, and an increase in private consumption outlays by no more than 26 percent.[2]

These figures have caused some alarm. Both advocates and critics of the welfare state are expressing concern about the future development of the national pension system.

There are now clear signs of a future crisis in the Swedish social security system. This system is mainly organized according to the PAYG principle (pay-as-you-go). The present level of taxation to finance pension benefits is about 20 % of the wage bill. Since Sweden is believed to have reached its level of taxation – the present level corresponds to 55 % of the GNP – all future increases in pension claims will be hard to meet. However, there are several tendensies indicating that pension claims will continue to increase. Both the *replacement ratio,* expressing the average level of pension benefits in comparison to the average level of earnings, and the *dependency ratio,* expressing the number of pensioners in comparison to the number of workers, are expected to increase. Let us give just a few figures to illustrate what situation Sweden now is facing.

First, there is an increasing proportion of elderly in the population. The number of individuals above the age of 65 in relation to the total number of individuals above the age of 16 was just around 15 % up to the early 1950s and is expected to become 35 % if the birth rate stays at its present level (1.7 child per woman). Should the Swedish birth rate decline to the present level in Denmark and Germany (1.4 child per person), the proportion of elderly will increase to around 45 %.[3]

In addition, there are pensioners in the age groups 16-64 years. At present their proportion is 9 %. Due to provisions for an early retirement among other things, this proportion is also expected to increase.

Secondly, participation rates in the work force are expected to decline. This tendency has been pronounced among male workers for a long time, but so far this tendency has been balanced by increasing participation rates

[1] Statistics Sweden. (SCB) "Inkomst och pensioner för pensionärer 16-64 år inkomståret 1984". *Pressmeddelande* nr 1986:30.

[2] Näringslivets Ekonomifakta, *Ekonomifaktas databank:* "Transfereringar till pensionärer", 1987-07-28.

[3] F. Snickars & S. Axelsson. *Om hundra år. Några framtidsbilder av befolkningen. Samhällsekonomi och välfärd under 2000-talet.* Statsrådsberedningen Ds SB 1984:2.

among women. It is now believed that this balancing factor soon will come to an end, and that aggregate participation rates then will start to decrease.[4]

Thirdly, there is a tendency towards shorter working hours. Although the total number of people employed has increased by 10 % since 1970, the total number of hours worked has gone down by 2 % in the same period.[5]

Fourth, one can expect a slower productivity growth in the future. In principle, a high rate of productivity growth would counterbalance all the other factors mentioned, and indeed, for a long time Sweden has had an exceptionally large growth rate. But this has become history. Sweden is now faced with a rather slow rate of growth in the industry sector; the forecast for the next ten years stops at 2 % annually.[6] In addition, services engage an increasing part of the total employment, and there the forecast is even gloomier. Almost 60 % of all services are publicly produced, mainly by local governments. In this part of the economy there are evidence of a decline in the productivity of labor. Since 1960, this decline has been 1.3 % annually.[7] Adding all these figures together one cannot escape the conclusion that a slow growth is very likely.

Against this background one could expect that Sweden would take steps to lower either the replacement ratio or the dependency ratio, or both. However, no such steps are in sight. As mentioned above the policy followed in recent years has rather gone the opposite way. Pension benefits and thereby the replacement ratio has been increased. The statuary pensionable age has been lowered, thereby increasing the dependency ratio. Voices are now raised in favour of the idea to shorten regular working hours by 25 %, from 8 to 6 hours per day. A consequence would be that the replacement ratio increases considerably.

In view of all this, it seems to us that early retirement should be taxed rather than subsidized. Why should costly public revenues be used to encourage people to lower their labor supply, and thereby diminish the tax base? We turn to this question in section V. Before that we give a short description of the Swedish pension system in section 2, and show how marginal pension benefits are related to earnings in section 3. The main purpuse of this analysis is to show what pension rights an individual will acquire by postponing retirement. Then, in section 4, we report on the Swedish way to promote an early retirement. Among other things, we show how these promotions have been used by various occupational groups.

---

[4]   Statistics Sweden (SCB), *Trender och prognoser. Inför 90-talet.* Information i prognosfrågor 1985:2.

[5]   Statistics Sweden (SCB). *National accounts.* 1986.

[6]   Ministry of finance, *Långtidsutredning '87,* SOU 1987:3.

[7]   R. Murray. *Den offentliga sektorn. Produktivetet och effektivitet,* Bilaga 21 till 1987 års långstidsutredning, Stockholm 1987.

2. Old Age and Disability Pensions in Sweden

In this chapter we give a brief description of the Swedish pension system. This system has three parts: national pension schemes, schemes negotiated in the labor market, and personal pension schemes.

2.1 National Pension Schemes

The national pension schemes with respect to old age and disability include a basic pension ("folkpension") and a supplementary pension ("ATP"). The benefits are price-indexed through the base amount (B) which is changed in accordance with inflation (the consumer price index, adjusted for the change in energy prices and indirect taxes). In 1986, B was 23300 SEK.

Basic Old Age Pension Scheme

The basic pension is the same for all individuals equal to $0,96 \cdot B$. If the individual has no or a low ATP-pension, an additional supplement of at most $0,48 \cdot B$ is granted. This benefit is reduced at the same rate as ATP increases. The lowest possible benefit is thus $1,44 \cdot B$ and for benefits from the ATP there is a 100 % marginal tax rate between 0,96 and 1,44 base amounts.

Supplementary Old Age Pension Scheme

Supplementary pension benefits are earnings-related and determined in the following way:

$$\text{ATP-benefit} = 0.6 \, [t/N] \, \hat{q} \qquad (1)$$

where

t = number of years worked with earnings exceeding 1 B for at least 3 years

$N = 30$

$t/N = 1$ for $t \geq 30$

$$\hat{q} = \sum_{1=1}^{15} q_i / 15$$

$q_i = y_i \, (1-\tau) - B. \qquad B \leq y_i (1-\tau) \leq 7.5 \, B$

y_i = gross earnings in the ith year belonging to the individual's fifteen best years in terms of earnings

$y_i (1-\tau)$ = net income in the ith year. Income taxes are disregarded.

τ = payroll tax(es).

Disability Pension Schemes

The disability pension schemes consists of a basic pension and an ATP-pension. It can be granted as a full pension, two thirds of a full pension or as half a pension.

The benefit from the basic pension is 0,96 base amounts. If there is no or a low benefit from the ATP, an additional supplement of 0,96 base amounts is granted. As in the case of an old age pension this additional suplement is reduced in correspondence with increases in the ATP pension benefit.

In principle, the benefit from the ATP scheme is counted in the same way as the benefit from the old age pension. However, the individual's "earning status" $\hat{q}$ is determined in a special way. q_i is determined by an assumed earnings profile based on either the average of the two highest earnings the last four years or the average of earnings since the age of 16. The method most favourable to the individual is chosen. t is counted as if the individual had been able to work until the age of 65.

Other Benefits

In addition to the old age or disability pension benefits pensioners are granted a housing allowance and some extra benefits in kind in the form of house cleaning, transportation etc. These benefits are means-tested.

Moreover, there are supplementary benefits in the case a pensioner is married or has children.

Finally, in the case of death, under-aged children and the widow are granted a pension benefit in proportion to the deceased's pension rights (basic pension + supplementary pension).

Financing

The basic pension is mainly financed by a payroll tax of at present 9.45 %. This tax covers about 85 % of the expenditures on benefits. The rest is covered by the state budget.

The ATP pension is financed by a payroll tax of at present 10.2 %. Earlier tax revenues exceeded the expenditures on benefits, and a fund was created. At present the tax covers only about 80 % of the expenditures, the rest being paid for by the interest earned by the fund.

These payroll taxes apply to the entire wage bill in all branches of employment, public as well as private. If all benefits in the national pension scheme were to be financed by a payroll tax in addition to the interest earned by the ATP fund, this tax would have to be about 21 %.

2.2 Negotiated Pension Schemes

Four negotiated pension schemes cover nearly all employees. These are pension schemes for white collar workers in the private sector ("ITP"), blue collar workers in the private sector ("STP"), central government employees, and local government employees. As a rule, 30 years are required to get a full pension with a proportional reduction for each missing year.

ITP for White Collar Workers in the Private Sector

The old age pension benefit in the ITP is proportional to earnings at the time of retirement. It compensates for 10 % of net incomes (that is earnings net of the pay roll tax) up to 7.5 base amounts, 65 % of net incomes between 7.5 and 20 base amounts and 32,5 % of net incomes between 20 and 30 base amounts. It is a funded system and financed by a negotiated fee in proportion to earnings.

STP for Blue Collar Workers in the Private Sector

The old age pension benefit in STP is determined by the average of the individual's three highest earnings in the period when he is between 55 and 59 years of age. The compensation is 10 % of net incomes up to 7.5 base amounts. Net incomes above 7.5 base amounts are not carrying any pension benefits. STP is a capital-reserve system and financed by a negotiated fee in proportion to earnings.

Pensions for Public Employees

The two negotiated pension schemes in the public sector show only minor differences. Individuals employed by the central government or the local governments get a pension benefit in proportion to the wage at the time of retirement. This pension benefit includes benefits from the national pension schemes and guarantees a compensation in total of 65 % of net incomes up to 20 base amounts and of 32,5 % of net incomes between 20 and 30 base amounts. These schemes are pay-as-you-go systems and financed out of the public budgets.

These rules apply to *old age*. In the case of *disability* the negotiated pension schemes provide benefits of a similar sort. Except for STP, the negotiated schemes also bring benefits to survivors – the widow and under-aged children.

2.3 Personal Pensions

There is as great a variety of personal pensions in Sweden as elsewhere. Premiums up to 1 base amount are deductible from taxable income in the income taxes. Received benefits are taxed as ordinary income.

3. Pensions in the Wage Structure

As we have seen, a large proportion of pension benefits in Sweden are earnings related. This does not mean, however, that accrued pension rights may be viewed as a *normal* part of an individual's remuneration from work. The fact is that most hours worked do not carry any pension rights at all. Hence, most of the time contributions to the pension schemes should be viewed as a pure tax. This also holds true for contributions made to the negotiated schemes.

3.1 The Value of Pension Rights

To simplify the discussion we now disregard other benefits than the old age pension benefit. This benefit has the form of an annuity from a certain age as long as the individual lives. Let the annuity be denoted b.

The value of acquired pension rights obviously depends on how many years the individual expects to receive pension benefits and how these benefits are discounted. If he expects to receive the annuity for k years and his rate of discount is r the present value of expected benefits at the age of retirement will be

$$b \sum_{i=1}^{k} (1+r)^{1-i} \tag{2}$$

For example, when $k = 15$ and $r = 0.02$ this value will be 11.33 b.

However, more discounting is needed. In order to make future benefits comparable to current contributions we must also take into account the time till the individual retires. If the retirement age is z, future benefits must be further discounted by the factor $(1+r)^{j-z}$, where j is the individual's present age.

The annuity will typically consist of two parts, one from the national pension scheme and one from the individual's negotiated pension scheme. We denote these parts b_1 and b_2, respectively. The present value of these annuities at age j may be written in the following way

$$\beta = \beta_{1j} + \beta_{2j}$$

$$= (b_1 + b_2)(1+r)^{j-z} \sum_{i=1}^{k} (1+r)^{1-i} \tag{3}$$

The question is how this value is affected if an individual decides to increase his supply of labor. We shall proceed in two steps. Our first step concerns the individual's decision to participate in the work force. The question is how this decision affects the individual's pension rights. Our second step concerns the individual's decision on working hours in a particular year when he already is participating in the work force. The same question will then be asked.

3.2 Participation

We now look at the decision to participate in the work force. An individual's alternative may be to stay at school, take a long vacation, or to retire early.

For the moment we assume that the individual has an exogenously given earnings status ($\hat{q}$), i.e. that his earnings status does not depend on his decision to participate or not in a particular year. (What we mean by an individual's earnings status has been explained in section 2.)

In this case the individual's pension rights will simply be proportional to the number of years he participates in the work force. However, at most thirty years are counted, and in order to have a particular year counted the individual must have earnings above 1 base amount.

Hence, if the individual already has worked thirty years, he will not aquire any new pension rights by working an extra year. On the other hand, if his working experience is shorter, the value of his pension rights will increase by

$$d\beta_{1j} = \frac{0.60}{30} \hat{q}_1 (1+r)^{j-z} \sum_{i=1}^{k} (1+r)^{1-i} \tag{4a}$$

in the national pension scheme, and by

$$d\beta_{2j} = \frac{x}{30} \hat{q}_2 (1+r)^{j-z} \sum_{i=1}^{k} (1+r)^{1-i} \tag{4b}$$

in the negotiated pension schemes.

In the latter case x will be different for different occupational groups. For public employees and white collar workers in the private sector x will be 5 and 10 %, respectively.[8] For blue collar workers in the private sector the negotiated supplementary pension is set equal to 10 % of an average of the individual's three highest annual earnings in the ages 55 to 59 years. Hence, except for these three years, x will be zero for such a person.

---

[8]   This figure is an approximation in the case of public employees. The correct formula for this category is

$$d\beta_{2j} = [\frac{0.65}{30} \hat{q}_2 - \frac{0.60}{30} \hat{q}_1 - 0.96\,B] (1+r)^{j-z} \sum_{i=1}^{k} (1+r)^{1-i}$$

3.3 Level of Earnings

We now turn to the individual's decision on working hours or other factors influencing his level of earnings in a particular year. This decision will influence his pension benefits to the extent that an increased supply of labor effects his earning status $(\hat{q})$.

It should be pointed out that different occupational groups have their earnings status determined differently depending on how their negotiated scheme is coordinated with the national pension scheme. In our discussion we start with the latter.

An individual's earnings status in the national pension scheme is determined by his earnings during his fifteen best years in terms of earnings, as explained in formula (1). For any year belonging to this category the individual will gain pension benefits by an increased labor supply in the following way

$$d\beta_{1j} = [\frac{0.60t}{30}(1+r)^{j-z} \sum_{i=1}^{k}(1+r)^{1-i}]\frac{\delta \hat{q}}{\delta y_j}dy_j \qquad (5)$$

$$t \leq 30, \ \hat{q} \leq 6.5\,\text{B}, \ 1\,\text{B} \leq y_j \leq 7.5\,\text{B}$$

where $(\delta\hat{q}/\delta y_j)dy_j$ measures the change in the individual's earnings status. We now disregard the effect from participation. For all other years it holds that $\delta\beta_{1j}/\delta y_j = 0$.

Ex post one can always tell if a particular year belongs to the individual's best fifteen years in terms of earnings or not. One can then go back and use the formula (5) to calculate how much pension benefits the individual was able to gain by earning more in this particular year.

However, at the time when the individual makes his decision to work he cannot be sure about the effect on his earnings status. Since he cannot know for sure what his future earnings will look like, he cannot know for sure whether the present year will be one of his best fifteen years in terms of earnings or not. Taking this uncertainty into account, $\delta\beta_{1j}/\delta y_j$ should be treated as a stochastical variable.

As we have stressed above, practically all employees get pension benefits in excess of the benefits acquired in the national pension scheme. Since these extra benefits are determined differently for different categories, we have to treat these categories separately.

For blue collar workers in the private sector negotiated pension rights can only be acquired when the individual is in the ages 55 to 59 years. An individual's earnings status during these years is set equal to

$$\hat{q}_2 = \sum_{i=1}^{3} q_i/3$$

where

$$q_i = y_i(1-\tau). \qquad y_i(1-\tau) \leq 7.5\,\text{B}$$

For a year belonging to the 55 to 59 years category the individual acquires the
following extra pension rights

$$d\beta_{2j}=0.10\,(1+r)^{j-z}\sum_{i=1}^{k}(1+r)^{(1-i)}\frac{\delta\hat{q}_2}{\delta y_j}dy_j \tag{6}$$

These rights are added to the rights determined by (5).

For white collar workers in the private sector, their earnings status in the
negotiated scheme is determined by the "final earnings", i.e. the wage received shortly before retirement. (The meaning of an individual's "final
earnings" is presently being debated and the subject of negotiations.) Let
$(1-t)y_{z-1}$ denote an individual's "final earnings". By increasing these earnings the individual will increase his pension rights by the amount

$$d\beta_{2,z-1}=(1-\tau)\frac{xt}{30}\sum_{i=0}^{k}(1+r)^{-i}dy_{z-1}\qquad\qquad t\le30 \tag{7}$$

where x is equal to

$$\begin{array}{lll}0.10 & \text{for} & (1-\tau)y_{z-1}\le7.5\,B\\[4pt]0.65 & \text{for} & 7.5\,B<(1-\tau)y_{z-1}\le20\,B\\[4pt]0.325 & \text{for} & 20\,B<(1-\tau)y_{z-1}\le30\,B\\[4pt]0 & \text{for} & 30\,B<(1-\tau)y_{z-1}\end{array} \tag{7a}$$

These pension rights are added to the rights determined by (5).

The situation for public employees is different. In most cases they will
not get any net benefits at all from the national pension scheme. Their annuity is determined as

$$b=\max\,(b_1,b_2)$$

where $b_2>b_1$ unless the individual has a decreasing level of earnings (in real
terms) towards the end of his working life. The monthly annuity received
from the negotiated scheme is 65 % of what the individual earns in December the year before retirement, provided that he has worked for thirty years.
Let $(1-\tau)w_{z-1}$ denote this wage. By earning more this particular *month* the
individual will increase his pension rights by the amount

$$d\beta_{2,z-1}=12\,(1-\tau)\frac{0.65\,t}{30}\sum_{i=1}^{k}(1+r)^{-i}dw_{z-1}\qquad\qquad t\le30 \tag{8}$$

What he earns all other months during his entire working life has no direct impact on his pension rights. However, in order to increase his Decem-
ber-wage, the individual might have to get promotions earlier in life. The formula (8) is not used without discreation, however. Only "normal" remunera-
tions are allowed to influence the individual's earning status.

This concludes our presentation of the Swedish pension system in its general terms. From this presentation one can see that there is a loose connection between an individual's earnings and his status in the pension system. While contributions to the system are made on all earnings, extra earnings will only occasionally bring an extra return in the form of pension rights. Hence, except in rare situations, the pension system has a negative effect on marginal net wages.

4. Provisions for an Early Retirement

Early retirement has alwys been a possibility for people who have a personal pension scheme or work in certain occupations. Nowadays, early retirement is offered in the national pension scheme to all Swedish employees and self-employed persons. There are three opportunities for an early retirement in this scheme. An individual can get (a) advanced withdrawals of his old age pension rights, (b) an "unemployment" pension, or (c) a partial (or part-time) pension.

So far these opportunities are restricted to the age group 60 to 64 years. *Table 1* shows how the participation rate has developed for men in this age group. For the whole group the participation rate has decreased from 79.5 percent in 1970 to 65.1 percent in 1985. In the ages 62, 63 and 64, the decrease is about 18 percentage points.

Table 1. Participation rates among men in the age groups 60 to 64 years. Percent

	Year			
Age	1970	1975	1980	1985
60	83.3	82.0	76.3	77.1
61	83.2	77.4	74.0	73.9
62	81.2	77.0	72.9	62.5
63	78.2	67.6	61.6	60.8
64	70.6	65.5	58.3	52.2
Total	79.5	74.0	69.0	65.1

Source: Statistics Sweden (SCB), *Labor force surveys.* Selected years.

Furthermore, there has been a sharp decline in working hours among those who actually participate in the labor force, see *Diagram 1.* The proportion of male workers working full-time has declined from over 70 to below 50 percent.

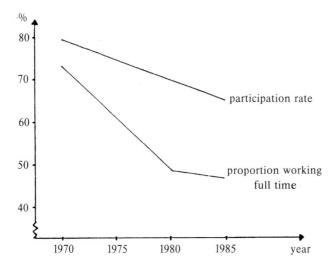

Diagram 1: Participation rates and the proportion working full time. Men aged 60-64 years.
Source: Statistics Sweden (SCB), *Labor force surveys.*

4.1 Advanced Withdrawals of Pension Rights

The first opportunity for an early retirement is to have advanced withdrawals of one's ordinary old age pension. This opportunity was introduced in 1976 and is offered on an actuarial basis. For each month of advanced withdrawal (before the age of 65) the pension benefit will be reduced permanently by 0.5 percentage points. Hence, an individual who chooses to have advanced withdrawals from the age of 60 will have his pension benefit reduced by 30 percent for the rest of his life. However, the individual may choose to have advanced withdrawals of only a part of his pension.[9]

Even negotiated pension benefits are affected in the case of advanced withdrawals.

One is not required to reduce the labor supply in order to get advanced withdrawals. The pension benefit can be added to one's income from employment. Hence, advanced withdrawals are not necessarily used to finance an early retirement. They can also be used to increase private consumption or private savings. In the latter case, one possibility is to buy a personal pension. Private insurance companies offer a very rich supply of pension plans for the purpose of satisfying a great variety of wishes from their clients. Advanced withdrawals allow the individual an easy way to take advantage of this

---

[9] There is also an opportunity to defer withdrawals after the age of 65. In this case the pension benefit will be permanently increased by 0.6 percentage points per month of deferred withdrawal (until the age of 70). An individual who uses this opportunity to its full extent will after the age of 70 receive a pension benefit that is 35 percent higher than the pension he would have received from the age of 65. Very few Swedes use this opportunity.

supply, at the same time as his total pension benefits are kept within a reasonable limit. However, the alternative to buy a personal pension with borrowed money may sometimes be even more advantageous. In this case benefits from the national pension scheme can be used to finance amortization payments in the future.

It turns out that very few Swedes have used the opportunity to have advanced withdrawals of their pension rights, although we can notice a slight increase over time, see *Table 2*.

Table 2. Number of individuals having advanced withdrawals of their pension rights

	1980		1984	
	Men	Women	Men	Women
Total number	6400	5600	9400	8000
Percent	2.8	2.3	3.9	3.1

Source: C-G Sjögren, Statistisk redovisning av utfallet inom systemet med rörlig pensionsålder. *PM 6 to the Pensions committee,* 1985.

4.2 "Unemployment" Pension

The number of people getting a disability pension is much larger. In 1984, no less than 27 percent of all men and women in the age group 60 to 64 years were receiving a disability pension. The proportion was somewhat higher for men than for women, 29.2 percent and 24.4 percent, respectively.[10]

These large numbers do not mean that Swedes have a bad health status. Since 1972, even perfectly healthy individuals are entitled to a disability pension, provided that they (a) are above the age of 60, (b) have some working experience and (c) are unable to find a suitable full-time employment. When suitable part-time jobs are available, the individual will be granted only one-half or two-thirds of the pension benefit.

Under the conditions stated the disability pension merely serves as an extension of the national unemployment insurance scheme. The opportunity of becoming a pensioner is directed towards individuals who otherwise are likely to be caught in a permanent state of unemployment. In those cases we use the term "unemployment" pension.

However, also other individuals may take advantage of this opportunity. In practice, it serves as a means to finance early retirement. An individual who wants to stop working altogether, or to shorten his work week, can make himself eligible for the disability pension. It will suffice that the employer (and the labor union) supports his wish by attesting that he will be laid off at least partially. If the labor market is tight, as has been the case in recent years, the pension benefit will then normally be granted. The individual may have to be on the dole for a while, but that does not mean that he must suffer a loss

---

[10] C.-G. Sjögren, Statistisk redovisning av utfallet inom systemet med rörlig pensionsålder, *PM 6 to the Pensions committee,* 1985.

of income. The wage forgone will in many cases be compensated for by severence payments etc.

As already mentioned, 27 percent of all individuals in the age group 60 to 64 years now receive a disability pension benefit. Bad health is the main reason, but if we look at the category of newly granted pension benefits after the age of 60, claimed unemployment has become an equally important reason to get the pension benefit. This is shown in *Table 3*.

Table 3. Newly granted disability pension benefits to individuals in the age group 60 to 64 years

Year	Due to bad health	Due to unemployment	Percent of total
1975	15644	1414	8.3
1980	14163	3604	20.3
1984	9876	9124	48.0

Source: See Table 2.

4.3 Partial Pension

The third opportunity for an early retirement provided in the Swedish social security system is to apply for a partial (or part-time) pension. This opportunity was introduced in 1976 as a separate pension scheme, financed by a payroll tax. As in the case of advanced withdrawals and the "unemployment" pension the partial pension is restricted to individuals 60 to 64 years of age.

Partial pension benefits are granted under two conditions. *First,* the individual must have a long working experience. He is required to have had earnings above a certain limit for at least ten years after the age of 45. *Secondly,* the individual must reduce his supply of labor by at least 5 hours per week, or in the case of self-employed persons by at least 50 percent. Anyhow, the individual must continue to work at least 17 hours per week. Hence, employees working less than 22 hours and self-employed persons working less than 34 hours are not eligible to a partial pension.

Up to a certain limit the partial pension benefit covers 65 percent of the income lost due to the reduction in working hours. If an individual has to move to a lower paid job the pension benefit is still calculated on his previous wage per hour.[11] The rate of compensation was lowered to 50 percent in 1981, but was again raised to 65 percent in 1987.

At the outset, the partial pension was offered only to employees. Self-employed persons were included in this pension scheme in 1981. The number of individuals receiving a partial pension benefit reached a maximum of 68000 in 1980. Since then the number has decreased to 41000, but is now expected to rise again, see *Table 4*.

---

[11] To be more precise, the individual's "actual" income from work is set equal to an average of his three highest incomes during the last five years. This average is inflation-proof. If the individual has been promoted to a better paid job in the period, his "actual" income will be raised proportionally.

Table 4. Number of persons receiving a partial pension benefit 1976 – 1985

Year	Men	Percent of individuals employed	Women	Percent of individuals employed
1976	10200	6.1	4400	2.1
1980	46800	30.1	21000	21.5
1985	24100	16.7	16800	15.6

Source: C-G Sjögren, Statistik rörande delpensioneringen, *PM 20 to the Pensions committee,* 1985.

The partial pension scheme obviously implies a subsidy to individuals who want an early retirement. But when this scheme was introduced the intention was not to bring about a reduction in the supply of labor. Instead, this scheme was thought of as a measure to prevent unemployment among elderly workers. It was believed that there are many elderly workers who have difficulties to meet the demands put on them in a full-time job, and who are too poor to reduce working hours at their own expense. For this category the partial pension scheme offers an alternative to an "unemployment" pension. They get an opportunity to remain in their usual occupation and to work in accordance with their ability. Moreover, it was felt that some elderly workers may need a period of part-time work in order to get used to their future life as a pensioner.

In practice, the partial scheme turned out somewhat differently. As can be seen in Table 5, this scheme has not exclusively or foremost been used by low paid workers in physically demanding jobs. The group taking most advantage of this pension scheme is female employees in insurance companies. In this category, every second person above the age of 60 are receiving a partial pension benefit.

Table 5. The proportion of individuals getting a partial pension benefit in various occupations

Occupation	Men		Women	
	1980	1984	1980	1984
White collar				
– academics	8.6	13.1	19.8	26.5
– civil servants	12.6	21.3	16.9	34.9
– private industry	26.8	25.4	26.7	28.0
– commerce	18.8	17.9	17.2	17.7
– banks	n.a.	n.a.	25.0	17.8
– insurance companies	n.a.	n.a.	17.4	51.6
Blue collar				
– foremen	18.9	18.8	n.a.	n.a.
– iron, metal industry	33.5	20.9	27.1	17.3
– building industry	11.2	18.6	n.a.	n.a.
– forrest industry	27.3	27.9	n.a.	n.a.
– engineering	21.3	23.0	15.2	21.9
– public sector	4.2	4.1	6.5	10.6

Source: See Table 2.

In the table a sample of labor unions with the highest degree of partial pensions is shown. In spite of the over all decrease in the number of partial pensioners, as shown in Table 4, applications from white collar employees continued to increase, while blue collar workers have reduced their applications. The reason might have been that the "unemployment" pension became comparatively more favorable when the compensation ratio in the partial pension scheme was lowered in 1981. Since white collar workers are less likely to get an "unemployment" pension benefit, they continued to demand the partial pension benefit.

It should be pointed out that Swedish employers have a rather favourable view on part-time work and that they have actively supported the partial pension scheme. One reason is that they have learned to get out more work per hour by part-time workers. Another reason is that Sweden has a law against dismissals; in principle, an employee cannot be dismissed as long as the employer can afford to keep him. Part-time work under the partial pension scheme may serve as a substitute to a dismissal.

4.4 Compensation Ratios

To choose between these provisions for an early retirement should not prove too difficult. Provided that an individual really wants to reduce his supply of labor, advanced withdrawals should be out of the question. In this case he would have to bear the income loss all by himself. On the other hand, if he makes use of the partial pension or is granted an "unemployment" pension benefit the income loss will to a large extent be covered by public means. His private cost will in these cases be much smaller.

The following example is illustrative. Suppose that a male worker has earned an average income all his life and that he at the age of 60 decides to reduce his supply of labor by 50 percent. His share of the income loss will in this case be:

	Before tax	After tax
Partial pension	35 %	14 %
Disability pension	32 %	12 %

In the case of a partial pension 65 percent of his income loss will be covered by the pension benefit. Taking the income tax into account no less than 86 percent will be covered by public means. In the case of a disability pension the proportion covered by the public is even larger. The disability pension benefit covers 68 percent (respectively 88 percent) of the income loss.[12] Hence, the opportunity to retire early should be hard to resists.

---

[12] The average amount of "pension points" in the Swedish national supplementary pension scheme for men at the age of 60 is 3.55. A person with this number of points gets a supplementary pension benefit equal to $0.60 \cdot 3.55 \cdot B$. In addition he gets the basic pension benefit which is $0.96 \cdot B$. Hence, his total pension benefit will be 3.09 B. If he is granted a half pension benefit this will be 1.545 B. In 1986, this amounted to 36000 SEK. At the same time, the individual in our example earns 4.55 B or 106.000 SEK when working full-time. Due to payroll taxes the employer has to pay 1.36 times more.

These figures refer to male workers of an average income. The compensation ratios differ for different categories of income, as shown in *Diagram 2.*

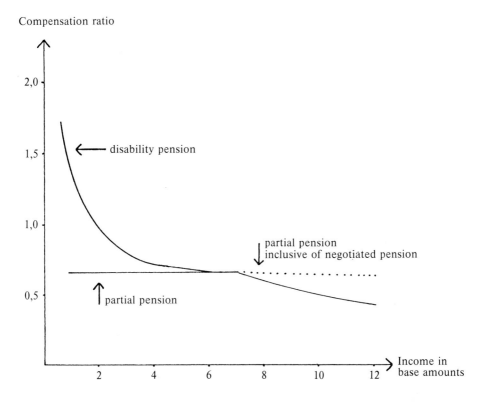

Compensation ratio

Diagram 2. How the compensation ratio varies with an individual's income. The individual is assumed to have a flat earnings profile.

For individuals at the lower end of the income scale it is universally true that the "unemployment" pension gives a higher compensation than the partial pension. For individuals at the higher end, however, the partial pension scheme may for some categories be more favorable. All public employees and white collar workers in the private sector will automatically get an extra compensation from their negotiated pension schemes in the case of a partial pension, but not in the case of an "unemployment" pension with one exception; white collar workers in the private sector get this extra benefit also in the case of an "unemployment" pension. This extra compensation is granted only for individuals above an income of 7.5 base amounts (= 174750 SEK in

1986). The reason is that the national pension scheme does not apply to incomes exceeding 7.5 base amounts.[13)

In these calculations we have not included any effect on the individual's old age pension. This is of no importance in the case of public employees. For this category there may be a reduction in the old age pension benefit from the national pension scheme, but any such reduction would automatically be compensated for by an increased pension benefit from the negotiated pension scheme. For example, in the case of an individual employed by the central government, the pension benefit is always determined by his level of earnings in December the year before he retires permanently. It does not matter if he works part-time and has a partial or "unemployment" pension benefit. His old age pension benefit will nevertheless be determined *as if* he had worked full-time.[14)

Blue collar workers have a different situation. For this category the negotiated supplementary pension benefit (STP) is a fixed amount determined by the level of earnings during the period when the individual is 55 to 59 years of age. Reductions in the pension benefit from the national pension scheme will therefore not be automatically compensated for. For these workers the private cost for an early retirement may be slightly higher than is shown in Diagram 2.

These observations seem to imply that most individuals should prefer the "unemployment" pension to the partial pension. However, we must keep in mind that some individuals are unlikely to become unemployed and therefore have a small chance of being granted a "unemployment" pension benefit, for example public employees, and that most people will have to go through some trouble before they are granted this benefit. The disability pension benefit is not granted without cause; it takes some time to make sure that an individual is genuinely unemployed; there may be income losses during the decision period. Some people may therefore prefer a partial pension benefit.

[13) The benefits from the negotiated pension schemes in the case of a partial pension and a disability pension granted on non-medical grounds are:

	Partial pension	*Disability pension*
White collar workers in the private sector	Nothing up to 7.5 B. 50% between 7.5 and 20 B, 25% between 20 and 30 B.	Public pension + negotiated pension 80% of income up to 7,5 B, 65% between 7,5 and 20 B, 32,5% between 20 and 30 B.
Public employees both central and local	See above	0
Blue collar workers in the private sector	0	0

B is the base amount.

[14) Advanced withdrawals are different also in this respect. An individual who chooses to have advanced withdrawals of his national pension benefits must accept that even the negotiated pension benefit will be permanently reduced.

In fact, quite a few individuals in higher income brackets (above 5 base amounts) are making use of the partial pension scheme. In 1982, no less than 40 percent of all newly granted partial pension benefits went to this category. There were even many who got extra benefits from their negotiated pension scheme. These extra benefits are restricted to individuals who earn more than 7.5 base amounts at the outset, i.e. before the reduction in working hours.

5. Discussion

In this final section we give some figures on the cost to society brought about by the Swedish way of promoting an early retirement. In addition, we raise the issue whether early retirement should be subsidized at all.

5.1 The Cost to Society

In 1986, public expenditures in the national pension scheme amounted to 100.2 billion SEK. This corresponds to 10.4 percent of GNP. However, only a small part of these expenditures were directed towards individuals in the age group 60 to 64 years. The expenditures on partial and disability pension benefits related to early retirements were about 1.3 billion SEK. A payroll tax of 0.28 percent would suffice to finance these expenditures.

This is not meant to say that the public budget was loaded with 1.3 billion SEK on account of early retirements. *First,* pension benefits are to some extent subsitutes to unemployment compensations. *Secondly,* the public budget also suffers losses of revenue due to early retirements. For example, a male worker of average income reducing his labor supply by 50 percent at the age of 60 will get a pension benefit of 35500 SEK and at the same time have his income tax reduced by 27700 SEK. For individuals in higher income brackets the government "pays" more in the form of tax reductions than in the form of pension benefits.

The public budget effect does not in itself signify a cost to society. Tax payments and pension benefits are nothing but transfers of income. Whether there is a cost to society or not depends on how people react to these transfers. How are savings and investments affected? What happens to the supply of labor and the functioning of the labor market? Will the distribution of consumer goods be disturbed? These are the factors determining the real cost to society, sometimes called be *excess burden* of transferring income through the public budget.

Various transfers differ in their excess burden. It is crucial not only what the transfer looks like and how it is financed, but also under what circumstances it takes place. For a particular transfer, the cost to society may be quite different depending on the general level of taxation, whether the business cycle is near its peak or bottom, etc.

In this paper we cannot go deep into these matters. We cannot do more than to give a few comments. *First,* since Sweden has reached a high level of taxation all transfers of income are costly from an economic point of view. There are studies indicating that the marginal cost of raising public funds in certain cases has passed 100 percent. The social cost to transfer 1 SEK has been estimated to be 3.00 SEK when it is financed by a proportional income tax, 2.30 SEK when it is financed by a payroll tax, and 1.50 SEK when it is financed by a tax which is proportional to the disposable income.[15] Hence, the excess burden in these cases is 200, 130 and 50 percent, respectively. The second of these numbers is most relevant in this context. Pension benefits are mainly financed by payroll taxes earmarked for this purpose.

Secondly, these estimates refer to a situation where the transfer has the form of a lump-sum. Pension benefits are certainly not of this kind. They give people an incentive to reduce the supply of labor (and perhaps to save less) and will therefore have an excess burden by themselves. The incentive to reduce working hours is very strong. As we have seen, there is a dramatic decline in the effective wage rate when a person reaches the age of 60 and becomes eligible to a pension benefit. For an employee working more than 22 hours per week the effective marginal wage rate drops by at least 70 percent. Including pension benefits forgone, the marginal tax on earnings from an extra hour of work increases to well over 85 percent.[16] This large tax wedge in the wage structure is bound to have a substantial impact on the supply of labor. We have seen the effect: a decreasing participation rate combined with shorter working hours. These changes involve an excess burden since highly valued work efforts are substituted for leisure of much lower value. The ratio between these values is about 7.8:1 at the margin.

In order to evaluate the excess burden one must bear in mind that there may be other factors than the tax wedge caused by pension benefits behind the decline in the supply of labor from the elderly. Furthermore, one has to take into account that this decline may induce younger workers to work more. Although we do not think so, for example there may be a balancing decrease in the rate of unemployment.

Finally and not least important, as far as these provisions for an early retirement actually have a negative effect on the supply of labor and earnings there will be a corresponding decrease in the tax base. This decrease may force the government to increase tax rates and thereby enlarge tax wedges all around the economy. As a consequence there would be a general increase in

---

[15] K. Andersson et. al.. *Finansteoretiska undersökningar, Lundaforskare under ledning av I. Hansson, I. Ståhl och L. Söderström om frågeställningar och forskningsbehov inom finansvetenskapen,* Riksbankens jubileumsfond 1986:2, Helsingborg 1986.

[16] Cf. note 12. The employer pays 1.36 x 106000: 1600 = 90.10 SEK per hour. The net income (after income tax) for an employee working full-time would be 66450 SEK or 41.53 SEK per hour. If the employee instead works half-time his net income will be 57200 SEK or 71.50 SEK per hour. Hence, by increasing his labor from 800 to 1600 hours his net income would increase by 9250 SEK or 11.56 SEK per hour. In comparison to what the employer has to pay the employee would keep only 12.8 percent.

the excess burden for tax financed public expenditures. At some point the economy would then run into a vicious circle where the tax base shrinks faster than rates are raised.

We do not think that Sweden actually has been caught in this vicious circle. We just want to point out that the Swedish mode of promoting early retirements has been a clear step in this direction. The cost to society is not only an increasing excess burden in the financing of present public expenditures. There will also be less scope for other expensive and perhaps more urgent policies in the future.

5.2 Towards a Neutral System

Our previous discussion has emphasized the excess burden inherent in many public transfer systems. This burden arises because private costs (or benefits) differ from the corresponding social cost (or benefit), for example in the supply of labor. In order to avoid the excess burden one should try to organize public transfers according to the *benefit principle,* meaning that each individual has to pay for his own benefits. Such a public transfer system may be called neutral; it does not cause any tax wedges (our subsidy wedges) in the structure of prices.

From this point of view the Swedish system of advanced (and deferred) withdrawals of pension rights seems ideal. Individuals are offered an opportunity to retire on an almost actuarial basis. The present value of acquired pension benefits from the old age pension schemes is not affected. Hence, it looks like a situation where private costs and social costs coincide.

This is not the whole story, however. There is one prerequisite missing. Actuarially fair advanced withdrawals do not guarantee neutrality with respect to early retirement unless the pension system in itself has this property. An individual's decision to retire early will otherwise give rise to financial external effects in the pension system as a whole. These effects may be positive as well as negative. In the former case neutrality requires that there is a subsidy linked to advanced withdrawals or in other words that such withdrawals may be made on better terms than in the case of actuarial fairness. In the latter case on the other hand, neutrality requires that there is a tax linked to advanced withdrawals.

Which should it be, a subsidy or a tax? In our presentation of the Swedish pension system it can be seen that individuals rarely acquire more pension rights than they pay for. This is particularly true for individuals above the age of 60. In most cases they have already participated in the work force for at least thirty years, and they are unlikely to get a sharp increase in their earnings status. At the same time they have to make full contributions to the system, payments being about 20 % of gross earning. Hence, it seems that a tax should be more appropriate than a subsidy in most cases.

Public employees are in the best position to acquire large pension rights by working after they have reached the age of 60. They get pension benefits according to the rules used in the negotiated scheme, which means that an individual in this group has his earnings status determined by his "final earnings" and not by the 15-years rule in the national scheme. Provided that his earnings increase (in real terms) and that he has not worked thirty years, he may acquire pension rights of the order of 40% of his gross earnings by working an extra year. This is certainly more than he has to contribute.

However, that public employees might be heavily subsidized when they continue to work, does not mean that they should be subsidized when they use the opportunity to have advanced withdrawals of pension rights. The crux of the matter is that public employees will be subsidized in the old age pension scheme even if they retire, provided that they do not retire entirely. As was stressed in our presentation of the Swedish system, a public employee's "final earnings" is not his actual earnings during his final year of duty but rather his *potential earnings,* given his wage rate in December the year before retirement. So, whether he actually works full-time or not has no direct effect on his pension rights. The only difference is that his contribution will be larger or smaller since payments nevertheless are made in proportion to *actual earnings.*

For private employees the situation is somewhat different. Since they get most of their pension benefits from the national pension scheme they must experience an extremely sharp increase in their earnings status in order to get subsidized pension rights during the ages 60 to 64 years. In 99 percent of all cases they will contribute more than they get out of the pension system (at the margin). Therefore, neutrality requires that they are taxed also when they do not work.

Our discussion thus indicates that the Swedish system of advanced (and deferred) withdrawals of old pension rights is less than ideal when these withdrawals are seen as a means to finance an early retirement. From the point of view of neutrality individuals are in most cases given this opportunity on too good terms.

A fortiori, the same holds true for the opportunity to finance an early retirement with a partial pension or an "unemployment" pension. The departure from neutrality is in these cases even larger. While at least privately employed individuals in most cases are taxed by the pension system when they decide to work, they are actually given money when they decide not to work. For public employees there will be a dubble subsidy when they decide not to work (full-time).

A policy like this seems hard to justify, in particular since the Swedish pension system anyhow has to be adjusted to an increasing dependency ratio, and possibly also an increasing replacement ratio. A more reasonable reaction to the financial strains one can expect in the future would be to encourage people to work rather than to retire early. But a switch to a neutral system would also be reasonable.

Let us conclude this paper by pointing out some steps one can take in order to make the Swedish pension system more neutral with respect to early retirements:

— Make pension benefits more earnings-related. Increases in the basic pension should be avoided.
— Have pension benefits determined by actual earnings rather than potential earnings. This is particularly important in the case of public employees.
— Abolish the partial pension scheme and be selective when people are granted an "unemployment" pension. When pension benefits are based on actual earnings and given a level in accordance with contributions, advanced (and deferred) withdrawals of pension rights may be made on actuarially fair terms.

These steps are justified as means to bring down the excess burden caused by the pension system. It should be pointed out that they also may be justified as means to achieve a more equitable system. The present system favors individuals who work relatively few years with high earnings and expect to live relatively long. This is not the situation we expect to be typical for a blue collar worker.

The Process of Retirement in Denmark: Trends, Public Discussion and Institutional Framework

J. H. Petersen

Contents

1. Setting the Stage

Acting in conformity with an implicit contract between the generations – as does a pay-as-you-go financed pension arrangement – depends on the credibility and the long-run political viability of the scheme in question. Thus, the implied taxation must be politically feasible. Future scheduled taxes should be within the limits of practical acceptability to the social security tax-paying population. Because the social security system is basically an unfunded pension programme its financial integrity would be endangered unless it commands strong taxpayer support. Excessively high social security taxes – levied in one form or another – could conceivably jeopardize the whole system. The social security system, must be constructed in such a way that it can function with whatever age-structure of the population which may emerge or can seriously be expected to emerge, and also so that it retains its capacity to function over the longer run. New legislative regulations have to be considered from this perspective.

The tax-rate needed to assure equilibrium is determined by the fundamental pay-as-you-go identity, i.e.

$$\tau_t Y_t L_t = \pi_i P_t$$

W. Schmähl (Ed.)
Redefining the Process of Retirement
© Springer-Verlag Berlin Heidelberg 1989

in which τ is the pension tax-rate, Y the average level of earnings, L the number of workers, π the average level of pension benefits and P the number of pensioners all related to period t.
   Rewriting the identity

$$\tau_t = (\pi_t/Y_t)\ (P_t/L_t)$$

the tax rate is seen to depend on the politically determined *replacement ratio* and the *dependency ratio* partly governed by the demographic development and partly by political decisions.

   Interpreting $(\pi_t\ P_t)$ as the total expenditures on all pensions and $(Y_t\ L_t)$ as the gross factor income, τ_t is estimated to app. 9.6 per cent in 1985. With the number of pensioners in receipt of all types of pensions (and therefore not comparable to the figures presented in tables 1 and 2) relative to the working population equal to app. 36 per cent, the replacement ratio equals app. 27 per cent. (The replacement ratio is not to be confused with the *compensation ratio* defined as the pension net of taxation relative to the previous income net of taxation). Compared to the sum of wages the pension expenditures amount to app. 15 per cent.

   Obviously, the future development is dependent on demographic processes and political decisions related to the pension age, the length of the average educational period, the replacement ratio etc. Let us first consider the expected demographic development in isolation.

2. Demographic Trends

Neglecting the institutional characteristics of the Danish pension system diagram 1 illustrates the development of the number of individuals above the age of 65 relative to the number of individuals in the age group 20 to 64. In the early 1950s there were app. 15 per cent of the adult population above the age of 65, gradually rising to app. 25 per cent in the early 1980s. If the birth rate increases from its present level (1.5 child per woman) to reach 1.7 in 1995 the Diagram shows a declining ratio during the years 1990 to 2003, followed by a rise resulting in an old-age dependency ratio of app. 35 per cent in 2025 (36 if the birth rate is assumed constant at 1.5 during the period).

   Even if the long-term assumptions concerning the future birth rate as well as the development of migration are subject to uncertainty, the number of individuals above 65 will rise both in absolute and in relative terms over the next 38 years. As seen from Table 1 the total dependency ratio exhibits a U-form over the period 1985 to 2025 caused by a continuous decline of the youth dependency ratio and a U-formed development of the old-age dependency ratio. Approximately, the total dependency ratio in 2025 is equal to the 1985 ratio, but the structure is completely different. In 1985 the youth dependency ratio contributes 63 per cent to the total, while in 2025 the contribution has been reduced to app. 50 per cent.

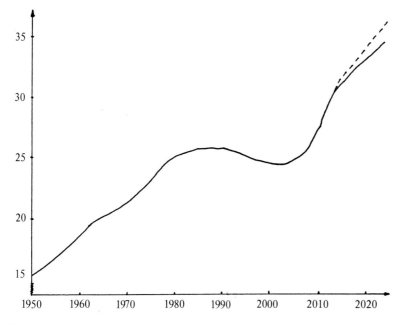

Diagram 1

Note:

The number of individuals above the age of 65 relative to the number of individuals in the age-group 20 to 64, 1950-2025. Actual data for the years 1950-1987. Forecasts for the period 1987 to 2025 made on the assumption that the birth rate will increase from the present 1.5 (alternative 1) or stay at its present level (alternative 2). Calculations are made on the basis of Danmark's Statistiks recent population forecast 1987 to 2025.

Since the per capita public expenditures on children and youth are low compared to the per capita public expenditures on pensioners and since it is political difficult to transfer resources from a shrinking to an expanding sector the demographic change will be a force working against the frictionless functioning of the pension system.

New institutional regulations have to be considered from this perspective. Even today measures have been implemented intensifying the problems suggested by the data of Table 1. This is seen from the development of age-specific participation rates.

Table 1. Number of persons (in thousands)   YDR   ODR   TDR

Year	< 20	20-64	65+	1:2	3:2	(1+3):2
	1	2	3			
1950	1406	2465	381	57.0	15.5	72.5
1960	1532	2554	480	60.0	18.8	78.8
1965	1546	2685	537	57.6	20.0	77.6
1970	1522	2787	598	54.6	21.5	76.1
1975	1516	2868	671	52.9	23.4	76.3
1980	1472	2915	735	50.5	25.2	75.7
1985	1349	2996	766	45.0	25.6	70.6
1990	1242	3094	797	40.1	25.8	65.9
1995	1191	3169	795	37.6	25.1	62.7
2000	1179	3193	782	36.9	24.5	61.4
2005	1195	3142	782	38.0	24.9	62.9
2010	1163	3051	830	38.1	27.2	65.3
2015	1088	2944	914	37.0	31.0	68.0
2020	1020	2876	950	35.5	33.0	68.5
2025	984	2785	971	35.3	34.9	70.2

Note: 1950-85: Actual data. From 1990 onward: forecast for the period 1987 to 2025 made on the assumption that the birth rate will increase from the present 1.5 to 1.7 as from 1995. Calculations are made on the basis of Danmark's Statistiks recent population forecast 1987 to 2025.

3. Trends Concerning Participation Rates

Prior to 1979 the employment surveys provide data on participation rates for selected age-groups. Diagram 2 illustrates the development for the older age-groups during the six years previous to 1979.

The general pattern over the last decades has been marked by a stable development for men and rising participation rates for women in all age-groups. The remarkable observation from Diagram 2 is the decline in participation rates for the age groups 60-64 and 65-69 from 1978 to 1979. Obviously, such a decline marking a significant change of the transition from employment to retirement must be explained in terms of an institutional change: the introduction of the voluntary, early retirement pay, cf. below.

After 1979 the labor force surveys provide data on age-specific participation rates. Even though data are available only for the years 1979 to 1984 an introductory cohort analysis is possible. The data at hand are illustrated for men in Diagram 3. The pattern is obvious: The younger the cohort, the earlier and the larger the decline in participation rates. The picture for women is a bit more complex, because it reflects a mix of two trends. The cohorts pass the age of 60 with participation rates rising from one cohort to the next, implying that the decline of the participation rates occur from a continuously higher level.

Another way of demonstrating the same phenomenon is to observe a cross-section picture of participation rates as related to age in 1984 and in 1979. This is shown by Diagram 4. For both sexes one observes a gradual decline from the age of 60. The figures for women show the 1984 data above the 1979 data for ages below 60 and below for ages above 60 reflecting the two trends at work.

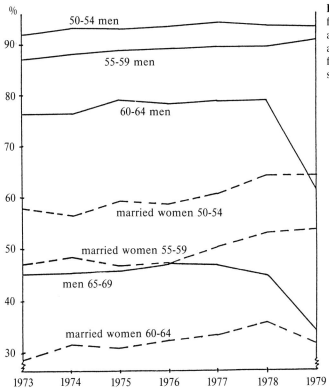

Diagram 2. Participation rates for men and women in the age groups 50-54, 55-59, 60-64 and 65-69, 1973-1979. Data from the employment surveys.

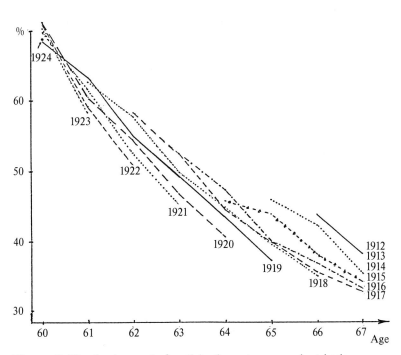

Diagram 3. The development of participation rates on a cohort basis.

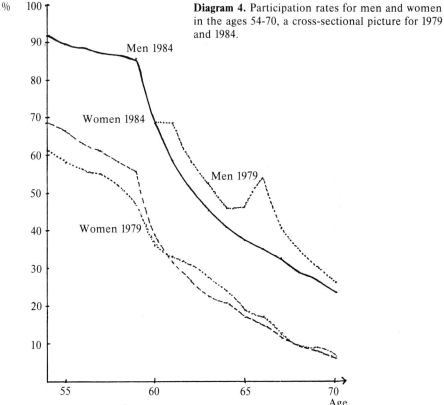

Diagram 4. Participation rates for men and women in the ages 54-70, a cross-sectional picture for 1979 and 1984.

Finally, Diagram 5 illustrates the relative share of men and women at different ages receiving pensions. Due to the possibilities for early retirement provided by a scheme outside of the pension system in the narrow sense the share of the population receiving a social pension reflects an incomplete picture. For the age group 60-66, therefore, two set of curves are presented. The dashed curves illustrate the share receiving pensions in the traditional sense, while the full drawn curves add the share in receipt of a voluntary early retirement pay. Obviously, the existence of the early retirement pay has a remarkable impact.

However it may be, a trend towards declining participation rates for individuals above 60 has marked the development since 1979. In 1986 54.7 per cent in the age-group 60 to 66 collected either a pension or an early retirement pay. On the average this corresponds to a de facto reduction of the statutory old-age pension age from 67 to 63. For an increasing number the retirement age now lies far below the once general retirement age of 67. Thus, a trend towards a reduced pension age has been developing over the last eight years.

Consequently, it seems reasonable to illuminate the development of dependency ratios on the assumption that the pension age will develop towards

60. The results are reported by Table 2. Compared to Table 1 the old- age dependency ratio has increased from 34.9 to 53.2 per cent, and the total dependency ratio from 70.2 to 93.3 per cent. With an unchanged replacement ratio this amounts to an increase of the social security tax-rate by app. 53 per cent.

Assuming the number of pensioners below the age of 60 relative to the population in the age-group 20-60 to be the same in 2025 as in 1985 (4.5 per cent) the pensioner ratio will be 60.4 per cent, i.e. an increase of app. 68 per cent compared to 1985.

In addition to this one has to be aware of a possible increase of the compensation ratio. The Danish pensions are not earnings related. Consequently, app. 50 per cent of the population has established private pension schemes of their own. If nothing else happens we will gradually develop a divided generation of pensioners with 50 per cent relying only on the public pension system, while the other 50 per cent will collect private, supplementary pensions. Obviously, such a development will imply a heavy political pressure for increases of the replacement ratio.

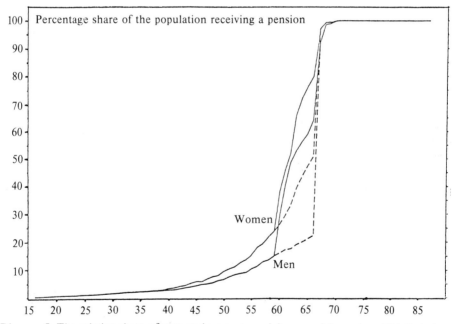

Diagram 5. The relative share of men and women receiving a social pension. Distributed according to age.
Source: Statistiske Efterretninger

Table 2. Number of persons (in thousands)

Year	< 20	20-59	60+	YDR	ODR	TDR
	1	2	3	1:2	3:2	(1+3):2
1990	1242	2848	1043	43.7	36.7	80.4
1995	1191	2931	1033	40.6	35.2	75.8
2000	1179	2939	1036	40.1	35.3	75.4
2005	1195	2835	1089	42.2	38.4	80.6
2010	1163	2698	1183	43.1	43.9	87.0
2015	1088	2630	1228	41.4	46.7	88.1
2020	1021	2563	1262	39.8	49.2	89.0
2025	984	2452	1304	40.1	53.2	93.3

4. Criteria of Eligibility in Danish Pension Policy

Denmark introduced old-age pensions in 1891, disability pensioning in 1921 and widow's pensioning in 1959. The main criterion of eligibility for old-age pensions has been age. Since 1946 a lower age has been stipulated for single women. In addition to that it has been possible to grant a pension in case of failing health or other exceptional circumstances. In 1977 a supplementary criterion was enacted: in case of particular social or labour market related circumstances a pension might be granted to individuals in the age-group 55 to 59. Eligibility for disability pensions has been conditioned by reduction of economic capacity irrespective of age, while widow's pensions has had certain age limitations as a supplementary condition. Single women above 50 were covered by the Act on widow's pensions too in case of failing health or other exceptional circumstances.

As from 1984 the distinctions between old-age, disability and widow's pensions have been abolished. They were replaced by a single act on social pensions including five forms of pensioning, cf. Diagram 6.

It is seen that an early retirement compared to the statutory age of 67 for old-age pensions is conditioned by a reduction of economic capacity, by failing health or by other social circumstances.

5. On the Concept of a Flexible Pension Age

One has always made use of a statutory fixed pension age in the old-age scheme. Conceptually an increased flexibility might be assured 1) by liberalizing the eligibility conditions of the pre-retirement pension schemes or 2) by giving the individual the option to decide his own retirement-age within limits. Alternative 1) assumes an evaluation of the health or social circumstances of the applicant, which is unnecessary in alternative 2). Obviously, it is the second option one has in mind in discussing a flexible pension age.

Thus, a flexible pension age is an arrangement based on a statutory fixed pension age, but with individual options to choose an earlier retirement age and consequently a lower life-long benefit or to defer the retirement in return for a higher life-long pension benefit. In the former case a smaller benefit is paid for a larger life-span, in the latter case a higher benefit is paid for a shorter life-span. If the pension is not reduced in case of earlier retirement flexibility actually means a general reduction of the pension age, and if the pension is not increased in case of a deferred pension no one will choose that option.

If the basis for calculating the benefit is the basic allowance, if the deductions and additions are calculated in an actuarial way, if the statutory age of eligibility is 67, and if we limit the age range to 60 to 70, we get the results reported by Table 3.

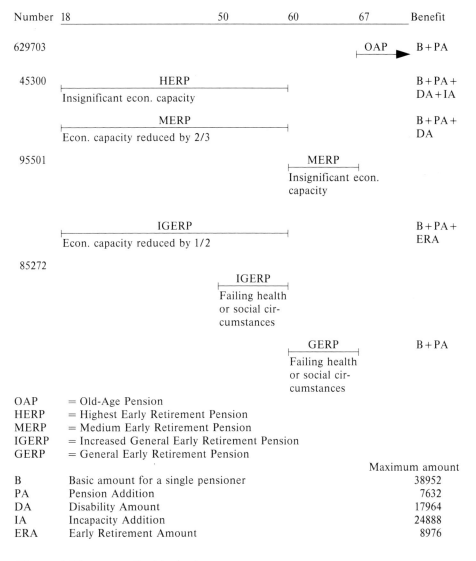

Number	18	50	60	67	Benefit
629703				OAP →	B + PA
45300	HERP Insignificant econ. capacity				B + PA + DA + IA
	MERP Econ. capacity reduced by 2/3				B + PA + DA
95501			MERP Insignificant econ. capacity		
	IGERP Econ. capacity reduced by 1/2				B + PA + ERA
85272			IGERP Failing health or social cir- cumstances		
			GERP Failing health or social cir- cumstances		B + PA

OAP   = Old-Age Pension
HERP   = Highest Early Retirement Pension
MERP   = Medium Early Retirement Pension
IGERP = Increased General Early Retirement Pension
GERP   = General Early Retirement Pension

		Maximum amount
B	Basic amount for a single pensioner	38952
PA	Pension Addition	7632
DA	Disability Amount	17964
IA	Incapacity Addition	24888
ERA	Early Retirement Amount	8976

Diagram 6. The present Danish pension system.

Table 3. Actuarial reduction and additional factors expressed a a per centage of the basic allowance

Age	Interest = 10 %	Interest = 14 %	The old-age pension act of 1975
70	129	135	130
69	118	122	120
68	109	110	110
67	100	100	100
66	92	91	–
65	85	83	–
64	79	75	–
63	72	68	–
62	67	62	–
61	62	56	–
60	57	50	–

As seen from the table the Danish old-age pension act of 1975 stipulated a set of additional factors in case of a deferred pension, while an earlier retirement was not possible. The additional factors were by and large actuarially fair, i.e. they worked in a neutral way. These so-called "waiting-additions" in case of a deferred pension were introduced in 1922. Related to changes of the statutory age limit the system of "waiting additions" has frequently been changed.

By the pension reform of 1984 the compensatory payments in case of a deferred pension were abolished. At the same time the flat rate basic allowances were replaced by a system according to which the basic amount is scaled down with rising incomes, but only in case of incomes originating from gainful employment. The objective was to stimulate the elderly to retire early from the labour market. Thus the objective was the same as the objective guiding the introduction of the early voluntary retirement pay implemented in 1979.

6. The Voluntary Early Retirement Pay Scheme

The voluntary early retirement pay was introduced from january the 1st 1979. The scheme is reserved for members of the unemployment funds. Consequently, it was made into law as a supplement to the Act on Labour Exchange and Unemployment Insurance.

Any member in the age-group 60 to 67 retiring from employment or from unemployment may apply for the benefit. The applicant is entitled, if 1) he has passed the age of 60, 2) he has been member of an unemployment fund for at least 10 years during the 15 years previous to the application, 3) he is qualified for unemployment daily allowances at the time of his application and 4) he has permanent residence in Denmark.

The benefit is terminated when the recipient attains the statutory age for old-age pensions. If he resumes work to a greater extent than allowed during the period in which he receives early retirement pay, cf. below, his later read-mission to the scheme is ruled out. Thus, the early retirement pay is an "once-only offer".

The recipient is not allowed to engage in gainful work for the first five weeks subsequent to being granted the benefit. During the period in which he is in receipt of an early retirement pay his gainful work, paid or unpaid, is limited to a maximum of 200 hours per year.

Having been full time insured for at least five years during the ten years previous to his application, including the 26 weeks immediately before, the benefit level is set equal to his daily allowances. From the time when his entitlement to daily allowances would have been terminated, in principle 2 1/2 year, the benefit is reduced to 80 per cent of the maximum daily allowances originally for the next two years. Subsequently, it was reduced to a maximum of 60 per cent. Later this maximum was raised to 70 per cent. By an amendment as from 1986, however, the reduction to 70 per cent has been repealed. The original three level scale has been replaced by two levels.

The scheme is administered by the unemployment funds. The recipients remain members of the fund and pay contributions at the same level as do unemployed on collecting daily allowances.

The recent and the current debate on employment of older workers, the retirement options and the transition from gainful employment to retirement is strongly influenced by the conditions of the labour market in the late 1970s and the 80s. Consequently, the most important objective of the voluntary early retirement pay is to give the elderly an incentive to early retirement for the purpose of providing additional job opportunities for the younger, i.e. a macro-motive. The scheme intends to guarantee that the retired person has had an attachment to the labour market and that he definitively retires from gainful employment, cf. the criteria of eligibility, the limiting condition of 200 working hours per year and the "once-only offer". The implication is an abrupt retirement similar to the one implied by the statutory age for old-age pensions.

The voluntary early retirement pay was designed not only to make an early retirement possible, but to deter part-time working.

Table 4 reports the benefit levels gross and net on the assumption that the previous income was 155.000 D.kr. app. corresponding to the wage of an unskilled worker. Benefits are stipulated as of april the 1st 1987.

Table 4. Benefit levels in the voluntary early retirement pay scheme compared to the previous income and the level of old-age pensions

Kr. per year	Full time work before the age of 60	Early retirement pay, first 2 1/2 year	Early retirement pay, after 2 1/2 year	Old-age pension
Gross	155000	107046	85637	46224
Net	85380	64293	53959	46224
Net compensation rate	–	75.3	63.2	54.1

The new act led to an immediate spurt in the number of persons receiving
early retirement pay with app. 48000 recipients in 1979 and more than the
double in 1986. The remarkable quantitative success is seen from Table 5.

Table 5. Recipients and the number of unemployment insured in the age-group 60 to 66

Year	Number of recipients	Number of insured	Ratio
1979	48064	97321	49
1980	53241	110649	48
1981	63253	133549	47
1982	78068	–	51
1983	81635	150958	54
1984	90841	156807	58
1985	96895	163999	59
1986	100600	166378	60

Source: Arbejdsdirektoratets Pressemeddelelser

By the introduction of the voluntary early retirement pay the age of eligibility for a public pension has in fact been reduced to the age of 60. In 10-15
years only a few groups will be excluded from the scheme and from that time
the qualifying age has definitively been reduced to 60. It might be argued
that the voluntary early retirement pay is a measure of labour market policy
triggered by the deteriorating economic conditions and aiming at a redistribution of the employment available. When a scheme like this, however, has
been implemented, experience shows that it is difficult to the point of the
impossible to do away with it when the economic conditions change. In particular as the scheme has been very popular and has been considered by the
unions as "the social reform of the century". One might term the scheme a
labour market measure, but in fact a fundamental change of the system of
pensioning has occurred. It is obvious that the longer possibilities exist for
early retirement, the greater will be the influence upon conceptions of the
age when retirement should take place.

The early retirement pay is not a contribution to a basic redefinition of
the process of retirement, if considered from the point of view of a flexible
and gradual adjustment from working life to a definitive retirement. The
scheme implies an abrupt retirement similar to the one implied by the statutory age of old-age pensions. Rather, it amounts to a decrease of the age of
eligibility giving the individual the choice of the time of retirement within
the age-bracket 60 to 66. The scheme has been marketed in terms of a positive employment policy and the issues of individual flexibility and gradual
retirement have deliberately been deemphasized. The overriding objective
refers to the employment level.

One recognizes the trade-off between a short-term objective in terms of
employment and the longer term impact when the scheme is considered
from the point of view of the demographic development to be expected. Because of the continuing high rates of unemployment, the short-term politi-

cal preferences are in favour of developing options for earlier retirement from gainful employment for the purpose of providing additional job-opportunities for the younger. In the long-run, however, a de facto reduction of the age of eligibility will increase the financing problems for the social security system.

7. The Public and Political Discussion

The original bill of the Social Democratic government on early retirement pay as well as the preparatory investigation certainly accomodated the entrenched ideas of the trade unions and the unemployment funds. Even though the unemployment funds are separate and independent organizations, they have historically grown out of the trade unions, and there are unbroken connections.

The voluntary early retirement pay was presented in terms of a positive employment policy and deemphasized the issues of individual flexibility and gradual retirement. Obviously, there is a desire on the part of the trade unions for reasons of organizational policy to prefer general and uniform solutions. Based on the argument that the scheme had to be administered by the unemployment funds and that only members were under their jurisdiction, it was recommended that the recipients remained members of the funds and continued their contributory payments.

The idea of the "once-only offer" was motivated by the employment objective and so was the limitation on the working hours allowed. Derived from the employment objective it was argued that the retirement pay had to replace the previous wage or the daily allowances. Therefore, the applicants' attachment to the labour force had to be effectively interrupted. To guarantee that the unemployed desiring to retire was not restricted by economic reasons, the benefit level was set equal to the daily allowances for the first 2 1/2 years. To attain a gradual adjustment towards the level of old-age pensions the level was to be reduced to 80 per cent for the next two years and subsequently to 60 per cent. (As mentioned above the reduction to 60 per cent was first changed to a reduction to 70 per cent and as from 1987 this third level of the benefit has been abolished.)

During the parliamentary debate in particular the Conservatives were critical. They emphasized that it was unacceptable that only members of the unemployment funds were covered, that the benefit level was unreasonable compared to other early retirement pension schemes, that the "once-only offer" was untolerable and that the main issue instead had to be the one of providing for greater flexibility so that the individuals themselves might decide on a gradual process of retirement. The Conservatives, therefore, moved an amendment on an early partial retirement pay covering all gainfully employed.

The second report by the Commission on the conditions of the elderly published in 1981 emphasized that self-determination relating to the retirement not only referred to the time of retirement but also to the extent of the working hours. The existing pension system including the early retirement pay excluded a part-time solution with a compensatory payment.

The Employers Confederation was very critical towards the new scheme, because it violated the time-honoured principle of universalism, discriminated to the advantage of the wage-earners, granted benefits in excess of the level of other early retirement pensions of the day, was an obstacle to part-time employment, stimulated rejection of the elderly from employment, was financed from employers' and employees' contributions, thus weakening the competitiveness of Danish industry etc.

Less than a month after the passage of the comprehensive reform – exclusive of the early retirement pay – of the pension system in 1984, the Minister of Social Affairs of the bourgeois coalition forming government in 1982 approved the establishment of an investigation on some remaining problems concerning the pension system.

One of the objectives was to provide opportunities for gradual retirement, greater flexibility and greater continuity. Potentially at least, the guiding ideas implied new emphasis on the value of personal choice and on public support to realize these choices. The scheme had to be worked out on the assumption that the organizations on the labour market would supplement the measure by bargains on part-time employment along with gradual retirement.

A bill on partial pensioning was introduced in may 1985. It was emphasized that the aim was to leave it to the single individual to decide his time of pensioning and his readjustment from working to leisure time in accordance with his desires and needs. The objectives were described in terms of self-determination, coherence, flexibility and continuity.

The Social Democratic spokesman critisized the extent of flexibility. The elderly would be enforced to enter and to leave the scheme, to increase and to decrease the working hours alternately, dependent on the needs of the employers. One cannot delegate the terms of working hours to individual arrangements, he argued. General bargains had to be settled by the organizations of the employers and the employees. Since the Trade Unions Congress (LO) had turned the ideas of the bill down it would simply not come to work. It was, he added, well known that LO was worried about the conceivable extension of part-time employment.

Thus, the bill on partial pensioning was very controversial. Actually, the bill was passed with 66 votes against 64 to be implemented from january the 1st 1987.

8. The Partial Pensioning Scheme

The partial pension scheme covers wage-earners and other persons with an occupational income in the age-group 60 to 66 who desire to reduce their working hours. Thus, independents and help-mates are covered as well. For non-wage-earners special regulations are stipulated by the Minister of Social Affairs.

A wage-earner qualifies for a partial pension, if 1) he has passed the age of 60, 2) he has permanent residence in Denmark, 3) he has paid contributions to the Supplementary Labour Market Pension scheme equal to at least 10 years full contributory payments during the 20 years previous to his application, and 4) he has been employed as a wage-earner for at least 9 month during the previous 12 months.

The eligibility is terminated when he attains the statutory age for old-age pensions. If he becomes sick or unemployed for 13 consecutive weeks he loses his entitlement, but if he resumes work later, he might be readmitted.

It is a condition that the average hours of work per week is reduced by at least 9 hours or 1/4 of the working hours during the 9 months previous to the application. Throughout the six months subsequent to the admission, and afterwards on a yearly basis, the average hours per week must at least amount to 15 and at most to 30. The placing of the working hours is a matter of agreement between the employer and the employee.

The benefit is calculated and regulated on the basis of a yearly stipulated "basic amount" equal to the maximum of the daily allowances in case of sickness. The yearly partial pension amounts to 1/39 of the basic amount per hours reduction in the working hours per week, i.e. a fixed amount independent from the current and the previous income.

When the benefit has been received for 2 1/2 year, it is reduced to 80 per cent of the amount mentioned. Similar to the scheme on early retirement pay the initially intended reduction of the benefit level to 70 per cent after 4 1/2 year was repealed before the Act came into force.

The scheme is administered by the Social Boards of the municipalities, but financed by the State.

The benefit level is illustrated by Table 6.

Table 6. Benefit level in the partial pension scheme compared to the previous income and the level of old-age pensions

Kr. per year	Full-time work before the age of 60	Part-time work = 20 hours per week + partial pension. First 2 1/2 year	Part-time work = 20 hours per week + partial pension. After 2 1/2 year	Old-age pensions
Gross	155000	131638	121208	46224
Net	85380	75777	70907	46224
Net compensation rate	–	88.8	83.0	54.1

Obviously, it is too early to evaluate the success or failure of the partial pension scheme. But the augmentation from january the 1st to the end of june 1987 suggests only a modest utilization. Only 1069 wage-earners and

1416 independents have been granted a partial pension. Compared to the
app. 48000 who were granted an early retirement pay during the first year, the
2495 recipients of a partial pension is an astonishing low figure.

One can only guess the reasons. The Ministry of Social Affairs in publishing the figures mentioned that the collective bargains covering app.
300000 wage-earners do not allow part-time work. Without full-time employment members of the corresponding unemployment funds have to give
up membership.

A spokesman for the Liberal Party suggested that the unions and the
unemployment funds attempt to thwart the scheme, because they prefer the
early retirement scheme. He argued in favour of an intervention by legislation. This, however, would be considered, in particular by the unions, as an
encroachment on the up till now recognized rights of the labour market organizations to decide on their own affairs, including the terms of the working
hours. During the recent election campaign the Minister of Labour announced a legislative initiative to entitle all wage-earners to part-time unemployment insurance irrespective of the trade unions. But after the election
the Social Democratic Party has proposed to abolish the partial pension
scheme, and possibly they will gain a majority in favour of this proposal.

9. Further Comments

As seen from the information given above there are three opportunities for
support in case of retirement previous to the statutory age of 67 for old-age
pensions. An individual might be eligible for (a) an early retirement pension
in one form or another, cf. Diagram 6, (b) an early retirement pay or (c) a partial pension. Since an early retirement pension is conditioned by a reduction
of the economic capacity, failing health or social circumstances, i.e. an individual evaluation by the public authorities, it is not embraced by the concept
of flexibility closely connected to the individual's self-determination.

The early retirement pay leaves it to the individual to determine his age
of retirement, but it is practically speaking conditioned by a complete retirement from the labour market. The partial pension, on the other hand, leaves
it to the individual to decide on the age from which he wants to reduce his
number of working hours and to negotiations between the employee and his
employer to determine the number of working hours within limits.

None of the schemes are directly linked to the old-age pension system
the benefit level determined on the basis of an amount taken over from the
schemes on daily allowances.

A direct comparison of the early retirement pay, the partial pension and
the old-age pension is not possible in nominal terms because of a differential
tax treatment. Nevertheless, Diagram 7 presents elements of a comparison.
The level of the old-age pension benefit for a single pensioner of 67 has been
converted to an equivalent amount on the assumption that the old-age pension was taxed similar to other incomes. The Diagram shows the actuarial va-

lues of the old-age pension in case of advanced and deferred withdrawals. It is a hypothetical construction since advanced withdrawals have never been possible, and deferred withdrawals accompanied by increased benefits were repealed in 1984.

The Diagram illustrates two curves for actuarial, equivalent old-age pensions, one based only on the basic amount and one on the basic allowance plus the pension addition. The dashed curve shows the two-level early retirement pay on the assumption that an early retirement pay is drawn from the age of 60. Similarly, the dotted curve illustrates the partial pension on the same assumption and based on the premise that the number of working hours has been reduced to 15 per week corresponding to the maximum partial pension.

It is seen from the diagram that the early retirement pay is above the actuarial old-age pension for all ages, while the second level of the maximum partial pension falls below the corresponding actuarial value over the age-range 63 to 67 if the actuarial value refers to the sum of the basic allowance and the pension addition.

Obviously, there are no incentives to defer withdrawal of the old-age pension beyond the age of 67.

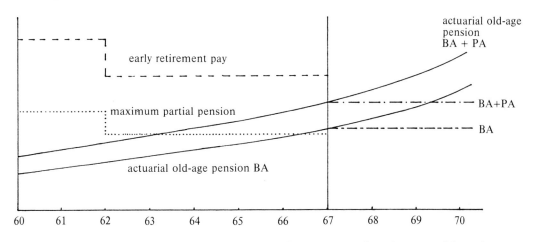

Diagram 7. Actuarial old-age pensions, early retirement pay and maximum partial pension.

Even though the second level of the maximum partial pension is below the equivalent value of the basic allowance it has to be remembered that the partial pension is received in addition to an income from gainful work. So is the basic allowance, however, if the income from gainful employment does not exceed a limit of 54800 kr. (1. april 1987). The equivalent yearly income assuming a number of working hours per week equal to 15 is app. 142000.

Diagram 8 illustrates the compensation ratios. Over the gross income range from 100000 to 200000 the percentage of the sum of the maximum partial pension and the income from gainful employment net of taxation relative to the net income decreases from app. 103 to 77.5 per cent, a total compensation in excess of the compensation ratio in case of early retirement declining from app. 92 to 62 per cent. If the compensation, however, is considered from the point of view of the net public payment relative to the private cost in terms of income foregone net of taxation, the maximum partial pension compensation is only in excess for lower incomes.

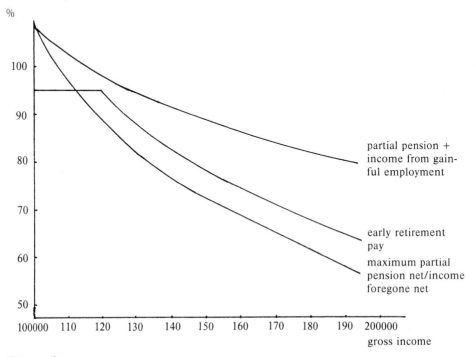

Diagram 8

10. Concluding Observations

The voluntary early retirement pay aims at giving the elderly an incentive to early and complete retirement for the purpose of providing additional job opportunities for the younger. Considered from the point of view of utilization is has been a quantitative success. The effect is a de facto reduction of the pension age. Apart from the individual's choice of the age of retirement the scheme deliberately deemphasizes individual flexibility and the possibility of a gradual transition from employment towards complete retirement.

The opportunities for gradual retirement, greater flexibility and greater continuity are important objectives of the partial pension scheme.

Even though differing in important respects the two schemes both provide incentives to a reduced labour supply and rising expenditures for the provision of the retired. As such they run counter to the longer-term objective of decreasing the pensioner quota to cope with the financial difficulties caused by an expected demographic development unfavourable to a pay-as-you-go financed pension system.

Ironically, the only element consistent with the longer-term objective: the increase of the old-age pension in case of a deferred withdrawal was repealed in 1984, and the efforts of the mid 1970s to develop a system of flexible pensioning based on actuarial principles were given up by the enactment in 1979 on early retirement pay.

This development mirrors the weight given to short-term objectives in political decision-making making it more difficult in the future to cope with the rising burden of pensioning. The longer favourable possibilities for early retirement exist, the greater will be the influence upon conceptions of the age when retirement should take place. Internalized norms might be difficult to change.

References

Andersen, B. R. (1981) Hvordan vil det offentlige pensionssystem udvikle sig fremover? Økonomi og Politik. p. 365-76

Betænkning nr. 755 (1977) Rapport om udvidet adgang til førtidig folkepension og fleksibel pensionsalder. København

Betænkning nr. 817 (1977) Udvalget til behandling af midaldrende og ældres beskæftigelsesproblemer på det private arbejdsmarked: Ældre og Arbejdsmarked. København

Betænkning nr. 835 (1978) Betænkning om efterløn, København

Betænkning nr. 898 (1980) Betænkning om førtidspension, København

Betænkning nr. 1028 Pensionsudvalget, Betænkning om delpension, samspilsproblemer, samordningsfradrag og førtidspensionering af tjenestemænd. København

Dansk Arbejdsgiverforening (1982) Førtidspension – en ny model. København

Hillestrøm, K. og I. Koch-Nielsen (1977) Ønsker om fleksibel pensionsalder og nedsat arbejdstid. Socialforskningsinstituttets meddelelser nr. 23. København

Olsen, H. (1984) Efterløn eller delpension, Socialforskningsinstituttets meddelelser, nr. 42. København

Platz, M., H. Olsen and T. Hansen (1983) Efterløn og beskæftigelse, Socialforskningsinstituttets meddelelser, nr. 122. København

Ældrekommissionens 1. delrapport (1980) Aldersforandringer-ældrepolitikkens forudsætninger. København

Ældrekommissionens 2. delrapport (1981) De ældres vilkår. København

Ældrekommissionens 3. delrapport (1982) Sammenhæng i ældrepolitikken. København

The Flexible Pensionable Age in Finland

H. Sundberg

We have in Finland two parallel pension schemes, the National Pension Scheme and the Employment Pension Scheme.

The National Pension Scheme provides a basic pension security to the entire population. There are three kinds of pension, invalidity pension, old-age pension and unemployment pension. Furthermore a special survivors' pension system is attached to the National Pension Scheme. It is a flat rate scheme. The pensions consist mainly of two parts, the basic part and the additional part. The basic part amounts this year (1988) to 346 FIM a month. It is paid to all pensioners. The additional part has a fixed maximum amount, this year 1,616 FIM or 1,532 FIM a month depending on the cost of living in the municipality where the pensioner resides. This maximum amount is, however, reduced, if the pensioner receives other kinds of pension, e.g. employment pension or work accident compensation. In addition to a national pension also several supplements might be paid, e.g. child supplement for each child under 16, housing allowance to beneficiaries with small income, helplessness supplement and front veterans' supplement. The national pensions and their supplements are adjusted from the beginning of every year according to the changes in the cost-of-living index.

The Employment Pension Scheme covers only those occupied in gainful work. The pensions are of the same kind as in the National Pension Scheme, i.e. invalidity pensions, old-age pensions, unemployment pensions and survivors' pensions. They are earnings-related. An insured person earns in pension as a rule 1,5 % of of the pensionable income for every year of insurance since he was 23 and until reaching the pensionable age, normally 65. The maximum pension is 60 %, but there are no limitations as to the amount of the pensionable income. The pension rights accrued and the pensions after they are granted are tied to a special pension index where both the changes in the cost-of-living index and the average changes of the wages and salaries are taken into account. The index adjustments are made from the beginning of every year. It is possible to improve this obligatory pension security by voluntary pension insurance. What is mentioned above relates to the private sector of the Employment Pension Scheme. The public sector of this scheme covers people employed by the State, the municipalities and the church. In this sector the pensions are a little higher (the maximum 66%) and there are also some differences in the qualifying conditions for the pensions.

W. Schmähl (Ed.)
Redifining the Process of Retirement
© Springer-Verlag Berlin Heidelberg 1989

The pensionable age in the National Pension Scheme has always been 65. The insured person has had a possibility to defer his old-age pension, in which case the amount of the pension has been increased. This possibility, however, has been of only small importance. On the other hand, no possibilities have existed for having the old-age pension in advance. Also in the private sector of the Employment Pension Scheme the pensionable age has been determined to 65. Still the employer has been able to arrange for his workers old-age protection also from an earlier age, usually from 60 or 63. Like in the National Pension Scheme it has also in the Employment Pension Scheme been possible for the insured person to defer his old-age pension, in which case the pension amount is increased on an acturial basis. However, no possibilities have existed for having the old-age pension before reaching the pensionable age.

This lack of flexibility has been stressed especially in two connections. When determining whether an insured person is disabled to such an extent, that he is entitled to an invalidity pension, also such factors are taken into account as the age of the claimant and his former occupation. The most important factor, however, has always been, whether the claimant's medical condition gives rise to the assumption, that he is unable to continue his work. In respect of these estimations some universal dissatisfaction has been discernible especially as concerns elderly people occupied for a long time in very hard work. There had been cases, where the doctor couldn't find any disease of importance, although the employer and the fellow workers held the claimant unable to perform his work. – The other and the most decisive factor was, however, that in the public sector of the Employment Pension Scheme a great many of specific pensionable ages had developed, where certain groups of workers were able to retire at ages between 50 and 63. Consequently the workers' organisations raised the question on having specific pensionable ages for workers in the private sector too.

When considering this question a State committee found it hardly feasible in a just and equitable way to determine the borders for the groups of workers entitled to old-age pension at a certain earlier age. As a matter of fact, the committee said, the ageing is a very individual process where the chronological age and the physiological age might differ to a high extent. It is also difficult to place a certain job or branch among those, which are to be considered very hard and exhausting as the nature of the work might undergo considerable changes because of the new machines and new working methods. The idea of specific pensionable ages was therefore abandoned. Instead new methods were proposed in order to bring about more flexibility in the pension schemes. As a result we have in Finland today the so called flexible pensionable age. For the moment this flexibility concerns the private sector only. Also in the public sector a solution have been found and the matter is going to the Parliament in a near future.

The new pensionable age is set into force by three separate measures: by introducing two kinds of pensions, i.e. the individual early pension and the part-time pension, and by opening a better possibility to get an advanced old-age pension.

Individual early pension is a kind of invalidity pension, where the qualifying conditions are moderated from what concerns ordinary invalidity pensions. Individual early pension is granted to a person, aged 55 or over, whose working capacity has deteriorated to such an extent that he cannot reasonably be expected to continue his work. When estimating the deterioration of working capacity there are to be taken into account besides the health conditions of the claimant also factors due to ageing, the length of working in the occupation, the physical and psychic attrition caused by the work and the individual working conditions. Furthermore is required, that the pensioner has no or very little gainful work any more and that he has stopped working not earlier than one year before the pension begins. The amount of the pension is the same as that of a full ordinary invalidity pension. The pension is granted both from the National Pension Scheme and the Employment Pension Scheme.

The individual early pension is, as already said, an invalidity pension. The claimant has to present a doctor's certificate on his health condition. It is, however, not required, that his health condition has an adequate causal connection to a disability for work, as is required for the ordinary invalidity pension. As a matter of fact the individual early pension does not require disability at all. It is enough, that all the factors mentioned above together have put the claimant in a situation, where he cannot reasonably be expected to continue his work. Another difference from the ordinary invalidity pension is, that for the individual early pension the question is only, whether the claimants' last work still can be held suitable to him. There should not be any estimation about other suitable work.

Advanced old-age pension. According to the new rules the insured person is also entitled to take out his old-age pension in advance, yet not before the age of 60. The pension amount is then permanently reduced by 0,5 % for every month of advancement. On the other hand the insured person might, as previously, postpone his old-age pension, in which case the pension amount is increased by 1 % for every month of deferment. The new rules concern the Employment Pension Scheme and the National Pension Scheme as well. The schemes operate separately and it is possible to have an advanced old-age pension from one scheme and an old-age pension at the normal pensionable age or a deferred pension from the other scheme.

When planning these new rules there were some doubts about the suitability of an advanced – and reduced – old-age pension. It seems to be very difficult to make rules concerning increase and decrease, which are fully neutral. Especially some supplements to the national pensions are not subject to the decrease, although their amount can be considerable. On the other hand the decrease concerns pension amounts, which the legislator has considered to be needed for accomplishing the protection intended. If a pension is decreased under an amount considered needed for giving a proper livelihood, the person concerned can ask for a supplement from the social welfare. Nevertheless the possibility of having old-age pension in advance was added to the system of flexible pensionable age, as it seems to be useful in some special cases, e.g. when of a married couple one has got a pension and the other wants to retire too.

Part-time pension concerns the Employment Pension Scheme only. Such a pension is granted to an insured person aged 60-64, who reduces his full-time work by at least 16 and at most 28 hours a week. The pension amounts to a certain portion of the decrease of income caused by the reduced working time. This portion varies between 44 and 60% depending on the pensioner's age at the beginning of the pension. The part-time pension, however, must not exceed 75% of the full employment pension accrued at the moment the part-time pension begins.

Originally the part-time pension was considered the most important part of the system of flexible pensionable age. The reduction of working time seemed to be a sound solution to many elderly workers who had met with difficulties in performing their previous work. By working part-time they were still in contact to their usual working surroundings and they could escape a feeling of loneliness typical of many other retired persons. On the other hand the possibility of having a part-time pension depends on the opportunity of getting part-time work. In this respect the situation was not very favourable. The situation was not improved by the facts, that this kind of person, for several reasons, was introduced one year later than the individual early pension and that the age limits for those both pensions differed.

The system of a flexible pensionable age came into force in two stages, the individual early pension and the new rules concerning advanced or deferred old-age pension from the beginning of 1986 and the part-time pension from the beginning of 1987.

In the beginning of 1986, when the legislation on individual early pension came into force, people took a very high interest in this new kind of pension. Claims could be presented already during the two last months in 1985. Then and during the three first months in 1986 there were more claims for this kind of pension than had been estimated for the whole year. But after that the situation was equalised. The insured person can get from the pension institution an advance decision on his right to an individual early pension if he leaves his work. This decision is binding the instituion, if the person concerned within 6 months shows that he has retired from work. There have, of course, been some cases, where the claimant has not fullfilled his claim, but they are not significant. The following Table shows the number of claims in the Employment Pension Scheme – the number being about the same also in the National Pension Scheme.

Table 1. The number of claims for individual early pension in 1985, 1986 and 1987 and the percentual part of actively insured persons, Employment Pension Scheme

| | 1985 | | 1986 | | 1987 | |
	Number of claims	% of insured	Number of claims	% of insured	Number of claims	% of insured
Men	1.055	1,1	6.160	6,2	4.211	4,5
Women	1.533	1,7	7.792	8,5	4.923	5,9
All	2.588	1,4	13.952	7,3	9.134	5,2

As there was a quite new kind of pension, it was only natural that not all claims were well founded. The percentage of denied claims, which as concerns ordinary invalidity pensions in this age group (55-64) varied between 5,5 and 6,4% was as concerns claims for individual early pension in 1986 30,4% and in 1987 30,2%. The percentage was, however much smaller in the group 60-64, being only 16,3% in 1986 and 14,9% in 1987.

The final result of the claims in the Employment Pension Scheme can be seen from the following:

Table 2. Individual early pensions granted in 1986 and in 1987, Employment Pension Scheme

	1986	1987
Men	3.612	3.549
Women	4.218	4.009
All	7.830	7.558

As can be seen there have been a slight decrease in the number of individual early pensions in 1987 as compared to the number of such pensions granted in 1986. The same reflections have been made also concerning the National Pension Scheme. It is, however, still very early to predict the future development. Up to now one serious obstacle has been the missing right to an individual early pension in the Employment Pension Scheme for the public sector. If this deficiency is removed from the beginning of next year, as are the odds for the moment, it seems natural, that there will be an increase in the number of individual early pensions also in the private sector.

One point of interest could be to check, whether these new individual early pension have caused a decrease of the number of the new ordinary invalidity pensions granted in 1986 and 1987.

Table 3. Number of new full invalidity pensions and individual early pensions granted in 1983 – 1987 in percent of insured persons in the same age group, Employment Pension Scheme, private sector

Age group	1983 Ordin. inv.p.	1984 Ordin. inv.p.	1985 Ordin. inv.p.	1986 Ordin. inv.p.	Indiv. early p.	1987 Ordin. inv.p.	Indiv. early p.
55 – 59	3,1	3,4	3,6	3,8	3,4	3,8	3,9
60 – 64	5,3	5,2	5,4	5,7	5,0	5,5	4,8

As can be seen, the number of new ordinary invalidity pensions have in the years 1986 and 1987 been about the same as before, although a new kind of invalidity pension was introduced. Naturally one cause to this might be, that the new individual early pensions filled a real gap in the security system. There are, however, other explanations too. One is the structural changes in the labour market. Another factor might be, that the age limit for unemployment pension (paid to elderly workers, who have been unemployed for a long time) was raised from 55 to 60.

When speaking of individual early pensions there is only small reason to use statistic data from both the Employment Pension Scheme and the National Pension Scheme, as the schemes co-operate and the insured persons as a rule get individual early pension from both schemes. The situation is, however, not quite the same as concerns old-age pension. Here it might be of interest to have statistics from both schemes. The situation in the National Pension Scheme looks as follows:

Table 4. New old-age pensions in 1986 and 1987, National Pension Scheme

	Men		Women		All	
	Pensions beginning at 65 or later	Advanced pensions	Pensions beginning at 65 or later	Advanced pensions	Pensions beginning at 65 or later	Advanced pensions
1986	18.464	721	26.026	4.580	44.490	5.571
1987	18.332	462	25.708	2.459	44.040	2.951

As can be seen, the number of advanced old-age pensions is rather high. One reason for that might be, that previously people lacked opportunities for having an advanced pension. The number seems to be on the decrease.

The statistics from the Employment Pension Scheme show also some interesting details on the extent to which the old-age pension has been advanced:

Table 5. New advanced old-age pensions in 1986 and 1987, Employment Pension Scheme, private sector

	Men		Women		All	
Age the year pension began	1986	1987	1986	1987	1986	1987
60	227	264	431	389	658	653
61	233	119	528	232	761	351
62	182	92	463	179	645	271
63	291	211	816	367	1107	578
64	281	137	727	314	1008	451
65	82	47	219	61	301	108
All together	1296	870	3184	1542	4480	2412

This table shows that there is among the women a significant rise in the number of new advanced pensions at the age 63. That might be due to the fact, that the normal pensionable age in the public sector is 63. The scope of the insured persons in the private sector of the Employment Pension Scheme numbers 2,7 million people as the National Pension Scheme covers the whole population, about 5 million people. Therefore the number of old-age pensions in this private sector of the Employment Pension Scheme is smaller too. The number of old-age pensions beginning at the age of 65 or later was in 1986 35.767 and in 1987 35.179.

Like in the National Pension Scheme also in the Employment Pension Scheme the number of advanced old-age pensions is much higher among the women. That in spite of the fact, that the advanced pensions to women are much smaller. The average advanced old-age pension in the private sector of the Employment Pension Scheme was at the end of 1987 to men 3.574 FIM a month and to women 979 FIM a month.

About the part-time pension is very little to report. Until now this kind of pension has gathered small interest only. At the end of 1987 the number of part-time pensions granted was 146. This is of course due to many reasons. The two main ones might be the lack of opportunities for part-time work and the fact that this kind of pension is available from a later age, than the individual early pension, which it was intended to interact with.

Although all informations on the new system of flexible pensionable age are not quite encouraging for the moment, we are in Finland convinced that we have chosen the right way and the system, perhaps with small amendments, will turn out very well.

American Patterns of Work and Retirement

R. V. Burkhauser and J. F. Quinn

Contents

1. Introduction

By most standards retirement policy in the United States has been a success. The Social Security system (Old-Age, Survivors, Disability, and Health Insurance, or OASDHI) provides a retirement pension and health benefits to most older workers and their families. The Supplemental Security Income Program guarantees a minimum income floor for those aged 65 and over regardless of past work histories. Federal tax policy encourages the creation of employer retirement pensions. The growth in both coverage and the size of benefits of this network of social insurance, social welfare, and employer pensions is in large part responsible for the dramatic increase in the well-being of older Americans.

Two major social indicators of this increase in well-being are the substantial drops in poverty and in the average retirement age of the elderly over the past four decades. The labor force participation rate of men 65 and over has dropped from nearly 1 in 2 in 1950 to only 1 in 6 today. At the same time,

W. Schmähl (Ed.)
Redifining the Process of Retirement
© Springer-Verlag Berlin Heidelberg 1989

the incidence of poverty among the elderly, which was twice the national average in 1969, has fallen steadily, and has been below that of the population as a whole since 1982 (Quinn (1987)).

Thus it is somewhat ironic that at the moment of its greatest success in reducing both deprivation and work effort, the American retirement system is embroiled in more controversy than at any time since its inception. Criticism over the growth of the federal government budget in general and social security in particular has increased dramatically. The result has been a period of general retrenchment in social welfare programs in the United States and social security has not been exempted.

To this long standing opposition to the growth of government expenditures comes an additional concern – the impact of the work disincentives embedded in the current retirement system. These disincentives have been criticized from two perspectives. The first is legal and reflects a changing view of what constitutes discrimination in the workplace. It argues that older workers should not be coerced to leave a job either explicitly via mandatory retirement rules or implicitly via age based retirement incentives.

The second is economic and reflects a change in the demographic structure of the labor force. It claims that the current system has reduced the work effort of older workers through the generosity of its benefits and the manner in which they are provided. While such an outcome may fit into an overall manpower strategy when unemployment rates are high it is much less reasonable during a time when labor is in short supply. And that time may be coming. The greying of the baby boom generation of the 1950s will mean a substantial aging of the work force in the 21st century. A much higher proportion of the employment pool will be older workers, and retirement policy must change if they are to be encouraged to retire later than they now do.

Thus, because of federal government budgetary excesses, changing views of age discrimination and concern over future economy wide manpower needs, United States policymakers have shifted from satisfied to increasingly concerned over the work effort of the aged.

This reversal in attitude has led to a series of changes in the retirement system in an attempt to cut costs and increase the work effort of older Americans. Yet the changes have been made with little appreciation of how the overall retirement system affects work decisions. This is especially true with respect to work before and after retirement.

Here we provide an overview of the growth in the United States retirement system. We discuss the nature of the work incentives that are embedded in our Social Security and employer pension programs, and describe the pattern of lifetime labor supply that the current system encourages. We then outline the reforms that have been proposed and enacted. Finally, we consider a small but significant group of older workers whose work patterns defy the traditional retirement stereotype of full time work followed by full time leisure. We show that work after retirement occurred in the 1970s despite employment disincentives. We suggest that these workers may offer a clue as to the effect of a future system that is more encouraging to work at older ages.

2. Trends in Expenditure, Poverty and Work

In this section, we discuss the growth of government social welfare expenditures in the United States. We show that while the non-Social Security component rose and fell with the macroeconomy and changes in the political climate, the Social Security component increased steadily. At the same time, employer pension coverage and benefits grew dramatically. These important structural changes were accompanied by decreases in both the poverty and labor force participation rates of older Americans.

2.1 Government Social Welfare Expenditures

United States social welfare expenditures have always been modest when compared to European standards. There is little political support in the U.S. for government transfer programs based on income alone. Instead, most government aid to the needy has been categorical, targeted at particular groups in need of aid.

During the 1960s and 1970s, considerable effort was focused on the lower end of the income distribution by a series of government programs labelled the "War on Poverty". This initiative has since slowed and in some cases, reversed. But one demographic group, the aged, has suffered very little retrenchment until just recently. The continuous growth in social security programs targeted primarily at the aged is a dominant force behind the expansion in the total Federal social welfare budget since 1950.

Table 1 shows how United States government social welfare expenditures in general and social security (OASDHI) expenditures in particular have changed over the past three and one-half decades. In 1950 total welfare expenditures equaled about five percent of Gross National Product. These expenditures include social insurance, public aid, health and medical, veteran (except education), housing, and other social welfare programs. The first social security programs (Old-Age and Survivors Insurance) were in place by 1940 but were still a trivial component of the social welfare budget ten years later.

Table 1 also tracks two important social indicators of the well-being of the aged, their rates of poverty and labor force participation. If normal retirement age for men is defined as the earliest age at which at least one half of men are out of the labor force – then in 1950 normal retirement for men did not occur until after age 68.

Although the concept of a poverty line was not officially recognized until 1964, Smolensky, Danziger, and Gottschalk (1988) have estimated poverty populations from earlier decennial Censuses. They deflate 1964 poverty thresholds back to 1949 and 1959 price levels to estimate their poverty counts. With such a measure, nearly two-thirds of men and women over the age of 65 were poor in 1950.

Table 1. Social indicators

Year	Social welfare expenditures[a] (billion)	Social welfare expenditures GNP	Non-OASDHI welfare expenditures GNP	OASDHI GNP	Poverty rates for those aged 65 and over	Male labor force Participation rates, by age[b]					
						55	60	63	65	68	70
1950	14.1	4.9	4.7	0.3	59.0	87.8	82.1	77.6	67.7	54.2	44.5
1960	34.3	6.8	4.6	2.2	36.2	89.9	83.2	75.7	53.6	39.4	33.2
1968	72.9	8.8	5.3	3.5	25.0	91.9	84.8	71.9	53.4	37.5	30.2
1972	129.9	11.8	7.4	4.4	18.6	90.7	82.1	66.5	45.2	33.8	27.1
1976	239.6	14.7	9.2	5.6	15.0	87.1	75.5	55.7	36.6	26.7	22.4
1980	369.1	13.8	8.1	5.7	15.7	84.9	74.0	52.3	35.2	24.1	21.3
1984	517.5	14.0	7.5	6.5	12.4	84.3	70.2	48.2	30.4	21.3	18.8

Sources: Columns 2-5:   Annual statistical supplements of the social security bulletin, Tables 1-3.

Column 6:   1950, 1960: Smolensky, Danziger and Gottschalk (1988), Table 3
                     1958-1984: U.S. Bureau of the Gensus (1986), Table 2.

Columns 7-12:   1950, 1960: decennial census
                     1968-1984: unpublished U.S. Department of Labor data

Notes: [a] Social welfare expenditures include all social insurance, public aid, health and medical, veteran (except education), housing, and other social welfare programs. These figures are based on data from social welfare expenditures under public programs published in Table 3 of the *Annual Statistical Supplement of the Social Security Bulletin,* 1987, and the analogous table in earlier years.

[b] The labor force participation rates for 1950 and 1960 are based on U.S. Bureau of Census labor force participation questions. For 1968 through 1980, they are based on Consumer Population Survey labor force participation questions.

Social welfare expenditures as a share of GNP rose steadily from 1950 to 1976, from five to nearly 15 percent. In the decade that followed political support for the non-social security components diminished, and since 1976 they have grown more slowly than GNP. But social security benefits continued to grow faster than GNP and by 1984 were 6.5 percent of GNP and almost one-half of all social welfare expenditures.

The poverty and labor force participation rates of the aged mirrored the surge of social security expenditures. Between 1950 and 1984 poverty rates of the elderly dropped from 64 to 12 percent, and the modal retirement age in the United States fell from age 68 to age 63.

Political leadership in the United States has swung between the Republican and Democratic parties over these years. But support for social security programs has not. Table 2 analyzes changes in social welfare and social security (as proportions of GNP) as well as poverty and labor force participation rates during the last seven Presidential administrations.

Table 2. Percentage changes in welfare proportions, poverty rates and labor force participation across presidential terms

Years	Percentage change in social welfare share of GNP[a]	Percentage change in non-social security welfare share of GNP[b]	Percentage change in social security share of GNP[c]	Percentage change in elderly poverty[d]	Age (Labor force participation)[e]					
					55	60	63	65	68	70
Eisenhower[f]										
1950-1960	39	-2	–	-39	2	1	-2	-21	-27	-25
Kennedy-Johnson										
1960-1968	29	15	59	-31	2	2	-5	0	-5	-9
Nixon-Ford										
1968-1976	67	74	60	-40	-5	-11	-23	-31	-29	-26
Carter										
1976-1980	-6	-12	2	5	-3	-2	-6	-4	-10	-5
Reagan										
1980-1984	1	-7	14	-21	-1	-5	-8	-15	-12	-12

Source: See Table 1.
Notes: [a] Percentage changes from Table 1, column 3.
   [b] Percentage changes from Table 1, column 4.
   [c] Percentage changes from Table 1, column 5.
   [d] Percentage changes from Table 1, column 6.
   [e] Percentage change from Table 1, Columns 7-12.
   [f] The Eisenhower Administration began in 1952, but our data are for 1950 and 1960.

At first blush, the results are somewhat surprising. The "War on Poverty", started during the eight years of Democratic presidential leadership under Kennedy and Johnson, yielded a 29 percent increase in social welfare expenditures' share of GNP, considerably less than the increase during the Republican administrations of Eisenhower and Nixon-Ford. The mystery of increasing overall expenditures is explained by separating them into social security and non-social security components. The non-social security component of the social welfare budget actually fell as a share of GNP during the 1950s, increased modestly in the 1960s, and expanded tremendously in the Nixon and Ford administrations as the full force of War on Poverty programs was felt during the recessionary years of the early 1970s.

Social security expenditures were the driving force behind increased social welfare expenditures in the 1950s as the first large numbers of workers began to receive retirement benefits. During the Kennedy and Johnson administrations social security expenditures continued to increase faster than GNP because the retired population increased, but also because the disability and health components of social security were developed. During the Republican administrations of Nixon and Ford increases in the size of social security benefits continued to add to expenditure growth.

The "golden" age of social welfare growth ended with the Ford administration. Under the Democratic leadership of the Carter administration, so-

cial welfare expenditures fell as a share of GNP. But as was the case in all except the Nixon-Ford years, non-social security expenditures grew more
slowly than social security expenditures. In fact, non-social security expenditures as a share of GNP fell by 12 percent in the Carter administration and
by 7 percent in the first Reagan term.

With the exception of a slight increase during the Carter years, the elderly poverty rate has fallen consistently since 1950. The decreases were very
large through 1976, and quite substantial also in the early 1980s. It is interesting to note that the latter occurred while the overall poverty rate rose from 13
to 14.4 percent.

Reductions in labor force participation during these years varied across
ages. The first great reduction in the work effort of those age 65 and above
occurred in the 1950s. Between 1960 and 1968 there were only modest falls in
labor force participation of those above age 65 and no change at all for men
age 65. Participation of those aged 55 and 60 actually grew during this period
of strong economic growth. Men aged 62 to 64 were first eligible for social security benefits in 1961 and their labor force participation fell modestly. Between 1968 and 1976 substantial reductions in labor force participation occurred at each age between 55 and 70 reported in Table 2. Since 1976 the
trend toward reduced work effort at older ages has persisted but at a slower
pace.

It is important to distinguish between increases in the growth of social
security expenditures because of changes in the share of the covered population reaching retirement age and because of changes in the level of benefits they receive. The growth in social security retirement expenditures during 1968-1976 was dominated by benefit increases. Table 3 shows the annual
social security benefit, in each year between 1959 and 1979 of a worker who
reached age 65, who had earned median social security covered earnings
over his or her lifetime and was married to a 65 year old non-working spouse.

Social security retirement benefits in the United States are based on
average earnings over a worker's lifetime and thus increase over time as
wages increase. But benefits also increase with changes in the benefit formula. Before 1974 this was done on an *ad hoc* basis by Congress. Since 1974
benefits have been adjusted automatically to offset inflation. As can be seen
in Table 3, between 1959 and 1968, the *ad hoc* increases in the benefit formula
together with the increase in the real earnings of subsequent cohorts of new
beneficiaries kept real social security benefits of the median earner approximately constant. But between 1968 and 1973 a major change in the formula
dramatically increased real social security benefits for new retirees. For the
median worker, real benefits increased by 47 percent during these five years
before benefit indexation. Real benefits increased slightly more during the
remainder of the decade because of a flaw in the formula which, in fact, over-
indexed benefits. While this error was quickly recognized, it was not correct-
ed until 1981.

Recent work by Anderson, Burkhauser, and Quinn (1986) and Burtless
(1986) argues that this unexpected increase in social security benefits may in

Table 3. Yearly social security benefits for a worker with median earnings, aged 65, with a 65-year-old dependent spouse

Year[a]	Yearly benefit (current dollars)	Yearly benefit (1979 dollars)	Percentage change in real terms from previous year
1959	$ 1,886	$ 4,702	--
1960	1,903	4,669	-0.7 %
1961	1,920	4,665	-0.1
1962	1,933	4,645	-0.4
1963	1,951	4,632	-0.3
1964	1,970	4,617	-0.3
1965	2,132	4,911	6.4
1966	2,157	4,830	-1.6
1967	2,186	4,758	-1.5
1968	2,218	4,634	-2.6
1969	2,546	5,048	8.9
1970	2,985	5,588	10.7
1971	3,342	5,997	7.3
1972	3,401	5,908	-1.4
1973	4,157	6,798	15.1
1974	4,238	6,245	-8.1
1975	4,799	6,480	3.8
1976	5,343	6,822	5.3
1977	5,878	7,050	3.4
1978	6,448	7,187	1.9
1979	7,009	7,009	-2.5
1959-68			-1.4
1968-73			46.7
1968-79			51.2

Source: Anderson, Burkhauser, and Quinn (1986).
[a]Assumes worker and wife are aged 65 on January 1. Benefits are based on social security rules as of January 1 of each year.

part explain the increased pace of labor force withdrawal of those 62 and over during the early 1970s. However, the 1970s were also a period of high unemployment and falling real wages in the United States. This may also have contributed to the drop in work effort.

2.2 Employer Pension Expenditures

Another major factor contributing to the observed trends in old age poverty and labor force participation may be the recent expansion of employer pensions. This growth can be measured in a number of ways. Table 4 shows the share of the work force covered by defined benefit pension plans, which base benefits on prior earnings or service. As we will see, they, like social security, have benefit rules which importantly influence the lifetime pattern of work.

Table 4. Growth of defined benefit pension plans, 1950-2000

Year	Pension coverage rate (percentage)	Retirees to work force ratio	Liabilities (billion of 1984 dollars)
1950	25.0	1.1	114
1955	32.4	2.2	161
1960	40.8	3.8	222
1965	42.9	5.4	360
1970	44.7	8.1	475
1975	46.5	11.1	620
1981	47.4	15.2	766
1990[a]	48.1	23.0	1203
2000[a]	48.4	31.8	1938

Sources: Ippolito (1986) Tables 5.1 and 5.2.
   [a] Estimated by Ippolito.

In 1950 one of four workers was covered by a defined benefit employer pension plan. By 1981, this had doubled to nearly one of two. For every one hundred active workers in the work force in 1950 there was one retired worker collecting a defined benefit employer pension. By 1981 that ratio had increased to 15 recipients per 100 workers. A final measure of growth is the real liabilities of the employer pension component of the retirement system. The value of real liabilities has increased over 500 percent between 1950 and 1981. Ycas and Grad (1987) report that while only 17 percent of married workers who first took social security benefits in 1941 had private pension income, 56 percent did so in 1982.

Unlike social security, most employer pension plans permit retirement before age 62. Hatch (1981) found that over half of workers with pensions have a normal retirement age before age 65. In addition, before 1960, two out of three plans required company consent for early retirement, but such permission is now rarely required. Nearly three out of every four workers covered by pension plans can retire by age 55. Both the size of the work force covered by employer pensions and the opportunity to retire at earlier ages have increased since 1950. And as we will see below, both social security and most employer pensions not only make retirement benefits available but also penalize those who choose not to take them.

3. A Life Cycle View of the United States Retirement System

Eligibility for Social Security and employer pension benefits has long been acknowledged as an important part of a worker's compensation package. Recent research has clarified the magnitudes of these components. Retirement benefits are promises of income streams in the future. As such, they are conveniently viewed as assets or as wealth, whose value equals the present discounted value of the future income flows. As one continues to work, the asset value of these future promises may rise or fall, depending on the details of the benefit calculation rules.

These changes in asset values are part of compensation – the return to working another year. If retirement income wealth is accruing, then true compensation exceeds the amount of traditionally defined earnings by the increase in wealth. On the other hand, if retirement wealth is decreasing with additional work, then the true return is less than the pay check implies.

In this section, we discuss the nature of the incentives built into our pension and social security systems. We show that the details of the benefit calculation rules encourage and discourage work at different times during the life cycle. The net result seems to be to encourage workers to remain on career jobs, but not forever. Penalties exist for those who leave employment either too early or too late.

3.1 Employer Pensions

Employer pension plans in the United States are generally of two types. Defined contribution plans establish a contribution rule. For instance, the employer and employee may each pay five percent of current salary into the pension fund. Contributions are invested and the benefit paid is based on the value of the funds at retirement. Because such plans are usually actuarially fair across retirement ages they play a relatively minor role in the retirement decision. The accrued value increases in accord with the contributions made in that year. But this is also true at younger ages. If workers who leave the firm have a right to the current wealth value of the pension, then (in this example) the accrual value of the pension would simply be a constant percent of salary at all ages. Defined contribution plans are really just forced saving plans. Their effect on work behavior should not be significantly different than that of other forms of wealth.

Defined benefit plans are a more complex form of savings and play a much more direct role in work decisions. And this is the type of pension that has grown in importance since 1950. Ippolito (1986) estimates that nearly 80 percent of pension covered workers have a defined benefit plan. These plans promise workers a benefit at retirement based on some agreed upon formula. Employees usually make no explicit contribution to the plan. A typical defined pension plan offers benefits beginning at some stated age to workers who have been with the firm for a given number of years. That benefit is usually based on some average of highest nominal earnings and/or years of service with the firm.

One method of calculating the accrual value of a pension is to estimate how the value of the pension plan changes with every year of tenure with the firm. After each year we calculate what the worker would get (in present discounted value terms) if he were to leave the firm at that time. This is called the current "quit value" of the pension. Positive accruals mean that true compensation exceeds the paycheck; negative accrual the opposite. Barnow and Ehrenberg (1979), Gordon and Blinder (1980), Kotlikoff and Wise (1985) and Gustman and Steinmeier (1987) have used this method to estimate pension accrual.

Tracing the "quit value" of a pension requires information on the worker's yearly earnings, the appropriate interest rate, the life expectancy of the worker, and the often quite complex pension plan rules. Kotlikoff and Wise (1985) show the sensitivity of lifetime patterns of accrual rates to changes in each of these parameters for workers with otherwise constant real wage growth. They use a pension plan with cliff vesting; that is, one in which workers lose all benefits unless they stay with the firm for ten years. Prior to 1987 this was the maximum number of years of tenure a firm could require of workers before vesting. The 1986 Tax Reform Act reduced the maximum to five years.

Kotlikoff and Wise also assume that the plan has an early retirement option with actuarially reduced yearly benefits. This is typical of most defined benefit plans. For simplicity benefits are assumed to be some fraction of final year's earnings and years of service, and there is no offset for social security. Finally they assume that the worker will definitely live to early retirement age and has a normal life expectancy thereafter.

They look at the ratio of pension accrual to salary in each year for workers who have constant growth in real wages. Under these assumptions, the constant share of wages implied in the previous defined contribution plan is now replaced by a path containing two major spikes.

For ease of explication, Kotlikoff and Wise assume work begins at age 30, early retirement is at age 55, and normal retirement is at age 65. Hence the first spike appears at age 40 when the worker has ten years of service with the firm. This is caused by cliff vesting. A worker who leaves the firm before ten years loses all pension benefits so the quit value of the pension is zero up to this point. Cliff vesting can also be a feature of a defined contribution plan and would cause the same type of spike.

Once the worker is vested, pension accrual is found to be a smoothly increasing percentage of salary up to the time when benefits can first be taken. This pattern is caused both by the continued aging of the worker (which moves him closer to the point that the promised benefits will be paid) and by the increase in years of service with the firm. The second peak in pension accrual occurs at the initial early retirement age.

Since most pension plans offer no additional service credit after normal retirement age, accrual is negative past that age and pension wealth falls for the great majority of workers. Those who continue to work lose retirement benefits which are not made up to them in the future. (This period is not shown on Figure 1 which stops at age 65.) The accrual rate between early and normal retirement is more varied. Pension regulations require plans that provide an early retirement option to reduce benefits by no more than that necessary to offset the additional years over which benefits can be expected to be paid. In other words, the reduced benefits must be at least actuarially fair. But in fact most defined benefit plans offer more than fair early retirement options.

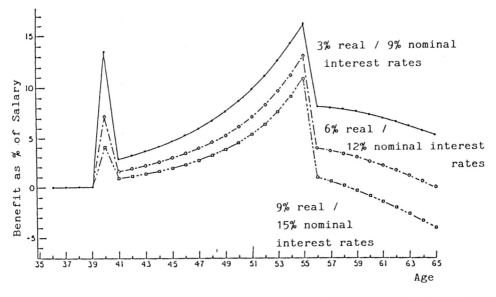

Fig. 1. Pension increments as a percentage of salary, by age, for a wage stream with 6% inflation discounted at real interest rates of 3%, 6%, and 9%.
Source: Kotlikoff and Wise (1985).

In Figure 1 all three assumptions about real wage growth and nominal interest rates yield peaks at the earliest retirement age but only the lowest line shows negative pension accrual immediately following early retirement age. The top two lines simply show smaller positive accrual after age 55. Actual accrual will depend on the size of the actuarial reduction factor and other details of the benefit calculation rules. Pension accrual will peak at early retirement age if the penalty for early retirement – which is the same as the reward for delayed retirements – is less than actuarially fair. But accruals may still stay positive because of wage growth and the effect of additional years of tenure with the firm. However, if the latter two factors are insufficient to compensate for the inadequate actuarial reward, accruals can actually turn negative after the initial early retirement age.

Hatch (1981) finds that the majority of retirement programs with early retirement options do in fact have better than actuarially fair reduction factors at all ages past early retirement. This means that pension compensation will fall after that age and could lead to total compensation being less than actual wage compensation. Note that for ease of exposition, Kotlikoff and Wise assume that benefits are based on a single year of earnings and that real wages grow at a constant rate. Most pension plans use more than one year in their calculations and it is likely that real wage growth slows at older ages. These two factors would make negative pension accrual more likely in all ages past the initial early retirement age. We find a preponderance of negative accrual rates using data from the Retirement History Study (Burkhauser and Quinn (1983a)).

3.2 The Spot vs. Implict Contract View of Pensions

There is considerable literature on the impact of pension incentives on the retirement decision. Most analysts now agree that pensions (and social security) penalize those who remain on the job "too late" by imposing pay cuts via losses in pension (and social security) wealth. A much smaller literature discusses the impact of these same mechanisms on labor supply decisions earlier in life. One view (the implicit contract view of pensions) suggests that pensions can also be used to insure that workers do not leave the job "too early".

Despite the fact that workers make no explicit payment into a defined pension fund, pensions are not a free gift from a firm to its workers. Rather, firms and workers recognize that promises to pay pension benefits are costly to the firm. This cost must be made up by the willingness of employees to receive smaller paychecks for a given amount of work. But there is profound disagreement among economists over the nature of this pension promise and the amount of reduced wages workers are willing to accept for it. Two contending theories of how competitive markets clear offer significantly different views of how workers value the pension promises of their firm and of how the resulting liability of these firms is determined.

In the previous section we discussed the quit value of a pension. The accrual value of the pension was measured as the difference between the pension's value if the worker quits today versus its value if the worker quits one year from now.

While this calculation is straightforward, its implications for work behavior are not. Neoclassical economic theory holds that a worker is paid the value of his marginal productivity to the firm. From a "spot" market view this means that the value of a worker's productivity in any one year is equal to total compensation in that year. But as we have seen, total compensation consists of both wage earnings and the accrued value of a pension associated with that extra work. But what is this accrued value? Because current pension legislation requires firms to back up their explicit defined pension promise to worker by holding funds in reserve to match the quit value of the pension, the accrual assumptions made in the previous section seem to be a reasonable way to measure it.

But as Kotlikoff and Wise point out, these accrued values and the assumption of spot labor markets imply a quite unlikely productivity relationship across a worker's work life with the firm. As Figure 1 shows, workers assumed to have constantly increasing real wages will have total compensation spikes at the year of vesting and once again at the point of early retirement eligibility. This seems incompatible with any reasonable pattern of productivity across a worker's tenure with a firm and suggests that a strict spot labor market model does not adequately explain the reality of pensions. A more complex model of labor market behavior is required to understand the role of pensions at younger ages.

Ippolito (1987) offers an alternative explanation of the pension contract. In the pure spot market case workers are assumed to be paid the value of their work in each period. Because the firm is able to fire them, workers value the pension promise only at its quit value, and it is the difference between these quit values that determines the accrued value in each period. But Ippolito argues that workers are willing to enter into implicit contracts with firms in which, for all years prior to the agreed upon retirement year, they forgo wages *in excess of* the quit value of their pensions. Workers are assumed to agree to this despite the fact that current federal legislation only requires firms to pay workers the quit value of their pension.

This type of model relaxes the single year requirement of equality between the value of a worker's productivity to the firm and his yearly compensation. Instead it requires that a worker's *lifetime* compensation from the firm equal *lifetime* productivity. [Becker and Stigler (1974) and Lazear (1979) provide earlier discussions of the importance of pensions in lifetime implicit contracts.]

The implications of this new view are significant. In the older spot market model, the worker is fully compensated each year. Part of the compensation is in the form of a paycheck, and the rest is "paid" as pension accrual. The pension accrual is delayed compensation, but the account is paid in full whenever the employee leaves. In the implicit contract view, on the other hand, the account is fully paid only if the employee remains until the agreed upon retirement age. Workers who quit before then receive pension rights that are worth less than the wages they had already foregone.

One common mechanism for this separation penalty is to determine annual pension benefits (due, say, at age 60) in terms of the *nominal* value of the last (or last several) year's earnings with the firm. Workers who leave the firm early then find that the real value of this pension promise diminishes as the cost of living rises. Those still working for the firm are protected against this erosion, since their "last year's earnings" rises with the price level.

In this model, pensions are seen as a mechanism to ensure that workers leave a job at a particular age. Negative pension accrual assures that workers will not stay too long and substantial losses in pension wealth assure that workers will not leave too soon. The loss in pension wealth workers who leave too soon suffer is not trivial. Ippolito (1987) shows that with an interest rate of 10 percent, a worker who quits a job 10 years from retirement will lose nearly two-thirds of his potential wealth.

3.3 Social Security

Much of the discussion concerning the value of pension wealth in the previous section is applicable to the retirement component of the social security program. We can estimate the accrual value of social security as we did for pensions.

In fact, this is precisely what was done by those estimating the impact of social security on retirement. Social security wealth and changes in that wealth as one continues to work are important components in the behavioral models of Burtless and Moffitt (1986), Fields and Mitchell (1984) and ourselves (Burkhauser and Quinn (1983)).

In the previous section the accrual value of pensions was discussed as a means of testing single-period versus multi-period models of labor market contracts. The emphasis was on how the pension plan alters work with a given firm. There is little or no discussion of how pensions affect overall work effort. Rather Ippolito argues that pensions encourage workers both to stay with a given firm up to retirement age and to leave thereafter. In contrast, the influence of social security on overall work patterns dominates the small amount of research on the effect of social security on younger workers.

Social security is similar to a defined benefit pension plan in that the government promises workers a benefit at retirement based on an agreed upon formula. Normal retirement benefits currently begin at age 65 with an early retirement option at age 62. For workers age 62 in 1987 retirement benefits are based on their highest 32 years of social security covered earnings. The number of years used in the average will increase by one year per year until it reaches 35 years in 1990. A major change in the formula occurred for those who were aged 62 or below in 1978. The highest earnings years used in the formulation of the benefit formulae were indexed to changes in the real wage rate. Note that this change in policy, if applied to defined benefit pension plans, would dramatically reduce the current penalty to those who leave their job before retirement age.

Social security differs from private pension plans, however, in at least one fundamental way. There is no requirement that the expected benefits paid to any single individual (or cohort) equal his payment into the plan.

If one assumes, as Kotlikoff and Wise do, that workers receive a constantly increasing wage rate and that they will work the same number of hours each year, then the accrual pattern of social security benefits would look much the same as that of a private pension. For the moment, if we ignore taxes and merely look at how present discounted benefits would change with one more year's work, the accrual pattern across the life of a person who begins to work in social security covered employment at age 20 can be traced.

As Figure 2 shows, accrual during the first 9 years is zero since social security requires 10 years of covered service before one is eligible to receive any benefits. The first peak in accrual would occur at age 30, representing the onset of a vested right to social security. Accrued benefits would then increase in the same manner as they did for private pensions since each year of work raises average monthly earnings and reduces the time between the current year and the year of early retirement. (Since 35 years of earnings are used in the average earnings calculations, the increase in average earnings associated with one more year of work will peak at age 55 since earnings are replacing zeros in the calculation before that. But depending on the discount rate chosen accrual rates may still rise to age 62). What happens to social se-

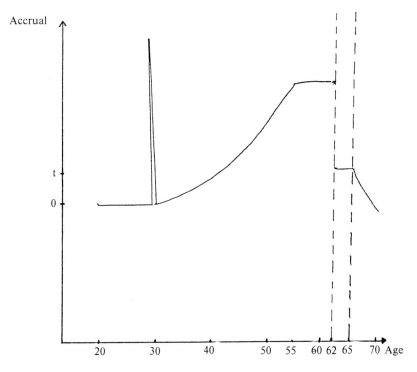

Fig. 2. Social Security Lifetime Accrual Path

curity accrual after age 62 is a matter of some debate. For example, Blinder, Gordon and Wise (1980) argue that at least for the period of the 1970s, the accrual rate for social security was positive past age 62, even after social security taxes are subtracted.

What marks the recent literature on social security is a shift away from the assumptions used in the estimation of the social security accrual path in Figure 2. Burkhauser and Turner (1982) argue that from a life time labor supply perspective in which workers can choose their individual work paths, it is irrelevant whether accrual rates are positive or negative after age 62. What is critical is whether these rates are higher or lower *than those in earlier years.* They argue that once one drops the assumption that workers must work the same amount of hours in all years, it can be shown that workers will shift out of hours which are relatively less rewarded and substitute work into the years that are more rewarded. Hence, if social security accrual rates peak at early retirement in the same way that private pensions do, this is sufficient to induce workers to work more at younger pre-social security retirement ages and less at older ages. Most economists would now agree that social security accural rates peak no later than age 62.

There is less consensus on when social security wealth peaks; that is, on when social security accural net of taxes turns negative. The small actuarial adjustments of those who postpone acceptance past age 65, suggest that it occurs at if not before this age. A first approximation is that today for a worker with average life expectancy, whose real earnings are increasing, taxes offset accrual and social security wealth is constant between age 62 and 65. It is rising, implying a wage subsidy, before age 62, and falling, implying a wage cut, after age 65.

4. Changing Retirement Incentives

4.1 Mandatory Retirement Rules

The 1977 Amendments to the Age Discrimination in Employment Act raised from 65 to 70 the age of earliest mandatory retirement for most workers. In 1986 mandatory retirement at any age was made illegal in all but a small number of jobs. The abolishment of mandatory retirement rules clearly increases the options available to many employees by permitting them to remain on their jobs. But there is little evidence that this change has had a significant effect on work effort.

Mandatory retirement rules were widespread in the early 1970s. We estimated that 43 percent of employed men aged 58 to 61 in 1969 faced mandatory retirement on the job they then held (Quinn and Burkhauser (1983)). But in addition we found that the great majority of such workers, 91 percent, were also eligible for an employer pension on that job. Hence the removal of mandatory retirement for most of these workers would still leave in place substantial disincentives to work.

As was discussed in the previous section, social security and pension accrual can importantly effect net wage compensation. We found that for full-time employed men age 63 to 65 in 1974, social security and private pensions dramatically altered wage compensation. For the median worker aged 63 or 64 eligible for social security but not employer pension benefits, social security accrual was positive and increased true compensation by around 10 percent of traditionally defined earnings (see Quinn and Burkhauser (1983)). But at age 65 the median worker suffered a negative accrual which reduced compensation by about a third. This dramatic change occurred because at that time the delayed retirement credit (the percentage supplement to future benefits following an additional year of work) fell at age 65, from eight percent to only one percent per year of delay. In 1981 the delayed retirement credit, after age 65 was increased to 3 percent per year of delay. For the median worker eligible for both social security and a private pension at age 63, compensation was augmented by about 10 percent, but was reduced by 3 percent at age 64, and by almost half at age 65. This suggests that attempts to increase work effort after age 65 that do not address the dramatic reductions in pension and social security wealth that occur around this age may be doomed to failure.

We also simulated the effect of raising the mandatory retirement age from 65 to 70 on a sample of fully employed men aged 62 to 64 in 1974 (Burkhauser and Quinn (1983b)). We asked what the work effort of these men would have been in 1975 if the law raising the mandatory retirement age had been in effect, and estimated that only about 50,000 additional men from that cohort would have been in the labor force. This would have raised the labor force participation rate of that group by about 2 percent, and would have been inconsequential in the aggregate economy.

4.2 Changing Social Security Rules

There is little doubt that the work incentives embedded in social security have altered the behavior of older Americans, although the size of the aggregate effect is hotly debated. In the early years of the 21st century, the costs of this policy in lost manpower will grow. The changing demographic structure makes policies that drive older men and women away from work more and more questionable. These considerations, together with the budget crises of the early 1980s, were at the heart of the 1983 Amendments to the Social Security Act which for the first time substantially reduced social security benefits.

It is worth noting that *current* social security beneficiaries were only slightly effected by the budget cuts and these cuts will have only very minor effects on program outlays over the next two decades. Bipartisan political support for social security made it impossible to phase cuts in any faster.

The amendments will change two features of the system. The first will increase work effort by reducing benefits. The second will increase work effort by increasing benefits. The gradual increase in the normal retirement age from 65 to 67 lowers the benefit of those who retire before age 67. But the increase in the annual reward for delayed receipt of benefits past age 65 from 3 to 8 percent per year increases the marginal return to work past age 65. These are important changes in the incentive structure. But it is unclear how much of an effect this will have on future work effort.

Social security benefits will continue to be offered at age 62. But for workers who choose to take such benefits, the actuarial reduction will reduce yearly benefits to 70 percent of normal benefits rather than the 80 percent that now exists. Two studies done before the actual rule changes were announced simulated the effect of similar proposals. Burtless and Moffitt (1985) find that delaying the normal retirement age will increase work effort, but estimate that the size of the effect will be relatively small. They suggest that if retirement age were increased to 68, this would increase the average retirement age by less than one-half year. Fields and Mitchell (1984), using a slightly different behavioral model, also find that the increase in work effort from such a change would be modest – on the order of two months on average.

Gustman and Steinmeier (1985) simulate three actual changes initiated by the 1983 Social Security Amendments – the increases in normal retirement age to 67, the increase in the delayed retirement credit after age 65 from 3 to 8 percent, and the decrease in the benefit reduction rate (the earnings test tax rate) from 50 to 33 percent. The effects are long run in that they assume that workers know these are the rules over their lifetime. But they do not allow other aspects of the retirement system to change; in particular, the details of private pension plan accrual are assumed to be unaltered.

Gustman and Steinmeier find a larger effect than the other studies. The percentage of men over age 65 working full time would increase, and the percentage working part-time would decrease. They find that the percentage of men aged 66 who work full-time would increase from 18.4 to 22.7 percent or by almost one-quarter of their previous rate, with similar if not larger increases to other age categories above age 65. While these are dramatic increases, they are from a small base so that overall effects on the labor market would still be small. They find more modest effects on retirement age prior to age 65. The majority of the impact on work effort is found to result from the increase in the delayed retirement credit rather than the postponement of normal retirement age.

4.3 Changes in Employer Pension Plans

Information on pension plans is more difficult to obtain since there are so many plans, each with its own rules. Hence it is more difficult to estimate the full effect of these plans on work behavior. Fields and Mitchell (1984) and we (Burkhauser and Quinn (1983)) have shown that negative pension accrual does influence the age at which a worker leaves a firm and that the age at which most pension plan accrual rates turn negative is at or before age 65. But because pension plans vary widely across the economy no one has estimated the impact of these plans on overall work effort.

Because employer pensions play an important part in the retirement decision of workers, simulations of the type discussed above can be dramatically effected by assumptions about how pensions accrual patterns will change over the next several decades. And it is unlikely that they will remain the same as is implicitly assumed by these simulations. The dramatic drops in social security accrual at age 65 will be substantially reduced once the 1983 Amendments are fully implemented. If firms continue to want to encourage their workers to leave the firm at or before age 65, they can simply increase the size of their negative pension accruals to offset this reduction. But if labor shortages begin to appear in the first part of the 21st century then it is also possible that firms will follow the lead of social security and reduce negative accruals at older ages.

5. Work After Retirement

Social Security and employer pension plans are now an integral part of the United States labor market. We have argued that the accrual patterns of defined benefit pensions may serve an important function. They ensure that workers neither stay too long nor leave too soon from their career job. Social security's accrual system also encourages workers to work more at younger ages and less later. Thus both components of the retirement system may have contributed to the current pattern of early retirement.

But as the age of exit from career jobs has fallen over the last several decades a less recognized phenomena has also occurred – work after retirement. Social security rules encourage workers to shift work from older ages in which the accrual rate is low (and sometimes negative) to younger ages when the accrual rate is higher. Employer pensions add to this incentive by encouraging workers to stay with a particular firm until retirement age and then to leave the firm. But how do older workers actually exit career jobs?

Quinn (1981), Gustman and Steinmeier (1984), and Hanoch and Honig (1985) have argued that the decision to leave full time work is not a simple one in which the alternative is complete retirement. Rather, they model the decision as one of full time work, part time work or no work. But the real work decision is even more varied. Exit from a full career job can occur not only in terms of hours of work but also in terms of alternative jobs. Because employer pensions are usually tied to a specific job, they most directly effect work at that job, but they generally do not restrict other employment. Hence our present retirement system offers one explanation for work after retirement.

Table 5 shows how older American workers in the Retirement History Study, a 10 year longitudinal survey of men and single women age 58 to 63 in 1969, exited from their career jobs. Workers were considered to be on their career job in 1969 if they were working full time and had worked on that job for at least 10 years. About three-quarters of those employed full time in 1969 had been so for 10 years or more. Of the 1,446 non-self employed males on career jobs, a little over 70 percent left them by 1975 and remained completely out of the work force for at least four years.

This traditional transition – from full time work to full time retirement – is still the most common way that workers depart. But it is by no means the

Table 5. Exit from full time career job, men aged 58-63 in 1969

Transition	Wage and salary	Self-employed
Part time on the same job	5	25
Part time on a new job	10	13
Full time on a new job	12	13
Out of labor force	73	49
Sample size	1446	241

Source: Retirement History Study.

only way. About five percent first dropped to part time status on the career job. But more surprisingly over 20 percent of older workers left a career job and then moved to new full time or part time employment. Work after retirement is one of the least explored aspects of the labor market in the United States.

Why workers leave their full time jobs to move to other work is not fully understood. It is interesting to note, however, that self-employed workers behave quite differently. Less than half of the self-employed moved directly from full time work to full retirement. The self employed are more likely to be able to control working conditions, especially hours of work. Almost one of every four self-employed men moved from full time to part time work on his career job. The remaining quarter moved to new full time or part time employment.

The movement to a new employer is not necessarily instantaneous. Table 6 shows that most non-self employed men who took new *full time* jobs did so within six months of leaving their full time career jobs. Seven in ten were on their new full time job within a year. The average time span between an exit from a full time career job to a new *part time* job was greater. About one in three started within six months of exit and one-half did so within a year. But for 30 percent of the sample, a new part time job was not taken until a full two years has elapsed.

Table 6. Time interval between career job and new job wage and salary men, aged 58-63 in 1969

	N = 151	N = 176
Months	Part time	Full time
0 – 6	31 %	55 %
7 – 12	15	16
13 – 18	12	10
19 – 24	11	8
25 – 30	10	5
31 – 36	7	5
37 – 42	9	2
43 – 48	4	2
Total	100	100

Source: Retirement History Study.

Work after retirement is not a rare event and the jobs are in most cases substantial. In Table 7 we follow those workers who took new jobs for two years after the transition. The majority were still working at the end of this period. Nearly 60 percent of those who simply reduced their hours of work on their career job were still working part time on that job two years later. About a quarter had left the labor force. The rest had either moved to another new job or had returned to full time work on their career job.

Table 7. Probability of labor activity two years after start of post-Career job wage and salary men, aged 58-63 in 1969

Post-career job	No change	Out of labor force	New Part time job	New Full time job	Return to Full time career job	N
Part time on the same job	57 %	26	7	1	9	82
Part Time on a new job	49	26	20	5	--	168
Full time on a new job	44	33	7	16	--	203

Source: Retirement History Study.
Note: The sample sizes are slightly larger than in Table 6 because we only required two
years of post-transition data here.

Of those who took new *part time* employment, half are still on that part time job two years later. About a quarter are no longer working and the rest are on another new job. For those who took a new full time job the pattern is similar, although they are slightly more likely to have left the labor force.

These findings indicate that older workers leave their career jobs in many different ways. While it is true that the majority do so in the traditional manner, directly from full time work to full time retirement, a significant percentage exit otherwise. As Gustman and Steinmeier (1984) and Honig and Hanoch (1985) suggest, some go from full to part time employment. This sometimes occurs by reducing hours on the career job. But it is far more likely to involve a new job, and considerably lower hourly pay.

The majority of workers who leave their career jobs in these unconventional ways remain in the work force for at least two years. This is a significant amount of time, suggesting that these transitional steps are important. Unfortunately, little is known about the postretirement behavior of workers. This is a fertile area for new research.

6. Conclusions

The retirement system in the United States has grown enormously in the past three and one-half decades. Social security programs have had almost universal support over this period and that support has been translated into substantial growth under both Democratic and Republican administrations. Even in the last decade, when growth relative to GNP was negative for non-social security programs, social security continued to expand.

Major cuts in social security liabilities did occur in 1983 but they will not affect current or near term beneficiaries. Rather these cuts will be borne by those retiring in the second decade of the 21st century. Even these cuts were

controversial and are by no means sure to occur. They were made in part because of a fear that the graying of America will lead to future labor shortages
and a belief that such cuts will increase work effort at older ages.

We argue that the current retirement system in the United States affects
work at all ages, and that one cannot appreciate its full impact without a life-
cycle view of both social security and employer pensions. The financial incentives in defined benefit pension plans encourage workers to stay on a career job until retirement age and to leave soon thereafter. Social security encourages workers to work longer hours than they otherwise would at younger ages and to leave the labor force at older ages. These schemes also influence the way that workers exit their career jobs. Negative pension accrual encourages an exit from a career job but not necessarily from the labor force.
Social security encourages both. In the face of these work constraints most
workers go from full time work on a career job to full time retirement. The
age at which this transition occurs has fallen dramatically over time. But a
substantial minority of transitions from career jobs are not to full retirement.
Although this has not been adequately studied, it is likely that recent social
security reforms reducing the penalty for continued work at older ages will
further encourage part time or even full time work after the end of a career
job.

References

Anderson, K. H., R. V. Burkhauser, and J. F. Quinn (1986) Do Retirement Dreams Come True:
    The Effect of Unanticipated Events on Retirement Plans. Industrial and Labor Relations
    Review 39, 4, pp. 518-526
Barnow, B. S. and R. G. Ehrenberg (1979) The Costs of Defined Benefit Pension Plans and
    Firm Adjustments. Quarterly Journal of Economics, pp. 523-540
Becker, G. S. and G. J. Stigler (1974) Law Enforcement, Malfeasance, and Compensation of
    Enforcers. Journal of Legal Studies 3, pp. 1-18
Blinder, A. S., R. Gordon, and D. E. Wise (1980) Reconsidering the Work Disincentive Effects
    of Social Security. National Tax Journal 33, pp. 431-442
Burkhauser, R. V. and J. F. Quinn (1983a) The Effect of Pension Plans on the Pattern of Life-
    Cycle Compensation. In: The Measure of Labor Cost, Jack E. Triplett (Ed.) Chicago: Uni-
    versity of Chicago Press, pp. 395-415
Burkhauser, R. V. and J. F. Quinn (1983b) Is Mandatory Retirement Overrated? Evidence from
    the 1970s. Journal of Human Resources 18, pp. 337-358
Burkhauser, R. V. and J. A. Turner (1982) Labor-Market Experience of the Almost Old and the
    Implications for Income Support. American Economic Review 72, pp. 304-308
Burtless, G. (1986) Social Security, Unanticipated Benefit Increases, and the Timing of Retire-
    ment. Review of Economic Studies 53, 176, pp. 781-805
Burtless, G. and R. A. Moffitt (1985) The Joint Choice of Retirement Age and Postretirement
    Hours of Work. Journal of Labor Economics 3, pp. 209-236
Burtless, G. and R. A. Moffit (1986) Social Security, Earnings Tests, and Age of Retirement.
    Public Finance Quarterly 14, pp. 3-27
Fields, G. S. and O. S. Mitchell (1984) Retirement, Pensions, and Social Security. Cambridge,
    MA: The MIT Press
Gordon, R. H. and A. S. Blinder (1980) Market Wages, Reservation Wages, and Retirement De-
    cisions. Journal of Public Economics, pp. 431-442

Gustman, A. A. and T. L. Steinmeier (1984) Partial Retirement and the Analysis of Retirement Behavior. Industrial and Labor Relations Review 37, pp. 403-415

Gustman, A. A. and T. L. Steinmeier (1985) The 1983 Social Security Reforms and Labor Supply Adjustments of Older Individuals in the Long Run. Journal of Labor Economics 3, pp. 237-253

Gustman, A. A. and T. L. Steinmeier (1987) An Analysis of Pension Benefits Formulas, Pension Wealth, and Incentives from Pensions. U.S. Department of Labor (B9P52726), mimeo

Hatch, S. (1981) Financial Retirement Incentives in Private Pension Plans, Urban Institute Report. Draft project report to the Department of Labor, J-9-P-0-0163

Honig, M. and G. Hanoch (1985) Partial Retirement as a Separate Mode of Retirement Behavior. Journal of Human Resources 20, pp. 21-46

Ippolito, R. A. (1986) Pensions, Economics, and Public Policy. Homewood, IL: Dow Jones-Irwin

Ippolito, R. A. (1987) The Implicit Pension Contract: Developments and New Directions. Journal of Human Resources 22, pp. 441-467

Kotlikoff, L. J. and David A. Wise (1985) Labor Compensation and the Structure of Private Pension Plans: Evidence for Contractual versus Spot Labor Markets. In: Pensions, Labor, and Individual Choice, David A. Wise (Ed.) Chicago: The University of Chicago Press

Lazear, E. P. (1979) Why Is There Mandatory Retirement? Journal of Political Economy 87, pp. 1261-1284

Quinn, J. F. (1981) The Extent and Correlates of Partial Retirement. The Gerontologist 21, pp. 634-643

Quinn, J. F. (1987) The Economic Status of the Elderly: Beware of the Mean. Review of Income and Wealth 33, pp. 63-82

Quinn, J. F. and R. V. Burkhauser (1983) Influencing Retirement Behavior: A Key Issue for Social Security. Journal of Policy Analysis and Management 3, pp. 1-13

Smolensky, E., S. Danziger, and P. Gottshalk (1988) The Declining Significance of Age in the United States: Trends in the Well-Being of Children and the Elderly since 1939. In: The Vulnerable, J. Palmer, T. Smeeding, and B. Torrey (Eds.) Washington, D.C.: The Urban Institute, pp. 29-54

Social Security Administration (1987) Annual Statistical Supplement. Washington, D.C.: U.S. Government Printing Office

U.S. Bureau of the Census (1986) Current Population Reports. Series P-60, No. 152. Characteristics of the Population Below the Poverty Level: 1984. Washington, D.C.: U.S. Government Printing Office

Ycas, M. and S. Grad (1987) Income of Retirement-Aged Persons, Social Security Bulletin 50, pp. 5-14

The Retirement Process in the United States: Mobility Among Full-Time Work, Partial Retirement, and Full Retirement

C. Reimers and M. Honig[1]

Contents

1. Introduction

The older American male's long-term trend toward withdrawal from the labor force has continued into the 1980's, though at a decelerating rate. At all ages over 57, male labor force participation during a year dropped by 3-4 percentage points from 1977 to 1982; whereas in the preceding 5 years it had dropped by 7-12 percentage points. While 87 percent of 55-57 year olds still worked sometime during 1982, the dropoff with advancing age was steep; only 60 percent of 62-64 year olds and 25 percent of 68-73 year olds worked at all in that year. The decline in participation from 1977 to 1982 by men over 65 came entirely at the expense of part-time work; the small fractions working substantially full-time remained stable. On the other hand, men aged 62-64 moved out of both full-time and part-time work; while men under age 62 shifted into part-time out of full-time work.[2]

---

[1] We thank George Sweeting for unusually able assistance and the conference participants, especially Winfried Schmähl, for helpful suggestions.

[2] U.S. Bureau of the Census (1973, 1978, 1983); authors' tabulations.

W. Schmähl (Ed.)
Redifining the Process of Retirement
© Springer-Verlag Berlin Heidelberg 1989

This trend toward non-participation has no obvious explanation. In the U.S. at present, private pensions provide incentives for many to leave their career jobs even before they become eligible to receive Social Security benefits at age 62. However, private pension rules do not require one to reduce one's earnings, if one can find another job that pays as well. The current Social Security rules (summarized in the Appendix) do encourage a reduction of earnings at age 65, to a level implying part-time work (but not *no* work) for most men. The actuarial adjustment for postponed benefit receipt between ages 62 and 65 is nearly fair on average. Therefore the rules, *if* they are well understood, should not encourage earnings reduction before age 65 – unless illiquidity is a problem or unless one's expected remaining lifetime is shorter than average. Burtless and Moffitt (1985, p. 225) calculated the distribution of age at "retirement" (defined as "a sudden and discontinuous drop in hours" to below 30 per week) for men aged 66-71 in 1977 who had already retired. They found that retirements peak at age 62 and again, even more, at 65. They argue that illiquidity of Social Security wealth is the most plausible reason for the peak at 62.

New Social Security rules, enacted in 1983 to be phased in beginning in 1987, will eventually reduce the incentive to stop working full-time at age 65 by making the actuarial adjustment fair on average after that age, too. Beginning in 2000 benefit levels will also gradually be reduced, until ultimately they will be 13 percent lower than at present, for equivalent individuals. (See the Appendix for an explanation of these rules.) Will these new rules induce more work after age 65? Will it be part-time or full-time? To what extent do labor market conditions and constraints on weekly hours create obstacles preventing older workers from working the amount they desire? Answers to such questions are important as policy makers try to cope with the changing age structure of the U.S. population.

Several recent careful studies of the effects of Social Security on retirement behavior in the U.S. estimate very small responses to changes in the Social Security rules (Burtless (1986), Burtless and Moffitt (1984, 1985), Hausman and Wise (1985)). It is noteworthy that these authors rely on a definition of retirement as a one-step action; while Gustman and Steinmeier (1985a, 1985b), who use a more complex model incorporating the possibility of partial retirement, find larger estimated effects of changes in Social Security. Diamond and Hausman (1984) also find fairly large effects despite using a single-step definition of retirement, but they use a different data set from the others. The question is clearly open to further investigation.

Almost all research so far has defined "retirement" as a *state* that one is either in or not in. This both reflects and reinforces a widely held view that retirement is a one-step, irreversible event. However, if retirement is in fact a *process* that occurs over an extended period of time rather than an *act* that occurs at a point in time, a model of retirement as a single act will fail to capture some of the ways older people respond to changes in circumstances. Estimates based on such models, therefore, may be misleading guides to policymaking. Without careful empirical study of people's actual behavior over time, we cannot understand what "retirement" is. Is there in fact an abrupt shift from full-time to no work, or an intervening period of part-time work, or several moves into and out of the labor force?

Several types of evidence cast doubt on the traditional one-step view of retirement. For instance, many older men in the U.S. work part-time. Part-time or part-year work rises with age after 55, reaching a peak of over 20 percent of men aged 65-67 in 1982.[3] Many men also refer to themselves as "partially retired" at some time during their later life. This, too, increases with age, peaking at 20 percent of men aged 65-69 during the years 1969-1979.[4] In a sample from the Retirement History Survey of 2542 men aged 58 to 73 in 1969-1979, we found that 37 percent spent some time in partial retirement (as defined by a relative earnings measure), while only 35 percent followed the "classic" path, moving from full employment to full retirement in one step.

Moreover, older workers do not simply reduce their work activity in one or two steps. Many who partially retire return to full-time employment and many others, who leave the labor force completely, re-enter later at various levels of activity. Fifteen percent of the individuals in the above-mentioned sample moved from full retirement back into the work force, or from partial retirement back to full-time work, at some point in their retirement process. Among the 2542 men in the sample, 710 new jobs were begun in the ten years after the start of the survey.

We are currently engaged in research that exploits the longitudinal Retirement History Survey to describe and analyze patterns of retirement behavior by older Americans, where retirement is explicitly viewed as a process that may last for several years and may involve several transitions out of and into the labor force and between full-time and part-time work. Besides a better understanding of the longitudinal labor-force behavior of older Americans, we hope to provide better estimates of the effects of Social Security, private pensions, and labor market conditions on the path and timing of the retirement process. As American policy makers struggle with the changing age structure of the population and its implications for future labor shortages and support of the elderly, major changes in the future Social Security rules have already been enacted in 1983. We would like to know to what extent older people may respond to these or other policy initiatives by continuing to work full time until an older age, or by working part time, or by re-entering the work force after a spell of time off. What factors (e.g., health, marital status, occupation) are associated with greater ability to make such adjustments? What policy changes are indicated to achieve a desired pattern of retirement behavior? The answers have implications for the long-term financing of the Social Security system as well as for the adequacy of supply of certain types of labor and the welfare of the elderly.

---

[3] U.S. Bureau of the Census (1983); authors' tabulations.
[4] Gustman and Steinmeier (1985a), Table 1, p. 30. Their sample consists of males who were not self-employed in their main job (the job held full-time at age 55), pooling all 6 waves of the Retirement History Survey (which was collected biennially, 1969-1979).

The goal of our research is to analyze transition probabilities among the states of non-retirement, partial retirement, and full retirement by estimating a continuous-time, multiple-spell, three-state duration model of the retirement process for American men and women. A fuller exposition of the model and issues of definition and measurement is in Honig and Reimers (1987). Our data are drawn from the longitudinal Retirement History Survey (RHS), a sample of married males and unmarried females aged 58-63 in 1969, who were interviewed biennially through 1979.[5] While estimates of the model are not yet available, in Section II we discuss our choice of relative monthly earnings as a measure of retirement behavior over time, and in Section III we present some preliminary findings for men. These explore the patterns of observed transitions among the discrete retirement states of full retirement, partial retirement, and non-retirement, including transitions to states of greater activity; and analyze the relationship between transition type and factors such as age, health, pension eligibility, occupation, industry, and peak lifetime earnings. Section IV contains some concluding remarks.

2. Defining Retirement States

Since the retirement process appears to be characterized by discrete jumps in earnings (Burtless and Moffitt (1984)) as well as by changes in job and occupation, it is most naturally handled by a model that examines transitions among states, rather than one that treats labor supply as a continuous variable. Moreover, because re-entry and increases in work activity are rather common, these upward transitions should be included in the analysis.

Retirement states may be defined by at least three criteria: self-reported status, hours of work, and earnings. The latter two are preferable to the first because they are based on measurable behavior in the labor market. Earnings have the advantage of capturing the effect of the retirement process on wages as well as on hours of work. Departure from the career job may involve loss of seniority rents and firm-specific human capital. In addition, increased demand for easier working conditions may involve a compensating wage differential for the same hours of work, which would not be detected in an hours of work definition.

Because some people have low earnings throughout their lives, an absolute earnings criterion would be inappropriate for defining retirement states. This is particularly true of women, many of whom work part time throughout their careers. We therefore define partial retirement as positive current monthly earnings less than 80 percent (in real terms) of maximum lifetime earnings (and, if the person was classified as non-retired in the previous month, a decline in nominal earnings of at least 20 percent from the previous month). We choose a ratio of current to peak real earnings of 0.8 to conform to the usual definition of part-time work as less than 35 hours per week,

---

[5]   For a description of these data, see Irelan (1976).

which is a little over 80 percent of average full-time hours. Even if a person is still working full-time hours, a decline in real earnings of 20 percent from the lifetime peak would reflect a major change in job or work activity. We require a month-to-month decline in nominal earnings of at least 20 percent to avoid generating spurious transitions from non-retirement to partial retirement due to changes in the price index or to minor fluctuations in reported earnings. A person is defined as non-retired if his current real monthly earnings are at least 80 percent of his maximum lifetime earnings; and, for one classified as partially retired in the previous month, if his real earnings rose by at least 20 percent from month to month. This prevents an ordinary wage increase on a continuing job from appearing to be a transition to a state of higher labor force activity.

Our method of defining retirement states differs from that adopted by Burkhauser and Quinn elsewhere in this volume. Whereas we define a man's status by his monthly earnings rate (relative to his lifetime peak), they focus on weekly hours worked and job tenure. They distinguish between a "career job," as defined by full-time hours and long tenure (at least ten years in 1969, at ages 58-63), and subsequent full-time jobs; by definition, one cannot return to a career job once one has retired from it. We, on the other hand, do not distinguish between "non-retirement" (i.e., high-earnings) jobs of differing durations, and we permit a person to return to non-retired status after a spell of partial or full retirement. Furthermore, they distinguish among post-retirement states by weekly hours of work alone (i.e., full-time, part-time, or none), ignoring the possibility of wages changing due to a change of job content or the loss of firm-specific skills, knowledge, and seniority. Our scheme, being based on relative monthly earnings, does take account of changes in rates of pay as well as in hours of work.

Moreover, Burkhauser and Quinn follow people for only four years after retirement from their career job, and count at most one subsequent job during that time. Their sample, also drawn from the RHS, is restricted to men who were still on their "career job" when they were aged 58-63, but left it within the next two years; thus, their sample excludes both early and late retirees. We, on the other hand, count all the transitions between retirement states during a ten-year period covering ages 58-73, including men who left their career job before age 58. Because of this difference in our samples, we find a slightly higher ratio of new jobs to sample size: $710/2542 = .28$ in our case; .24 in theirs.

Because the interviews were conducted biennially, most previous analysts of the RHS have used a two-year time period. This has major limitations for analysis of the retirement process. Measured levels of work activity and earnings are sensitive to the time unit chosen: the longer the time unit, the smoother the earnings path and the more time people will appear to spend in partial retirement rather than alternating between full retirement and full-time work. A two-year period obscures much of the mobility that occurs; the shorter the time unit, the more movement will be observed among discrete states.

We therefore constructed a monthly work history for each individual, from which we determined the timing of transitions among the three states of non-retirement, partial retirement, and full retirement, and the durations of spells in each state, to the nearest month. For example, a transition from full-time work in May to full retirement in June is classified as such, not as a partial retirement during the entire year. Our use of a month as our time unit reveals in more detail than in previous studies the different patterns of work activity by older people. For example, we will be able to see whether the Social Security benefit reduction based on a monthly earnings test (in effect during the survey years) led to "cycling" between periods of full-time and no work.[6] When we examine month-to-month transitions of the 2542 men in our RHS sample, we find a higher ratio of upward (i.e., from full retirement to partial or non-retirement, or from partial to non-retirement) to downward (i.e., from non-retirement to partial or full retirement, or from partial to full retirement) transitions (683/2622=.26) than are apparent in the two-year transitions (310/2049=.15). A two-year time period smooths the fluctuations in labor suply behavior and allows the long-term trend toward full retirement to dominate the observed pattern. Much of the detail of retirement behavior is thus obscured.

3. Results: Correlates of Transition Types

At this point in our research we can report some preliminary statistics for the men in our sample, showing how the six types of transition between non-retirement, partial retirement, and full retirement are correlated with a change of employer, with age, health, private pension eligibility, industry, occupation, and peak lifetime earnings.

3.1 Changes of Employer

Transitions between non-retirement and partial retirement may involve changes of employer or changes of hours and/or wages with the same employer. The vast majority of these transitions occur within the same firm. This is not surprising when we recall that these men are moving directly between non-retirement and partial retirement within a month, without an intervening spell out of a job. Eighty-seven percent of the 545 men making a transition directly from non-retirement to partial retirement do so within the firm they had been working for. Of the 227 men who move directly from partial retirement to non-retirement, 95 percent do so while continuing with the same employer.

---

[6]   The monthly earnings test in Social Security, in which full monthly benefits were payable for months with earnings below the maximum regardless of annual earnings, was eliminated to reduce such planned movements. Annual earnings may still be reduced by part-year employment, however.

Of a total of 710 jobs with *new* employers obtained by the 2542 men in our sample, 74 percent involve a change of retirement state, while the remaining 26 percent involve a change of employer without a change in retirement status. Sixty-three percent represent moves out of full retirement, while only 11 percent involve transitions between non-retirement and partial retirement.

Table 1 shows these jobs with new employers, broken down by age and type of transition. Somewhat surprisingly, 51 percent of the moves to new employers were by men over age 65. Most of these were moves out of full retirement to partial retirement. Re-entry is not, as is often assumed, primarily a phenomenon associated with the younger age groups entering the "retirement years." If the re-entry from full retirement simply reflected a one- or two-month gap between two full-time jobs such as prime-age workers might experience, we would expect the age pattern to resemble that for the "non-retirement to non-retirement" job changes. These are cases where a non-retired person goes from one job to another within a month, with no observed unemployment in between.

Table 1. New employers, by age and type of transition: men aged 58-73, 1969-1979 (sample size: 2542)

Age		Down Transitions NR to PR[a]	Lateral Transitions PR to PR[a]	NR to NR[a]	Up Transitions FR to PR[a]	FR to NR[a]	PR to NR[a]	Total
58-61	N	29	29	29	29	16	6	138
	%	21.0	21.0	21.0	21.0	11.6	4.3	100%
62-64	N	21	58	22	86	21	3	211
	%	10.0	27.5	10.4	40.8	10.0	1.4	100%
65-70	N	20	36	4	258	16	3	337
	%	5.9	10.7	1.2	76.6	4.7	0.9	100%
71+[b]	N	0	5	0	18	1	0	24
	%	0	20.8	0	75.0	4.2	0	100%
Total	N	70	128	55	391	54	12	710
	%	9.9	18.0	7.7	55.1	7.6	1.7	100%

[a] NR = Non-retirement (current/peak monthly earnings > .8)
    PR = Partial retirement (0 < current/peak monthly earnings < .8)
    FR = Full retirement (current monthly earnings = 0)
[b] Imprecise estimate due to small sample in this age group.
Note: Since the RHS sample is unevenly distributed by age, the age distributions of new jobs (i.e., the percentages of column totals) have no significance.

3.2 Age

Table 2 presents the distribution of types of retirement transitions by age, where transitions may occur within a firm as well as with a change of employer. Due to the aging of the RHS panel, the number of observations in each age bracket is unrepresentative of the population. Therefore Table 2 cannot tell us about the age distribution of a particular transition (i.e., percentages of column totals are distorted). However, we *can* compare the distributions of transition types across age groups. The majority of transitions are downward at all ages, but there is a relative increase in upward moves by those aged 65-70. Only 16 percent of the transitions by 62-64 year olds are upward, while 22 percent of the transitions by 65-70 years olds are upward. This is because more men are fully retired by this age, and any transition from full retirement must of course be upward.

Table 2. Distribution of transition types 1969-79: males, by age

Age		Down transitions			Up transitions			Total
		NR to PR[a]	NR to FR[a]	PR to FR[a]	PR to NR[a]	FR to PR[a]	FR to NR[a]	
58-61	N	185	147	54	88	33	22	529
	%	35.0	27.8	10.2	16.6	6.2	4.2	100%
62-64	N	254	536	268	97	87	21	1263
	%	20.1	42.4	21.2	7.7	6.9	1.7	100%
65-70	N	101	512	528	40	258	16	1455
	%	6.9	35.2	36.3	2.7	17.7	1.1	100%

[a] NR = Non-retirement PR = Partial retirement FR = Full retirement

Not surprisingly, 63 percent of the transitions by 58-61 year olds involve downward moves *out of non*-retirement, while 72 percent of the transitions by 65-70 year olds are moves *into full* retirement. What is somewhat surprising is that the percentage of non-retirees moving to full retirement increases so dramatically between ages 58-61 and 62-64. Twice as many of the transitions by 62-64 year olds are from non-retirement to full retirement (42 percent) as are from non-retirement to partial retirement (20 percent). This might be attributed to Social Security eligibility at age 62; but, as was pointed out above, receipt of benefits does not require a complete stoppage of work.

We see the expected age-related shifts in destination of transition, given the original state. Of 58-61 year old non-retirees who appreciably reduce their earnings rate, the majority (56 percent) move directly into a partial retirement job; while 68 percent of 62-64 year old (and 84 percent of 65-70 year old) non-retirees who move "down" stop work entirely for at least one month. Partial retirees who change states are much more likely to move up, the younger they are. Of moves out of partial retirement, 62 percent are to non-retirement at ages 58-61; whereas 27 percent are to non-retirement at ages 62-64, and only 7 percent are to non-retirement at ages 65-70. Similarly, men who go back to work after a period of full retirement are much less likely to move into non-retirement (i.e., earn over 80 percent of their lifetime peak monthly earnings), the older they are.

3.3 Health

Table 3 shows the proportion of those making each transition who report that a health limitation affects their ability to work, for each age group. Health is strongly associated with retirement state and transition type. In each age group, about 20 percent of those who remain in non-retirement or who move from non-retirement to partial retirement report poor health; while, over all ages combined, about 30 percent of those moving down from non-retirement to full retirement have a health limitation. However, this last proportion diminishes with age, from 35 percent at ages 58-64 to 26 percent at ages 65-70.

Table 3. Proportion with health limitation, by age and type of transition: men aged 58-70, 1969-1979

Age	Transitions from NR to:			Transitions from PR to:			Transitions from FR to:		
	NR[a]	PR[a]	FR[a]	NR[a]	PR[a]	FR[a]	NR[a]	PR[a]	FR[a]
58-61	.19	.19	.35	.20	.26	.26	.23	.36	.70
62-64	.20	.20	.35	.21	.28	.43	.14	.33	.57
65-70	.18	.18	.26	.17	.28	.36	.19	.38	.48
All Ages:	.20	.19	.31	.20	.27	.31	.18	.36	.51

[a] NR = Non-retirement (current/peak monthly earnings > .8)
PR = Partial retirement (0 < current/peak monthly earnings < .8)
FR = Full retirement (current monthly earnings = 0)

For the partially retired, those moving to non-retirement are the least likely (20 percent) to be in poor health; while 27 percent of those who stay in partial retirement report a health limitation. These proportions do not change much with age. However, the proportion of those moving from partial retirement to full retirement who have a health limitation does vary with age. It is much higher after age 61 than at younger ages, being 26 percent at ages 58-61 and 43 percent at ages 62-64.

The fully retired who move up to non-retirement are also among the groups least likely (about 20 percent) to have health problems. In contrast, about 35 percent of those who move from full retirement to partial retirement, and half of those who remain fully retired from one month to the next, are in poor health. The influence of health on remaining in full retirement also diminishes with age: 70 percent of the 58-61 years olds who remain fully retired report a health limitation, while only 48 percent of the 65-70 year olds do. This strong interaction of health with age is not observed for those who stay in partial retirement or non-retirement, nor for upward transitions, nor for downward moves from non-retirement to partial retirement.

These patterns suggest that health is not an important factor in decisions to move directly from non-retirement to partial retirement rather than remain non-retired. For the partially retired, however, poor health apparently

deters a move back to non-retirement, and encourages a move into full retirement (at least after age 62). Health status is also strongly associated with
decisions about moving from non-retirement to full retirement and about
returning to work, and how much, after full retirement. This association of
health with the decision to become, or remain, fully retired is strongest for
the younger men, and diminishes with advancing age as other considerations become more important.

3.4 Pensions

Table 4 shows the relation between private pension eligibility and transitions
among retirement states, for different age groups. Eligibility increases more
dramatically at age 62 than at age 65. Non-retirees of all ages who move directly into full retirement are most likely to have a pension from an employer. Among non-retirees under age 65, those who move to partial retirement
are *less* likely to have a pension than those who remain non-retired. However, after age 65 pensions are not associated with the choice between partial
retirement and continued non-retirement, for non-retirees.

Table 4. Proportion eligible to receive private pension, by age and type of transition: men
aged 58-70, 1969-1979

Age	Transitions from NR to:			Transitions from PR to:			Transitions from FR to:		
	NR[a]	PR[a]	FR[a]	NR[a]	PR[a]	FR[a]	NR[a]	PR[a]	FR[a]
58-61	.28	.18	.38	.26	.16	.20	.09	.21	.30
62-64	.54	.45	.66	.39	.34	.43	.43	.40	.52
65-70	.59	.57	.75	.40	.50	.59	.56	.59	.65
All ages:	.44	.38	.67	.34	.36	.52	.35	.51	.60

[a] NR = Non-retirement (current/peak monthly earnings $> .8$)
     PR = Partial retirement ($0 <$ current/peak monthly earnings $< .8$)
     FR = Full retirement (current monthly earnings $= 0$)

Partial retirement is, in general, associated with lower rates of pension
eligibility. Before age 65, those remaining partially retired are less likely to
have a pension than other partial retirees. Among partial retirees younger
than 62, pensions are, surprisingly, most common for those who move back
to non-retirement. After age 62 the effect of pensions makes more sense; the
partial retirees most likely to be eligible for a pension are those who move
into full retirement. For partial retirees beyond age 65, pensions are positively associated with moves to full retirement and negatively associated with
moves to non-retirement.

Full retirees who go back to work are those less likely to have a pension, at all ages. For full retirees, after age 62 there is little association between pension availability and the choice between partial retirement and non-retirement. In the youngest age group, however, those who move from full retirement back to non-retirement are least likely to have a pension.

Thus, we can conclude that private pensions encourage full retirement, while men without a pension more often resort to partial retirement to maintain income as they age. This association of partial retirement with the absence of a pension may in part reflect the behavior of the self-employed, who are less likely to have pensions and who have more flexibility about working hours and duties.

3.5 Industry and Occupation

Table 5 indicates the distribution of each type of downward transition among the major industry groups and between blue collar and white collar occupations. We see that men who move directly from non-retirement into full retirement are disproportionately employed in manufacturing, especially at ages 58-61; while those who move into partial retirement, or from partial to full retirement, are unusually likely to be in services and trade. Men who are still working after age 65 are less likely to be in manufacturing and more likely to be in services and trade than younger workers. This shift between sectors occurs almost entirely among those who move into and out of partial retirement.

Table 5. Proportion in each industry and occupation group, by age and type of downward transition: men aged 58-70, 1969-1979

| | Proportion of those making given transition who were in: | | | | | | | | | | | |
| | Manufacturing | | | Services | | | Trade | | | Blue Collar Occ. | | |
Age	NR to PR	NR to FR	PR to FR	NR to PR	NR to FR	PR to FR	NR to PR	NR to FR	PR to FR	NR to PR	NR to FR	PR to FR
58-61	.58	.73	.52	.25	.17	.28	.14	.09	.15	.71	.70	.80
62-64	.59	.68	.51	.26	.21	.27	.13	.09	.16	.65	.67	.74
65-70	.43	.67	.44	.29	.24	.32	.24	.07	.17	.45	.62	.69

NR = Non-retirement
PR = Partial retirement
FR = Full retirement

Blue collar workers tend to retire earlier than men in white collar jobs. The frequency of manual occupations among transitions out of non-retirement declines with age. Moreover, regardless of age, blue collar jobs are more common among those who move from partial to full retirement than

among non-retirees. Until age 65 there is no occupational difference between non-retirees who stop working, temporarily or permanently, and
those who move into a partial retirement job without a break; but men over
65 who move from non-retirement to partial retirement are more likely to be
white collar workers than are those who leave the work force.

3.6 Lifetime Peak Earnings

In Table 6 we see further evidence that partial retirement is concentrated
among particular groups of workers. In transitions down from non-retirement, for example, lifetime peak monthly earnings are higher for those moving into partial retirement than full retirement. This pattern is consistent
across age groups, with the dollar differential increasing with age. Similarly,
among those re-entering the labor force, lifetime peak earnings are higher
for men moving into partial retirement. This is true as well for those remaining in a given retirement state; lifetime peak earnings are higher for those in
partial retirement than in either full retirement or non-retirement.
        We can also infer from Table 6 that higher lifetime earnings are associat-
ed with later withdrawal from the labor force. Average peak earnings of those
remaining non-retired or moving from partial to non-retirement rise with
age. The same thing happens to average peak earnings of those who stay fully
retired or who move from partial to full retirement, because high earners are
disproportionately added to these groups as they become older.
        The patterns in Tables 5 and 6 show that partial retirement is more prev-
alent among higher paid, white collar workers in services and trade. This suggests that blue collar and manufacturing workers may have fewer opportunities for part-time work and perhaps, more generous pensions relative to
earnings, so that they are more likely to follow the stereotypical pattern of an
abrupt and permanent withdrawal from the labor force. They also retire at
younger ages than white collar workers and those employed in the trade and
service sectors.

Table 6. Mean of lifetime peak monthly earnings, by age and type of transition: men aged
58-70, 1969-1979

Age	Transitions from NR to:			Transitions from PR to:			Transitions from FR to:		
	NR[a]	PR[a]	FR[a]	NR[a]	PR[a]	FR[a]	NR[a]	PR[a]	FR[a]
58-61	$ 753	$ 856	$ 795	$ 689	$ 829	$ 673	$ 675	$ 782	$ 654
62-64	769	847	756	657	844	812	771	922	693
65-70	861	871	774	827	850	840	755	814	752
All ages:	772	852	769	699	841	816	724	827	735

[a] NR = Non-retirement (current/peak monthly earnings > .8)
     PR = Partial retirement (0 < current/peak monthly earnings < .8)
     FR = Full retirement (current monthly earnings = 0)

4. Concluding Remarks

Retirement has often been viewed as an "either-or" proposition: either one is working full-time or not at all, with the transition occurring in the early sixties for Americans. It has become increasingly clear, however, that retirement in the U.S. is a more complex phenomenon. In particular, significant numbers of older workers are spending time in the intermediate state of partial retirement. Moreover, older workers do not simply reduce their work activity in one or two steps. Many who partially retire return to full-time employment and many others, who leave the labor force completely, re-enter later at various levels of activity.

Despite considerable work in this area, the exact path and timing of retirement is still not well understood. We hope to provide a better understanding of the longitudinal labor-force behavior of older Americans by analyzing retirement as a process that may extend over several years and may involve several transitions – either "up" or "down" – between full-time work, partial retirement, and no work.

Several issues in public policy involve the extent to which older workers may adjust their earnings levels. Legislated future declines in real Social Security benefits, resulting from increases in the age of eligibility for full benefits beginning in the year 2000, assume a larger role for earnings over the "normal" retirement years, as well as increased private savings and pension income. As private pension vesting becomes more widespread, an increasing fraction of the older work force will face incentives for early retirement from their career job which, with the substantial increases in longevity in recent years, will increase the span of the "retirement years" to two or three decades. The ability of older persons to maintain consumption over this extended period, and their ability to respond to unforeseen changes in income or needs, have become policy issues of considerable importance.

The tabulations reported in this paper suggest that health, pensions, earnings, occupation, and industry affect the pattern and timing of the retirement process. We do not yet know to what extent these apparent associations are the result of correlation among these factors, rather than independent effects. More research is needed to measure the degree to which such factors as health, age, pensions, Social Security, industrial and occupational structure enhance or diminish the earnings flexibility of older people. These magnitudes have implications for the adequacy of supply of certain types of labor as the numbers of new young entrants to the U.S. labor market decline, and for the costs of current programs and proposed reforms, as well as for the welfare of elderly Americans.

Appendix: Current Social Security Rules and the 1983 Amendments

Current Rules in 1986

Social Security benefits are currently financed by a payroll tax of 14.3 percent on annual earnings up to a maximum of $42,000 (1986 dollars), divided equally between employers and employees. Benefits are indexed to the Consumer Price Index.

Under current Social Security rules, the normal retirement age of eligibility for a full benefit is 65. One may, however, receive reduced benefits at ages 62-64 if one's earnings are low enough (see below concerning the earnings test). The benefit reduction is 5/9 percent for each month between initial benefit receipt and age 65. Thus, one can get 80 percent of the full benefit at age 62, or 86.7 percent at age 63, or 93.3 percent at age 64. Moreover, if one begins receiving benefits before age 65 and then earns enough to have them reduced in any month, at age 65 one's benefit is recomputed (increased) as if one had begun receiving benefits one month later. Since benefits increase by 7 to 8 percent per year if receipt is postponed, the adjustment is actuarially nearly fair (for the average person) in the age range 62-64. (Life expectancies at age 65 are 14 years for men and 18 years for women, and benefits are automatically indexed for inflation.) Moreover, if one does not take reduced benefits, one's earnings during these years enter the benefit computation formula and may increase the benefit one receives at age 65.

Apart from illiquidity effects, therefore, the current Social Security rules are roughly neutral with respect to the choice of retirement age up to age 65, for the average person. However, those who have reason to believe their life expectancy is below average – e.g., blacks, males, smokers – will have an incentive to retire at 62, even apart from problems with illiquidity of Social Security wealth. Those who have reason to believe their life expectancy is above average and who have no liquidity problems, on the other hand, will be induced to postpone benefit receipt until age 65, whether or not they stop working full-time. Since a person can always postpone receipt of benefits even though they have stopped working, a greater-than-fair actuarial adjustment does not provide incentives to postpone retirement itself.

From age 65 on, however, benefits are increased by only 1/4 percent for each month in which no benefit is received. This is only 3 percent per year, which is considerably less than actuarially fair. Clearly, the current rules encourage retirement at age 65, even for those with no liquidity constraints and above average life expectancy.

After age 70 one's earnings do not affect the benefit received, but until that age benefit receipt is subject to an earnings test. The benefit is reduced $1 for every $2 of annual earnings above $5760 (if one is under 65) or $7800 (if one is 65 to 69). Future benefits are then adjusted upward beginning at age 65, being recomputed as if the initial benefit receipt had started one month later. After age 65 benefits are increased on the next birthday, by 1/4 percent per month (3 percent per year) that no benefit is received.

Before age 65, when the actuarial adjustment is close to fair, the average person's Social Security wealth is unaffected by benefit loss due to the earnings test. (In fact, if one receives partial benefits for some months, they increase slightly the present value of one's lifetime benefit stream.) Thus, the earnings test should not affect labor supply between ages 62 and 65 for persons with average life expectancy. For those with below average life expectancy or over 65, for whom the actuarial adjustment is less than fair, the earnings test encourages a reduction of work effort to keep annual earnings below $5760. It is neutral with respect to the choice between part-time and no work, however.

For most people, Social Security benefits are exempt from income tax, but for persons with rather high incomes (over $25,000 for an individual or $32,000 for a married couple), a portion of Social Security benefits are taxed. Depending upon one's income from other sources, this may have the effect of reducing the level of earnings that are exempt from the earnings test, and of reducing benefits for earnings above a certain amount even after age 70, with (of course) no actuarial adjustment. Some people may have incentives to reduce their labor supply as a result.

Summary: Apart from increasing lifetime wealth (thus encouraging a reduction of work at all ages), and apart from liquidity considerations, current Social Security rules are neutral for the average person's labor supply decision up to age 65. They encourage persons with below average life expectancy to retire (i.e., to reduce annual earnings to $5760) at age 62. They encourage everyone else to retire at 65, and to earn no more than $7800 a year at ages 65-69. After age 70, they are completely neutral for everyone (apart from effects of taxing benefits of high-income groups).

The 1983 Amendments

Major amendments passed in 1983 will gradually raise the "normal" retirement age, at which full benefits are payable, from 65 to 67. The age will increase by 2 months per year for persons born in 1938-1943 and again for persons born in 1955-1960. A reduced benefit will still be available at age 62. The benefit will be reduced 5/9 percent for each of the first 36 months (6.7 percent per year for 3 years) that benefits are received before the age of full eligibility (as at present), plus 5/12 percent for each of up to 24 months (5 percent per year for 2 years) of earlier benefit receipt.

The benefit increase for delaying retirement beyond the "normal" age will also be gradually raised, from 1/4 percent to 2/3 percent for each month (i.e., from 3 percent to 8 percent per year) that no benefit is received between the age of full eligibility and age 70. This increase in the actuarial adjustment for delayed retirement will begin with persons born in 1925 (reaching 65 in 1990) and proceed by increments of 1/24 percent every two years, until the cohorts born in 1943 or later (reaching 65 in 2008 and after) will get the full 8 percent per year for postponing benefits up to age 70. There will continue to be no actuarial adjustment for non-receipt of benefits after age 70, but this does not matter. Since benefit receipt is unaffected by earnings after age 70, no one over 69 would fail to receive benefits.

Starting in 1990, the earnings test benefit reduction will be lowered to $1 for every $3 of earnings above the exempt amount, for persons between the age of eligibility for full benefits and age 70. With a fair actuarial adjustment, however (assuming people understand it!), the earnings test should not affect labor supply – apart from liquidity problems.

When the 1983 amendments take full effect, those born in 1960 and later face a 13 percent cut in lifetime benefits, relative to those born before 1938. This wealth effect should increase their labor supply at all ages. They will be able to get 70 percent of their full benefit at age 62, 75 percent at 63, 80 percent at 64, 86.7 percent at 65, 93.3 percent at 66, 100 percent at 67, 108 percent at 68, 116 percent at 69, and 124 percent at 70. As now, benefits will not be affected by earnings after age 70. Thus the actuarial adjustment for non-receipt of benefits will be approximately fair for the average person (assuming no further increases in life expectancy in the meantime) from age 62 on, and the Social Security rules will be neutral with respect to the choice of retirement age and age of benefit receipt for such a person. Persons for whom liquidity constraints are a problem or who have below the current average life expectancy will still have incentives to retire at 62 and to keep their earnings below $5760 (1986 dollars, adjusted for future aggregate wage growth) until age 70. Persons with above the current average life expectancy (presumably the majority by then) and no liquidity constraints will have an incentive to postpone receipt of benefits until age 70, but the rules will be neutral with respect to their choice of retirement age. (Recall that, since a person can always stop working and still postpone receipt of benefits, a greater-than-fair actuarial adjustment does not affect the choice of retirement age – only the age of benefit receipt.)

Summary: The wealth effect of the 1983 amendments should increase labor supply and thus postpone the desired retirement age. The changes in actuarial adjustments should remove the present incentives to retire at 65, thus further postponing retirement age and increasing labor supply after "retirement" in the 65-69 age group. Persons who face liquidity problems or very short life expectancies will still want to retire at 62, but otherwise the rules will be neutral (apart from the wealth effect).

References

Burtless, G. (1986) Social Security, Unanticipated Benefit Increases, and the Timing of Retirement. Review of Economic Studies 53, pp. 781-805

Burtless, G. and R. A. Moffitt (1984) The Effect of Social Security Benefits on the Labor Supply of the Aged. In: Henry J. Aaron and Gary Burtless (Eds.) Retirement and Economic Behavior (Washington, DC: Brookings Institution), pp. 135-174

Burtless, G. and R. A. Moffitt (1985) The Joint Choice of Retirement Age and Postretirement Hours of Work. Journal of Labor Economics 3, no. 2, pp. 209-236

Diamond, P. A. and J. A. Hausman (1984) The Retirement and Unemployment Behavior of Older Men. In: Henry J. Aaron and Gary Burtless (Eds.) Retirement and Economic Behavior (Washington, DC: Brookings Institution), pp. 97-134

Gustman, A. L. and T. L. Steinmeier (1985 a) A Disaggregated, Structural Analysis of Retirement by Race, Difficulty of Work and Health. Unpub. ms. (Dartmouth College)

Gustman, A. L. and T. L. Steinmeier (1985 b) The 1983 Social Security Reforms and Labor Supply Adjustments of Older Individuals in the Long Run. Journal of Labor Economics 3, no. 2, pp. 237-253

Hanoch, G. and M. Honig (1983), Retirement, Wages, and Labor Supply of the Elderly. Journal of Labor Economics 1, no. 2, pp. 131-151

Hausman, J. A. and D. A. Wise (1985) Social Security, Health Status, and Retirement. In: David A. Wise (Ed.) Pensions, Labor, and Individual Choice (Chicago, IL: NBER, University of Chicago Press), pp. 159-191

Honig, M. (1985) Partial Retirement Among Women. Journal of Human Resources 20, pp. 613-621

Honig, M. and G. Hanoch (1985) Partial Retirement as a Separate Mode of Retirement Behavior. Journal of Human Resources 20, pp. 21-46

Honig, M. and C. Reimers (1987) The Labor Market Mobility of Older Workers. Unpub. ms. (Hunter College, C.U.N.Y.)

Irelan, L. M. (1976) Retirement History Study: Introduction. In: Almost 65: Baseline Data from the Retirement History Study, Office of Research and Statistics, Department of Health, Education, and Welfare, GPO

U.S. Bureau of the Census (1973, 1978, 1983) Current Population Survey: March Annual Demographic Microdata Files

Early Retirement: The Problems of "Instrument Substitution" and "Cost Shifting" and Their Implications for Restructuring the Process of Retirement

B. Casey[1]

Contents

1. Introduction

The deterioration of the labour market in all OECD countries since the oil price shock of 1973 has brought with it a massive increase in early retirement. This is a result not only of discouraged older job seekers leaving the labour market for the more socially acceptable "alternative role" of early retiree, or, of persons eligible for disability benefits finding themselves forced by lack of work to exercise that option, but also of conscious policies by governments, backed by employers and trade unions (Casey and Bruche (1983), Casey (1984a), ISSA (1985)).

Initially these policies took the form of permitting the older unemployed to retire either *de facto* (by dropping the need to engage in active job search) or *de jure,* usually with a higher than normal level of replacement in-

[1] A first draft of this paper was presented at the Workshop "Preparation for Retirement – Variations and Approaches in the Field of Early Retirement" at the International Week of Gerontological Events organized by the Israeli Gerontological Society in Jerusalem 24-30 August 1986. A second version was presented to the WZB and Nordic Council Joint Conference on "Social Policy and Labour Markets" held at Bergen, 30 June 1987. I should like to thank Xavier Gaullier, Steve Nesbitt and participants at the Jerusalem workshop for their comments on the first draft, participants at the Bergen and Berlin conferences for their comments on the second and third drafts and Martin Rein for the initial discussion we had on the issues this paper covers.

W. Schmähl (Ed.)
Redifining the Process of Retirement
© Springer-Verlag Berlin Heidelberg 1989

come. Sometimes, as in France and Belgium, it was the unemployment compensation system that had the responsibility and bore the costs of such provisions, sometimes the disability pension system was made more accommodating, as in Sweden and the Netherlands, sometimes special provisions in the old age pension system existed or were created, as in Germany or Austria. In the course of time these provisions were added to, and this in three important ways. First, they came increasingly to concentrate not only upon the already unemployed but upon older workers still in employment. Enterprises faced with the need to restructure and reduce their labour forces, as well as or instead of resorting to traditional "last in first out" dismissal practices, started to shift the burden of redundancies to older workers for whom relatively generous provisions were available. In this they received at the least tacit support of trade unions, anxious to protect their "core members", of governments, concerned about the political dangers of high levels of youth unemployment, of public opinion who shared the view that "the old had had their turn and now should stand aside to make way for others" and of some older workers themselves, who valued the opportunity to leave work somewhat earlier. Second, they were often supplemented by private arrangements. Enterprises seeking to dispose of high cost workers whose productivity and adaptability they considered sub-optimal but who, thanks to the labour law or collective agreements of many centres also enjoyed a high degree of protection against dismissal, were willing to top up unemployment benefits or early/public pensions with dismissal compensation payments or early occupational pensions. Moreover, in those countries where publicly financed early retirement provisions were less generous or less developed, the relative importance of such private provisions increased and indeed they often served as substitutes for the public provisions elsewhere. This appears to be the case in Britain and in the USA. Third, their labour market policy objectives received official government sanction in the form of the introduction of special programmes which explicitly sought to encourage early retirement when the retiree was replaced by a registered unemployed person. This was the case in Britain, Belgium, France and, most recently, Germany (Casey (1985)).

Although this paper is concerned primarily with the question of early retirement, it seeks to generalise lessons drawn from its study to the question of raising the age of retirement and the question of promoting gradual retirement. The next section (2) explains the concepts of "instrument substitution" and "cost shifting" and considers in more detail with reference to recent German experiences the concept of "public-private cost shifting". Section 3 looks at the implications of "instrument substitution" and "cost shifting" for efforts to curb early retirement, lift the pension age and institute gradual retirement. The concluding section (4) comprises some more general comments.

2. "Instrument Substitution" and "Cost Shifting"

An overview, such as is provided in Table 1, shows a wide variety of means for facilitating early retirement with a wide variety of sources, both public and private, of financing them. When we consider the chronological developments in particular countries, which the table does not really show, we often find that within any one country the relative importance of particular provisions has changed. Initially, this reflected nothing more than newly opened avenues for early retirement, less restrictive in their eligibility criteria or more generous in terms of the compensation they offered, supplanting more restrictive or less generous provisions. Thus, in the Netherlands, the introduction of the so-called VUT early retirement provisions in collective agreements (1.XV)[2] at the end of the 1970s, as well as opening up additional opportunities for premature withdrawal from the labour force, seems to have reduced slightly the incidence of early retirement on the grounds of disability (1.XIV). Subsequently, following a liberalisation of dismissal procedures permitting the burden of dismissals to be placed upon older persons having access to extended unemployment benefits (1.XVI) that occurred in 1982, a further increase in early retirement went hand in hand with a relatively greater share being facilitated in this last fashion (van den Bosch and Petersen (1983)). In the same way, in France in the 1970s provisions were brought in under the unemployment compensation system to enable early retirement at 60, initially for persons becoming unemployed, later also for those voluntarily deciding to leave work (1.VI). There are some indications that the introduction of these schemes halted, and indeed reversed, a rise in the incidence of claims for an early age pension on the grounds of disability (1.V) (Lynes (1985)). With the enactment, in 1983, of a more or less general right to an unreduced age pension at 60 the early retirement provisions under the unemployment compensation system were closed for new entries. Equally, in Belgium a special early retirement scheme with a replacement condition which had been operating since 1976 (1.III) was replaced in 1983 by a somewhat similar scheme operated under the terms of the age pension system (1.IV). This phenomenon of one provision succeeding or displacing another I call "instrument substitution". "Instrument substitution" can, as we have seen, be the consequence of deliberate policy, it can also be an unintended consequence of administrative actions, collective bargaining developments or changing labour market conditions.

---

[2] The roman numerals refer to Table 1 where the provision is described.

Table 1. Principal forms of early retirement

	Normal age for receipt of unreduced retirement benefits		Early retirement					
			Regulated by	Entitlement	Minimum age	Benefit	Financing[a]	Extent
Austria	Men 63 Women 60	I	Government	Persons unemployed at least 1 year	Men 60 Women 55	Full old age pension	Pension fund	moderate, c 10,000 beneficiaries at end 1985
Belgium	Men 65 Women 60	II	Government/ social partners	Persons made redundant	Men 60 Women 55 (exceptionally 55 and 50)	Unemployment benefit + ¹/₂ diff. between this and last wages (= c 80 % last wages)	Unemployment insurance fund, enterprise (the supplement)	Large c 90,000 beneficiaries at end 1984
		III	Government	All subject to agreement by enterprise to replace with unemployed person	Men 60 Women 65	Unemployment benefit + ¹/₂ diff. between this and last wages (= c 80 % last wages)	Unemployment insurance fund, state (the supplement)	Moderate, c 45,000 beneficiaries at end 1982, c 8,000 new awards per year
			———————————— (operative until 1983) ————————————					
		IV	Government	All subject to agreement by enterprise to replace with unemployed person	Men 60	Full old age pension	Pension fund	Moderate, c 5,000 new awards per year
			———————————— (operative since 1983) ————————————					
France	65 until April 1983	V	Government/ social partners	Persons unfit for work	None	Full old age pension	Pension fund	Moderate, c 20 % of all pensions awarded
		VI	Government/ social partners	Persons involuntarily unemployed and, since 1977, persons retiring voluntarily	60	70 % last gross wages	Unemployment insurance fund	Very extensive, c 430,000 beneficiaries at end 1983
			———————————— (operative 1972 – April 1983) ————————————					
	60 since 1983	VII	Government	All, subject to agreement by enterprise to replace with unemployed person	55	65 – 70 % last gross wages	State	Extensive, 25 % of eligible persons, c 200,000 beneficiaries at end 1986
			———————————— (operative 1982 – 1983) ————————————					
		VIII	Government	Persons made redundant by enterprises in difficulties	55	65 – 70 % last gross wages	State	Moderate, c 165,000 beneficiaries at end 1986

Table 1. (continued)

	Normal age for receipt of unreduced retirement benefits		Early retirement					
			Regulated by	Entitlement	Minimum age	Benefit	Financing[a]	Extent
Germany (F. R.)	Men 63 Women 60 disabled Men 60	IX	Government	Persons unemployed at least 1 year	60	Full old age pension	Government but pension until 63 & unemployment benefit can be recouped from enterprise if person made unemployed at 59 and firm not in difficulties	Moderate, c 40,000 persons per year
		X	Government/ collective agreement	All, if collective agreement	58	65 – 75 % last gross wages	Enterprise, but $^1/_3$ subsidy from state	Relatively small, take up rate 30 % in industries where collective agreement concluded, c 45,000 beneficiaries after 2 years
		XI	Government	Persons with work incapacity, labour market chances taken into account in assessing incapacity	None	Work incapacity pension, approx. equivalent to old age pension	Pension fund	Very extensive, principal form of retirement for blue collar workers, usually from about 55
Great Britain	Men 65 Women 60	XII	Government	All, subject to agreement by enterprise to replace with unemployed person	Men 63 Women 59 Disabled Men 60	Flat rate allowance, level depends on family circumstances	State	10 % of eligible persons, c 90,000 beneficiaries at end 1985
		XIII	Enterprises	Persons made redundant	Usually over 55	Early occupational pension and/ or lump sum payments	Enterprise	Limited to large enterprises
Netherlands	65	XIV	Government/ social partners	Persons with at least 15 % medical disability & poor labour market chances	None	75 % of last income	Disability insurance fund	Extensive, over $^1/_2$ of insured 60 – 65 & $^1/_3$ of 55 – 59 year olds in receipt of pension
		XV	Industry-level collective agreements	Normally at least 10 years' service required	60 – 61	80 – 85 % of last income	Various, normally deducted from negotiated wage increase	Moderately extensive, c 20,000 beneficiaries = 4 % of population aged 60 – 64
		XVI	Government	Persons becoming unemployed	57 $^1/_2$	75 % of last gross wages	Unemployment insurance fund for first year then state	Moderately extensive, c 50,000, beneficiaries at end 1985

Table 1. (continued)

| | Normal age for receipt of unreduced retirement benefits | Early retirement | | | | | |
		Regulated by	Entitlement	Minimum age	Benefit	Financing[a])	Extent
Sweden	65	XVII Government	Persons with work incapacity, labour market chances taken into account in assessing incapacity	None	Full old age pension	Pension fund	Extensive, over $\frac{1}{4}$ of insured population aged 50 – 65, 10 % aged 50 – 59 in receipt of pension
		XVIII Government	Persons unemployed at least 1 $\frac{3}{4}$ years	60	Full old age pension	Pension fund	Moderate, c 4 % of insured population aged 60 – 65 in receipt of pension
USA	65	XIX Government	All persons	62	Old age pension reduced by 6,6 % per year of early liquidation	Pension fund	Extensive, c 46 % of insured 62 – 64 year olds
		XX Government	Persons with work incapacity	None	Old age pension based on past earnings	Disability pension fund	Moderate c 6 % insured 55 – 59 & 10 % insured 60 – 64 year olds
		XXI Enterprises	Persons made redundant	Usually aged over 55	Early occupational pension and/ or lump sum	Enterprise	Limited to large enterprises

[a]) The word 'fund' is used very loosely here. It does not necessarily refer to a 'fund-based' financing system; many of the systems described here are, in fact, 'pay-as-you-go' systems. Rather it is used as a shorthand for 'the authorities/source of financing' for the old age, disability or unemployment insurance system.

"Instrument substitution" frequently has a further element to it, in so far as it involves responsibility for the costs of early retirement being shifted from one body to another. Thus, the lowering of the normal pension age in France represented a transferral of the costs of meeting future "early" retirement from the unemployment insurance system to the public pension funds. The same applies to the substitution of one early retirement scheme with a replacement condition with another such scheme in Belgium in 1983. These are both examples of what I call "cost shifting". As we shall go on to see, "cost shifting" can be the product of intended, deliberate action, but it can equally be unintended or unforeseen.

"Cost shifting" itself can have a number of dimensions. In the examples just given, costs were shifted from one public authority to another, and this I call "public-public cost shifting". In the Dutch example, the shift in part of the burden of early retirement from the disability pension system to employer and employee financed collectively agreed provisions represented a (not necessarily intended or foreseen) shift from a public authority to the private sector. However, the subsequent increase in the relative importance of early retirement under the unemployment benefits system meant a (equally not necessarily intended) shifting from the private sector back to (another) public authority. These were cases of what I call "public-private" and "private-public cost shifting".

"Public-public cost shifting", whilst not affecting *per se* the "public-private" mix in the financing of early retirement is not an unimportant phenomenon. At least in much of continental Europe there is no integrated social security system according to which all benefits are financed by a single contribution paid to a single fund. The British "national insurance" system is probably the closest to an integrated model. In continental Europe, unemployment insurance might be paid out of one fund, with its own contributions, unemployment benefit (for persons whose insurance benefit has been exhausted) by another (often the central government out of tax revenue), age pensions by another fund with its own contributions, and disability pensions by yet another. Sometimes, indeed frequently, these funds receive exchequer grants, both as a contribution to a share of costs and as a top-up to cope with unexpected deficits. Each fund, however, has a fair degree of autonomy. Their separate identities mean they do not always appear as components of state expenditure (and might therefore give an incomplete picture of the size of this and the borrowing requirement), but also, in so far as any one of them is in deficit, it might seek to bring its finances into order at the expense of another.

A good example of this, in the field of early retirement, has been argued to have occurred in Sweden. There, one reason advanced for the growth in early retirement under the disability pensions provision (1.XVII) in the course of the 1970s was not only the simultaneous liberalisation of eligibility conditions allowing labour market chances as much as medical conditions to be taken into account in assessing disability but even more so the attempt by the sickness insurance funds to reduce the high incidence of long term sickness amongst older persons by reclassifying them as disabled. In this case they became the responsibility of the public pension funds (Hetzler and Eriksson (1981)). Moreover, in public expenditure terms as a whole the exercise was beneficial. Benefits paid to the sick under the sickness insurance scheme are considerably higher than those paid under the disability and old age pension schemes. More explicit in its objectives of the pursuit of savings was the recasting of the early retirement scheme with a replacement condition in Belgium. Benefits paid under the earlier, unemployment insurance system/exchequer financed scheme were higher than those paid under the current, age pension system financed scheme (Casey (1985)).

Because it would also involve substantial "cost shifting", the reduction in the normal pension age from 65 to 60 in France was not considered by the government planning its introduction as a reform which would result in an intolerable increase in public expenditure. Provisions for early retirement already in existence meant that the number of additional retirements at 60 would be rather small. The cost of paying pensions to them would largely be offset by the fact that the average level of benefits applicable to retirees under the ("basic" and "complementary") age pension system was lower than that applicable to early retirees under the unemployment benefits system. The unemployment benefits fund would be substantially relieved, the age pension funds would incur additional burdens (Merceau (1982)). In fact, the "complementary" pension funds insisted on receiving a special indemnification from the government to meet their new obligations over the first seven years, and this indemnification is paid for out of exchequer sources (Lynes (1985)).

2.1 "Public-Private Cost Shifting"

"Public-private cost shifting" must be interpreted as going one step further, since it involves not only an individual public financing source reducing its costs, but also an attempt to transfer these costs away from the public purse altogether. Given the prevailing climate of fiscal restraint and the perceived need for retrenchment of public expenditure, coupled with the particular fears about the growing burden of (age) pension payments, it is not surprising that "public-private" cost shifting has been contemplated, albeit, as we shall see, to a much lesser extent practised.

An example of a step in this direction is given in Germany. There one, although by no means quantitatively the most important, route to early retirement was the provision whereby those persons aged 60 who had been unemployed for at least a year could draw an early unreduced age pension (1.IX). As well as encouraging employers to shift the burden of redundancies onto eligible persons, the provisions were utilised by companies to permit a rejuvenation of their workforces and to provide early retirement at 59 as an employee benefit. Most of the costs were borne by the public purse (by the unemployed insurance funds and the public pension funds). The enterprise's share was limited to the costs of a topping-up payment to state benefits, this being a voluntary item which was usually the product of collective bargaining. In 1981 (with effect from 1982) the government sought to oblige enterprises dismissing long service workers to reimburse the unemployment insurance funds for the costs of the benefit these paid out, in other words to shift part of the cost of early retirement from the public to the private.[3] Exempted were enterprises in difficulties; so where large scale redundancies or rejuvenation was necessary for the enterprise's survival, it was still the public purse which bore the costs. Given that the following years the number of such early retirements remained undiminished, and that the level of reimbursements was very low, this attempt at "public-private cost shifting" largely failed (Hempel (1984)).

---

[3]   Very similar proposals were made by the Swedish in 1982 with respect to the almost identical "A case" scheme (1.XVIII) (see Arbetsmarknadsdepartementet, 1983). They have not, as yet, been implemented.

However, in 1984 the Government went further. It introduced a new early retirement law, permitting early retirement on a new "bridging payment" at age 58 (1.X) (Casey (1985)). The costs of this early retirement were to be met by enterprises and, it was hoped, by employees in the form of lower than otherwise negotiated pay rises. If the enterprise replaced the early retiree with an unemployed person, it received a subsidy towards the cost of the "bridging payment", but this was worth only about one third of the cost. At the same time, enterprises dismissing long service 59 year-olds were now required to reimburse not only unemployment insurance payments made to them but also the cost of early age pension benefits until the person reached normal pension age (63 for men).

This appears to be a very striking case of attempted "public-private cost shifting". Its effects, however, are somewhat ambiguous. There has been no apparent fall-off in the number of early retirements under the old provisions and no significant increase in the level of reimbursements made (Puth (1986)). In part this reflects the exemptions for enterprises in difficulties that existed and had now been made more generous. Thus, the early retirees under the new provision appear to have been the product of additional early retirements, facilitated by an *additional* instrument, rather than the product of the same number of early retirements as before but facilitated by an *alternative* instrument. Moreover, whilst producing some small net saving for the public purse as a whole, the principal effect of the new provision was to shift costs between various public authorities. There were major savings for the public pension funds, since the new provision took over support for a number of persons who would otherwise have drawn disability pensions, but there were increased costs for the unemployment insurance fund, which paid the subsidy to enterprises (Hellberger (1984)). Our own calculations indicate there was also a significant negative impact on the exchequer, which lost corporate tax revenue as enterprises set their additional costs against tax liabilities.[4]

3. The Implications of "Instrument Substitution" and "Cost Shifting"

In this section we shall follow up some of the implications of the concepts of "instrument substitution" and "cost shifting", concerning ourselves particularly with those concerning efforts to reduce public expenditure on early retirement and on retirement in general, and efforts to encourage gradual retirement in general.

---

[4] Together with Bernd Reissert of the Science Centre Berlin, I undertook a cost estimating exercise rather similar to that used by Hellberger. However, unlike Hellberger's, this exercise included consideration of the consequences for corporate tax receipts (which flow to the exchequer) of any cost increases resulting from use of the new provision reducing company profits.

3.1 Early Retirement

Our investigations of "instrument substitution" and "cost shifting" lead us
first to ask whether efforts to reduce the costs to the public purse by cutting
back on early retirement schemes might fail to produce the desired results,
even as far as public expenditure is concerned.

The decision of the French government not to extend the life of the early retirement "solidarity contract" provisions (an early retirement scheme
with a replacement condition) (1.VII) is to be explained in part by their very
high cost. However, other, indeed as generous, publicly financed provisions
aimed at enabling older workers made redundant to retire early (1.VIII) remained in existence. Whilst eligibility criteria of the two programmes are not
identical, the experience we have of enterprises' ability to functionalise labour market and social security policy instruments to serve their ends (for il-
lustrations of this with respect to the French "solidarity contracts" see
(Frank el al (1982)) suggests that enterprises might well have reacted to the
removal of the first provision by increasing substantially their exploitation of
the second. The statistics do show this. The number of persons receiving benefits under the scheme for compensating older redundant workers more
than doubled between 1983 and 1986, to reach a level almost as high as that
recorded under the first scheme at its peak in 1983. By analogy, we would also
argue that the liberal interpretation of disability under the legislation of
many countries also provides an exit that might be increasingly exploited
should other means of early retirement be abolished or made more restrictive. Despite a considerable variety of schemes in Germany, early retirement
on the grounds of disability (1.XI) is by far the most important means of with-
drawing from working life in that country (on disability pensioning in Germany and elsewhere see Haveman et al (1984)).

Second, should government succeed, by legislative or other means, in
reducing the volume of early retirement facilitated by public programmes,
they will by no means reduce pro rata the overall volume of early retirement.
One of the outstanding impressions of an international survey of early retirement is the way in which in Britain and America, where public provision is
relatively less developed and less generous than in continental Europe, private provision in the form of dismissal compensation payments and early,
unreduced occupational pensions are relatively more developed and more
generous.

Third, to the extent that "public-private cost shifting" reduces the absolute volume of early retirement, it too is not without its problems. For
example, enterprises engage in age-selective dismissals because the major
share of the costs is externally borne. Without the availability of these provisions, or were the costs internalised, they might well act differently. The
redundancies would still be made but different, presumably younger, workers would be affected. In this case we are back to the situation described earlier, whereby "public-private cost shifting" becomes "public-public cost shifting". The cost to the public purse might be rather lower, but the political

costs might be higher. Similarly, if the ability of enterprises to externalise the cost of their disposing of their older, less productive labour is constrained, this too might have negative implications for their competitiveness and ultimately their employment levels which cannot be ignored.

3.2 Raising the Retirement Age

The most frequently adduced counter to the argument that we are experiencing an inexorable slide to a lowering of the "normal" retirement age, be this "normal" *de facto* or *de jure,* is that in America legislative steps were taken in 1983 to raise the age for receipt of a full old age pension. This raising, by steps from age 65 to 67, to take effect by 2027. Simultaneously the size of the actuarial reduction in benefits applied to persons who liquidate an age pension at 62 (1.XIX) is to be increased, as is the actuarial enhancement applied to those staying in work after the normal retirement age. The extent to which any earnings lead to a reduction in benefits is also being diminished. The principal objective of this reform, enacted in 1983, was to slow the growth of age pension expenditure; it sought to do this by removing disincentives to continued work, thereby reversing the trend towards ever earlier retirement.

What, however, the Greenspan Commission, whose report initiated this move apparently failed to do when considering the impact of its suggestions was to look beyond their impact on the old age pension finances. As the Congress subsequently noted, lifting the age of receipt of unreduced age pension benefits might have as a consequence an increase in the number of older persons seeking or claiming disability benefits (1.XX) (GAO (1986)). We would go further and suggest that there might also be extra demands made on the unemployment insurance system or on other alternative sources of social security/welfare benefits. In other words, an exercise in public expenditure reduction might end up, at least in part, as an exercise in "public-public cost shifting". One public fund might be relieved, but only at the (partial) expense of another, and although the pressure on the public purse is reduced, it is reduced by less than was anticipated.

In Belgium, again motivated primarily by budgetary considerations, but also justifying it in terms of bringing greater sexual equality into the social security system, the government recently proposed lifting the normal age of retirement for women from 60 to 65 – the age currently applicable to men. A pension at 60 for both sexes would also be possible, and if 45 years contributions had been paid this age pension would not be subject to any reduction. In delivering an "advice" on this proposal, the bipartite National Labour Council did what the Greenspan Commission failed to do and undertook a thorough investigation of (although it did not use these terms) its "instrument substitution" and "public-private cost shifting" implications. The Council considered the impact of the government's plan on the "bridging pension" scheme (1.II), on the unemployment insurance system (as far as this was concerned both with the older unemployed and other unemployed), on the disability pension scheme and on the age pension scheme itself. It concluded that since many women would continue to retire early through the "bridging pension" scheme, since some of those staying in work over 60 would "take jobs away" from the unemployed, and since some persons retiring at 60 would receive no reduction in pension, total costs to the public purse would rise considerably. Savings resulting from reduced calls upon the invalidity pension system, from the retention of some older women in work and from setting 45 rather than 40 years as the full contributions requirement for women would not match these. The net fiscal impact would be negative. Accordingly, the Council recommended the government not to proceed with its proposal (NAR (1987)).

Any consideration of the possible consequences of raising the pension age cannot however stop at its implications in terms of "public-public cost shifting". The National Labour Council's "advice" also took account of the cost to employers of contributing their share to the "bridging pensions". Many women would continue, voluntarily or involuntarily, to retire at 60 and, if possible, would seek to claim benefits under the "bridging pension" scheme rather than to claim a less generous, reduced age pension. When employers' costs were included in the estimates, in other words once the "public-private cost shifting" component was added to the "public-public cost shifting" component, the government's proposals were held yet more unacceptable.

Returning to the case of the 1983 reform of the American Social Security Act, we would suggest that, so long as employers feel they have good reason to encourage the departure of older workers, they are likely to make adjustments to their occupational pension schemes to offset, to a greater or lesser degree, the reductions in benefits available from the public old age pension system (Boaz (1987)).

Finally, even if it is the case that "public-private cost shifting", whether with respect to the costs of early or normal retirement, satisfies the end of reducing public expenditure, such "public-private cost shifting" raises its own problems. Private arrangements remain employment based and must themselves be financed. Unless, and this seems empirically unlikely, enterprises manage to shift the entire cost of them onto employees, then their existence constitutes, either explicitly or implicitly, a tax upon labour. It seems, prima facie, hard to distinguish the consequences of such a tax from the taxes imposed by social security systems, albeit that the former appear to have been shouldered voluntarily whilst the latter are statutory. Furthermore, the control and reversal of the growth of non-wage labour costs has now been identified by policy makers and academics as much an object of concern as the control and reversal of the growth of public expenditure, especially expenditure on retirement provision (OECD (1986)).

3.3 Gradual Retirement

Plans to cut down on opportunities for publicly financed early retirement and even to increase the age at which a full public pension can be claimed are on the agenda of many governments, even if few have as yet realised them and many have, in fact, succumbed to the short term, political pressures resulting from sustained high unemployment to introduce yet more early retirement options. Many social policy analysts, on the other hand, have been advocating an alternative approach to the management of retirement – the introduction of opportunities for gradual/phased or partial retirement. The merits, or otherwise, of such a retirement form, and its compatibility with many of the objectives both of reducing the retirement age and or raising it, have been discussed extensively elsewhere (Casey and Bruche (1983), Casey (1986)).[5] An understanding of the concepts of "instrument substitution" and "cost shifting" enables us to see what the preconditions for its successful introduction are and why some of the attempts of both governments and enterprises to promote gradual retirement opportunities have not been as successful as they might have been.

    Table 2 lists and describes some of the principal gradual retirement programmes and schemes which have been in existence for sufficiently long that experience of their operation is available.[6] The most extensive and best known gradual retirement scheme is the Swedish one (2.VII). Until the early 1980s commentary on it was almost exclusively in terms of its success. Since its introduction in 1976 the number of workers taking advantage of its provisions increased steadily and in relation to the eligible labour force was large. Indeed, the existence of the gradual retirement programme was seen as one reason why the incidence of full early retirement was relatively low in Sweden in the second half of the 1970s (Riksforsakringsverket (1984)). Between 1980 and 1985, however, the number of new entrants fell seventy per cent. This cannot simply be ascribed to the cutback in the replacement rate afforded by the partial retirement benefit whereby as of 1981 only 50 rather than 65 per cent of earnings for non-worked hours were made up. Due to Sweden's progressive tax structure, net of tax income of someone working part time would have fallen only from 85 to 80 per cent of net of tax income from full time working. Much more important an explanation, we would suggest, is

---

[5]   They can be summed up as: helping to avoid the problems of "pension shock"; adjusting work to the reduced capabilities of certain older workers – to the advantage both of those trying to remain in work and those seeking work; facilitating labour force reductions and/or creating spaces for the otherwise unemployed; enabling early retirees to contribute to their own income instead of relying exclusively on transfer payments and allowing enterprises to retain persons with valuable skills who they might otherwise lose entirely.

[6]   See also the papers by Petersen and Sundberg in this volume which discus similar programmes in Denmark and Finland.

Table 2. Principal forms of gradual retirement

Country	Level and form of regulation	Eligibility	Duration	Size of worktime reduction (% of normal worktime)	Manner of realization	Degree of wage compensation (% of previous gross wage)	Financing	Extent
France	I Company level collective agreements or management initiatives	Voluntary, no or limited seniority requirements	Commence: usually at 60; end: with requirement at 65	On basis of age – 5 – 11 % at 60 10 – 50 % at 64	Usual stipulation: reduction of weekly worktime or additional holiday; when taken to be negotiated with superior	With small working reduction, usually full wage compensation (100 %); with 50 % worktime reduction, usually 75 % of last wage	Enterprise	Very limited, since retirement at 60 possible
	II Government programme	Subject to employer consenting to refill vacancies created	Commence: 55; end: 60 (pensionable age)	50 % of normal hours	Not known	80 % of last gross wages	Enterprise for time worked, state tops up to 80 % if vacancy filled	Limited, 2000 persons
Germany FR	II Company and industry agreements	Voluntary, usually seniority requirements	Commence: 58 – 60; end: 63 (pensionable age)	Sometimes progressive; usually 50 % of normal hours	Various	Between full and half wages for time not worked	Enterprise	Limited (no studies available)
Great Britain	IV Company level management initiatives and (increasingly) collective agreements	Usually obligatory, normally without seniority requirements	Commence: maximum 2, usually 1 or 1/2 year before retirement (i.e. usually 63/64); end: with retirement at 65	Increase over duration program – 20 % 1 or 2 years before retirement, 40 – 80 % in last few months of working life	Usual stipulation: days per week, in some cases actual days of week specified	Always full wage compensation (100 %)	Enterprise	14 % of 400 surveyed firms (1977)
	V Government programme	Voluntary; enterprise must fill part-time vacancy with unemployed person	1 or 2 years before normal pensionable age	50 % of normal hours	Usually 1/2 days or 1/2 weeks	No wage compensation; special flat-rate grant to part-time retirees	Government, from labor market policy budget	Very small – 250 participants

Table 2. (continued)

Country	Level and form of regulation	Eligibility	Duration	Size of worktime reduction (% of normal worktime)	Manner of realization	Degree of wage compensation (% of previous gross wage)	Financing	Extent
Netherlands	VI Industry-wide collective agreements; in large companies, company agreements	Part of negotiated terms and conditions, but no obligation to participate; usually seniority requirement	Commence: usually at 62 or 63, sometimes 60; end: with retirement at 65	On basis of age - 5 - 10 % at commencement to max. 31 % (75 days) at end	Not usually stipulated, but requirement to give notice in advance and obtain agreement of superior; where no agreement exists, employer decides	Frequently full wage compensation (100 %), sometimes 75 %	Enterprise	In 36 of 87 industry agreements covering 2,500 employees: 14 agreements have reduction of less than 30 days per year
Sweden	VII Statutory right for all salary and wage earners and, since 1980, the self-employed	Right to partial pension if at least 10 years of pension contributions paid; employers not obliged to offer part-time work	Commence: 60; end: 65 (or under different conditions, 70)	Can be decided by participant; for majority of partial pensioners 50 %	Not stipulated; studies show 33 % work fewer days per week, 29 % shorter days, 27 % alternate weeks	When working halftime, about 80 % of last net income	Employer contributions to special fund: 0.5 % of total wage bill	28 % of eligible persons at end 1980
United States	VIII Company level management initiatives	Voluntary	Voluntary	Too varied to say	Too varied to say	Usually no wage compensation; only hours worked paid; benefit coverage may be continued	Enterprise (unless benefits continue to be provided, costs very limited; no wage compensation)	7 % of surveyed firms offer part-time options for older workers

that as the pressure on Swedish industry (including public administration and services) to restructure grew more intense in the 1980s, gradual retirement was no longer a viable option. Social policy considerations, which encouraged employers to accommodate to requests for gradual retirement, were increasingly displaced by economic policy considerations which encouraged them to get rid of older workers entirely. Furthermore, the appropriate instruments were there. Thus at the same time that new entries to gradual retirement were falling dramatically, new entries to full early retirement were increasing dramatically. The number of new "A cases" more than quadrupled.

The virtual disappearance of enterprise level gradual retirement schemes in France (2.I) in the late 1970s has been attributed by all commentators to the extension of the full early retirement provisions (SEDES (1979)). The income replacement rates available to full and partial retirement often differed very little. Not only did this induce "instrument substitution", there were strong incentives for employers to encourage this to occur. Enterprises bore the costs of the gradual retirement schemes, the unemployment insurance system the costs of full early retirement. Here was an opportunity for "private-public cost shifting".

Finally, we can consider the absolute failure of those gradual retirement programmes with a replacement condition operated in Britain (2.V) and France (2.II) in the last years in much the same light. Not only were they, particularly the British one, hedged round with a mass of restrictive conditions which made their implementation very difficult for employers (Casey (1984b)), they also existed alongside and in competition with full early retirement programmes – the "solidarity contracts" in France, the "job release" scheme (1.XII) in Britain. Given that the after tax income of a full early retiree in France was at about 85 per cent of his after tax earnings from full-time work, only 5 percentage points higher than that of a full early retiree, and given that employees often topped up the public benefits payable to the latter whilst they did not top up those payable to the former, there was little if any incentive on the worker's side to opt for gradual rather than full early retirement. Equally, in Britain the very restrictive replacement conditions attached to the part time "job release" scheme were such as to encourage employers to strongly prefer the full time scheme if they were prepared to sanction such early retirement at all, whilst as far as workers were concerned, full early retirement was rarely prejudicial to final salary-related occupational pension entitlements but partial retirement very often was.

4. Concluding Comments

Insofar as we have a conclusion, it is one of advising caution in efforts to control the growth of early retirement or to revise in an upward direction the age of normal pensioning. The public social security systems of most industrialised countries developed in an *ad hoc*, non-integrated fashion, and this process was accelerated and intensified by the labour market problems of the past decade and a half, particularly by the problems experienced by older workers (Pfaff (1985)). What has occurred in the public domain has been paralleled in the private domain, indeed there have been causal relationships in both directions, and this has increased the complexity and lack of transparency of the total social welfare system (Rein and Rainwater (1986)). It has meant that, *at least latently,* there is a high degree of substitutability of instruments facilitating retirement before the normal pension age has been reached, and that the adjustment of any single instrument cannot be considered only in its own right. The more we think through the consequences of making changes, the less attractive these changes are likely to be.

Equally, efforts to restructure the retirement process to smooth the process of withdrawal by introducing or extending opportunities for gradual retirement will largely be frustrated if they fail to take account of the workings of simultaneously existing opportunities for full, early retirement. Policy makers both public and private, will have to make adjustments to these latter programmes and schemes if they are successfully to implement the former.[7]

Finally, the most important lesson we draw from our analysis of "instrument substitution" and "cost shifting" is that it probably does little good trying to tackle the problem of the costs of early retirement itself, without first trying to tackle the problem of labour market slack which brought the early retirement about.

References

Arbetsmarknadsdepartementet (1983) Strukturbidrag – Ökat Arbetsgivaransvar vid Äldreavgångar. Ds A 1983:18, Liber, Stockholm

Boaz, R. (1987) The 1983 Amendments to the Social Security Act: Will They Delay Retirement? A Summary of the Evidence. In: The Gerontologist, Vol. 27, No. 2, (Spring), pp. 151-155

Casey, B. (1984a) Recent Trends in Retirement Policies and Practices in Europe and the USA: an alternative strategy. In: Robinson, P., J. Livingston and J. Birren (Eds.) Aging and Technological Advances, Plenum Press, New York, pp. 125-137. Reprinted in Mendelsohn, R. (Ed.) Finance of Old Age, Centre for Federal Financial Relations, Australian National University, Canberra, 1986, pp. 121-132

An overview of programmes directed to the exclusion of older workers and a suggestion for

Casey, B. (1984b), Governmental Measures Promoting Part Time Work for Young Persons: case studies from Belgium, France, Great Britain, FR Germany and Sweden. Discussion Paper 11M/LMP 84-18, Wissenschaftszentrum Berlin

Casey, B. (1985) Early Retirement Schemes with a Replacement Condition: Programmes and experiences in Belgium, France, Great Britain and the Federal Republic of Germany. Discussion Paper IIM/LMP 85-6 a, Wissenschaftszentrum Berlin (also in German)

Casey, B. (1986) Some Implications for Policy. In: Ageing International, Vol. XIII, No. 4 (Autumn/Winter), pp. 35-36

---

[7] Petersen's paper in this volume provides further evidence in support of this argument.

Casey, B. and G. Bruche (1983) Work or Retirement? Labour Market and Social Policy for Ol-
    der Workers in France, Great Britain, The Netherlands, Sweden and the USA. Gower, Al-
    dershot (also in German)
Frank, D., R. Hara, G. Magnier and O. Villey (1982) Entreprises et contrats de solidarité de pré-
    retraite démission. In: Travail et Emploi, No. 13 (Juillet-Septembre) pp. 75-89
GAO (1986) Retirement Before Age 65: Trends, Costs, and National Issues, Report to the
    Chairman, Select Committee on Aging of the House of Representatives, US General Ac-
    counting Office. GAO/HRD-86-86, Washington DC
Haveman, R., V. Halberstadt, and R. Burkhauser (1984) Public Policy Toward Disabled Work-
    ers. Cornell Univ. Press, Ithaca, NY
Hellberger, C. (1984) Kosten und Beschäftigungseffekte des Vorruhestands: Zwei Analysen zu
    dem Modell der Bundesregierung. Sonderforschungsbereich 3 (Arbeitspapier Nr. 135).
    J.W. Goethe-Universität Frankfurt und Universität Mannheim
Hempel, F. (1984), 59er-Regelung geändert, in Bundesarbeitsblatt, No. 7-8, pp. 8-12
Hetzler, A. and K. Eriksson (1981) Ökad Förtids Pensionering: En rättscoiologisk analys. Ekna,
    Lund
ISSA (1985), Social Security, Unemployment and Premature Retirement. International Social
    Security Association. Studies and Research No. 22, Geneva
Lynes, T. (1985) Paying for Pensions: The French Experience. Suntory-Toyota International
    Centre for Economics and Related Disciplines, London School of Economics
Merceau, F. (1982) La retraite à 60 ans. In: Droit Social, No. 6 (Juin), pp. 452-464
NAR (1987) Veralgemening van de pensiongerechtigde leeftijd op 65 jaar. Nationale Arbeids-
    raad (Advies Nr. 858), Brussel (also in French)
OECD (1986) Labour Market Flexibility: Report of a High Level Group of Experts to the Se-
    cretary General. Organisation for Economic Cooperation and Development, Paris, 1986
Pfaff, M. (1985) "Summing-up" in ISSA (1985), op.cit
Rein, M. and L. Rainwater (Eds.) The Public Private Interplay in Social Protection, a Compara-
    tive Study. Sharpe, White Plains, 1986
Riksförsäkringsverket (1984) Delpension och rörlig pensionsåldor: en uppföljning och utvär-
    dering. Stockholm
Puth, J. (1986) Anmerkungen zum Vorruhestand. In: Arbeit und Sozialpolitik, No. 3, pp. 75-76
SEDES (1979) Les conventions et accords de préretraite. In: Revue Française des Affaires So-
    ciales. An. 33, No. 2, pp. 133-160
van den Bosch, F. and C. Petersen (1983) Een economische analyse van de non-participatie-
    graad: de invloed van arbeidsongeschiktheid. In: van den Bosch, F. and C. Petersen (Eds.)
    Economie en arbeidsongeschicktheid: Analyse en beleid, Kluwer, Deventer, pp. 149-164

Seniority-Based Wage System and Postponed Retirement

L. Bellmann

Contents

1. Introduction

Demographic ageing is often measured by age dependency ratios i.e. the number of individuals 60 years or more old in relation to those individuals between 20 and 60 years old. An official projection for the Federal Republic of Germany predicts that the age dependency ratio will increase from 38.5 % in 1985 to 81.2 % in 2030. This challanges the existing retirement system. Assuming for instance a pay-as-you-go method of financing an earnings-related pension system, a doubling of the retirees ratio would also require a doubling of the contribution rate (leaving the benefit level unaltered). For the Federal Republic of Germany this would mean an increase of the contribution rate from 18.5 % to 37 %, shared in equal parts by employers and employees. Schmähl (1987) has discussed as measures to avoid this an increase of the labour-force participation rate and the prolongation of the employment phase. An increase of the labour-force participation rate would temporarily lower the pension burden, but also raise it later, while "in times of high employment – and only then it is a realistic option – an average one-year prolongation of the employment phase would reduce, for example, in the Federal Republic of Germany, the otherwise necessary contribution rate by 3 percentage points – through an increase in the number of contributors and a decrease in the number of pensioneers" (Schmähl (1987), p. 28). The aim of this paper is to discuss the strategy to postpone the retirement age under the additional assumption of a seniority wage system. This raises a problem, because the additional contributors are overpaid from the perspective of an implicit contract between the worker and the firm.

W. Schmähl (Ed.)
Redifining the Process of Retirement
© Springer-Verlag Berlin Heidelberg 1989

The paper deals with microeconomic explanations of the seniority based wage-system. In the second, third and fourth section several theories and in the fifth section the empirical status of seniority wage systems are considered. The selection of the theories was determined by the interest to study the worker's retirement decison. Arai (1982) and Bellmann (1986) survey the relevant literature more completely. The focus of the discussion of the theories is on potential problems of the implementation of a retirement system, which gives the allowance to the workers to choose their retirement age. Constraining the worker's choice is clearly inefficient in the standard specific human capital model, which is presented in the third section. However, both Lazear's shirking model and the model of Carmichael, who considers the effect of transaction costs in conjunction with investment in specific human capital, argue in favor of a mandatory retirement date. The reason therefore is that at the end of the working life the worker's wage profile lies above the value of his marginal productivity profile thus c.p. creating incentives for him to postpone his retirement age. If then, the workers are allowed to postpone their retirement date, in Lazear's shirking model this is at the firm's expense, since the condition is violated that the present values of the wage and the marginal productivity profiles are equal. In Carmichael's model the same behavior of the workers does not cause losses for the firm directly, but the younger worker's job prospects change for the worse. The arguments are presented in detail in the second and fourth section.

2. Productivity Enhancing Seniority-Wage Profiles

An upward sloping wage profile can be viewed as an incentive system; the worker is effectively promised a reward in the future for good behavior today. Therefore Lazear (1979, 1981) assumes that the worker's wage profile does not coincide with his productivity profile. Figure 1 shows that a worker receives a wage less than his marginal productivity at the beginning of his working life. For simplicity I subsequently assume a constant productivity and abstract from worker's time preferences. In this simple model the area between the wage profile, w, and the productivity profile, v, for tenure interval $\hat{t}$ to $\bar{t}$ can be interpreted as a bond, posted by the worker, which he gets back during the rest of his working life (i.e. in the tenure interval $\bar{t}$ up to the retirement date T), provided he does not shirk. Under the stated assumptions the area of both triangles must be equal.

The worker receives a rent if the stays with the firm. The value of this rent, R, is determined by the worker's reservation wage, $\bar{w}$. The curve of the reservation wage is difficult to derive theoretically. However, it seems plausible to assume that at the point in time the worker enters the firm his wage equals his reservation wage and that at the retirement date, T, the reservation wage equals the productivity, since this is the optimal date to leave the firm. This is shown in Figure 2. The worker looses a wage stream of $R(t^+)$, if he is detected shirking at t^+.

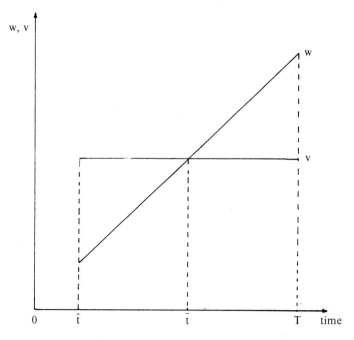

Fig. 1. Wage and productivity profile in Lazear's shirking model.
Source: Lazear (1981), p. 607

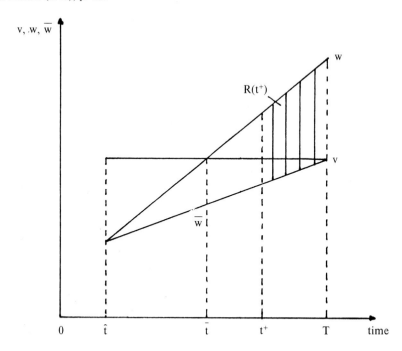

Fig. 2. Wage, productivity and reservation wage profile in Lazear's shirking model.
Source: Lazear (1981), p. 609

The model may be critisized, because of large incentives implied for the firms to break the contract after $\bar{t}$ years of tenure. Then the firm's gain amounts to the area between w and v. Lazear (1979) himself argues that the market contains informations whether a certain firm cheats or not. Then dishonest firms cannot attract workers, if they offer the same wage profile than honest firms. But a smaller slope of the wage profile will clearly enhance the probability of worker's shirking and impose additional costs on these dishonest firms, which will price them out of the market in the long run.

Central for the discussion of the question, whether the worker should be allowed to postpone his retirement date T, is the rationale for a mandatory retirement rule. For a given reservation wage profile $\overline{w}$ the retirement date T is optimal for the worker *ex-ante*. But the worker will decide at T to postpone his retirement, because his wage w exceeds his reservation wage $\overline{w}$ at T. The payment scheme adopted produces a superior wage profile which the worker prefers ex-ante. That is, altough both parties agree on a contract at $\hat{t}$, which specifies a wage path that meets the zero-profit condition, since the present value of the wage profile is equal to that of the productivity profile, *ex-post* the worker is interested in a prolongation of his contract. It is worth noting that the firm is also interested to modify the contract after $\bar{t}$, since after that point in time the wage profile is above the productivity profile and the firm can gain form dismissing the tenured worker and substituting him by a younger worker. Therefore I should consider the question, whether both parties will find a bargaining solution.

Exactly that seems to be difficult, because the worker must agree on a drastic wage reduction. Such a reduction is necessary, since during the years before the retirement date, the firm has to pay back the money the worker has initially posted as a bond. But after the retirement date the firm is not any longer obliged to do this. In addition to that the wage reduction must cover productivity differences between the time the worker was younger and the time he retires. I abstract from this productivity differences in the paper, but they play a prominent rôle in the literature (Wagner (1986), p. 32).

However, the wage reductions mentioned up to now seem to pose rather technical problems. That is not the case, when looking at the extent the wages should be reduced. If it is not possible to determine the exact productivity of a worker, he has a reason to suspect that the firm cheats on the contract by offering a very low wage for the time between the "mandatory" retirement date and the date the worker has chosen for his own retirement. Certainly the firm must trade off the gain from a low wage compared to the productivity of the worker against the danger of bad reputation, which makes it more difficult to hire new worker with the given slope of the wage profile.

There yet remains an other problem. If the worker has completed his contract with the firm at the "mandatory" retirement date T and if the wage he receives is equal to his productivity, he will not be encouraged any longer to work at full effort, since there is no rent he could loose. Therefore, self-employment work and easily controllable work are best suited for older workers.

Following Hutchens (1986) it seems irrational for the worker to shirk for instance at t^+, because he will loose the rent $R(t^+)$, whereas at the retirement date T he will loose only w-v. Therefore, he will wait up to the last possible moment, if he intends to shirk. A payment scheme like the one depicted in Figure 3 will be superior to that proposed by Lazear, since its end payment, which is decisive for the probability a worker shirks, is higher than for the strictly monoton increasing wage profile. Then the worker can deliberately choose the point in time he wishes to retire. However, the model may be critisized, because of e.g. structural change gives rise to new job offers for the worker and increases the value of his marginal productivity. Thus the firm could not be secure that the last possible moment for the worker to shirk is T. Instead, he might shirk before T, when he has decided to quit anyway. Therefore, I cannot fully accept the critique of Hutchens, although being very comfortable for our problems of postponed retirement.

Additionally some authors argue that upward sloping wage profiles are not sufficient to inhibit the worker from shirking. Then, the firms might pay a wage premium so that loss of employment would be costly to a worker. Workers at these firms would be afraid that, if they were caught shirking, they would loose the premium via termination. But if all employers try to use wage premia to forstall shirking, they will raise the market wage above its clearing level. Unemployment will result and the penalty for shirking be-

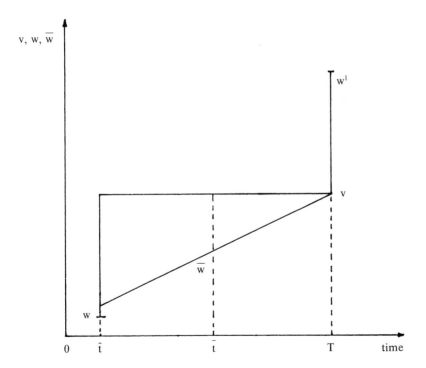

Fig. 3. Wage profiles in Hutchens' Shirking Model
Source: Hutchens (1986), p. 445

comes a spell without wage income as terminated workers seek new jobs
(Yellen (1984), Dickens et al. (1986)). Bellmann (1988) elaborates the argument that the firms cannot costlessly detect the worker's shirking, but em-
ploy supervisors in order to control the employees.

3. Standard Specific Human Capital Model

The model proposed by Becker (1962) argues that the training costs during
the training period are paid by the worker and the firm and consequently
both parties share the return to that human capital investment. Therefore, in
the training period the worker receives a wage, which is below his alternative
wage. In the post-training period he is compensated by a wage above the alternative wage. That is, the present values of the two areas in Figure 4, which
indicate the worker's investment cost, A1, and his return, B1, must be equal.
In addition to that the investment of the firm, A2, and her return, B2, are depicted in this figure. Therefore, the value of the marginal productivity of the
worker lies under his wage during the training period and later above the
worker's wage. By sharing the costs and benefits of the investment, both parties are encouraged to stay together after the end of the training period. But
the worker quits, if he gets an offer above w_2, although the value of his marginal productivity is v_2 and thus a social loss of $v_2 - w_2$ is created. This point is
investigated in the next section in detail.

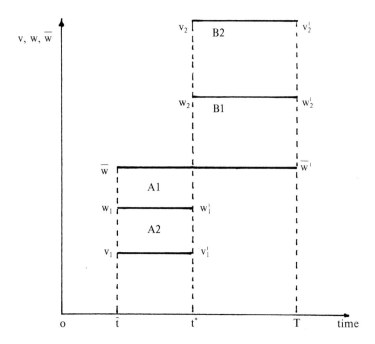

Fig. 4. Wage and productivity profile in the standard Human Capital Model

If the worker postpones his retirement after the point in time T, the return to the human capital investment will increase. Extensions of this simple model could include a depreciation of the specific human capital stock, which will depress the return. The social security system would alter the curve of the alternative wage $\overline{w}$ (Burkhauser and Quinn (1983), Genosko (1983)). These extensions will lead to an upper limit of the retirement date. However a mandatory retirement date would be efficient only by chance in the specific human capital model. Note that only if the value of the marginal productivity v_2 v_2' falls under the worker's wage w_2 w_2', it is inefficient to prolong the working life. Therefore specific human capital investment tends to protect jobs, because training costs can be regared upon as sunk costs by the firm. Those young workers, who just enter the labor market are, if at all, positively affected when older workers postpone retirement, because in future the firms might expect a longer post-training period, during which their investment costs can amortize.

This result is challanged by Carmichael's specific human capital model, which critizises the standard model presented in this section, because the parties internalize only their share of the return, and do not consider the effect of a seperation on the other party.

4. Specific Human Capital, Transaction Costs and the Enforcement of Contracts

Long-term contracts are often attributed to the existence of transaction costs (Williamson (1975)). However, this need not be the case, because transaction – specific rents create a host of noncooperative considerations having to do with the division of rents between the parties. Therefore, it may be difficult to reach the cooperative solution in a Prisoner's Dilemma situation. The theory of repeated games derives conditions under which the threat of dissolution of a contract can in principle inhibt both parties to extract the other's gains and thus lead to a self-enforcing agreement (Telser (1980)). In practice however tendencies toward opportunism remain as the end-period approaches. Other possibilities to enforce contracts include the monitoring of the behavior of the parties, as briefly mentioned in the last section, or the use of bonds, as in Lazear's model, or the reliance on reputations as bonding equivalents or the definition of "grievance procedures" under which various conflicts are handled by arbitration as they arise (Rosen (1984), p. 987). In what follows I will sketch out the idea of Carmichael's model about seniority-wage profiles, which induce optimal turnover in the presence of transaction costs and investment in firm-specific human capital.

Carmichael (1983) assumes that a worker enters the firm for one period of training, after which his firm-specific productivity is increased. Also after one period the worker knows his job satisfaction and the firm know the worker's actual productivity. The exchange of this private informations would require transaction costs. On the basis of their information, the firm and the worker may or may not stay together for the next period. After the second period the worker retires. The worker's contractual wages are w_1 and w_2 for the first and second period respectively, his alternative wage is $\overline{w}$. Thus the first period wage equals $\overline{w}$-c, where c is the cost of training. Sometime in the second period the worker receives a promotion, and then he earns the wage w_2 +B from this point in time until he retires. Thereby promotion is made depend upon the worker's seniority by the assumption that the firm's implicit contract with its workers specifies that the number of high wage jobs is fixed.

A contract, which specifies w_1 and w_2 is self-enforcing, if two conditions are met: Firstly, the worker has to pay the full cost of the investment into specific human capital. This was already mentioned, when specifying the first-period wage as $w_1 = \overline{w} - c$. Secondly, the wage differential a promoted worker receives, B, must be high enough to second-period wage, in order that the worker's post-training productivity is greater than his second-period wage. The first condition assumes that the worker internalize the full losses of a seperation when he quits, whereas the second condition does the same for the firm when she dismisses the worker. The firm can only save w_2 through a layoff but the costs are v_2, since the job will simply revert to the worker one rung down on the seniority ladder. The "third party", which gains from any seperation, is therfore madeup of all the less senior workers, whose seniority is increased as a result. Figure 5 illustrates the wage and the productivity profiles.

If the worker is allowed to postpone his retirement date, he would not do this *ex-ante,* when he enters the firm, but *ex-post,* when he was promoted and his wage w_2 +B exceeds his alternative wage $\overline{w}$, he will postpone his retirement. In contrast to Lazear's model this behavior does not cause direct problems for the firm. There is an easy adjustment available, because the less senior workers could be promoted later in their working lives.

It is important to note that in Carmichael's model a worker can always calculate the date he will be promoted, since this depends on the number of workers, who will stay with the firm during the post-training period, whose number can be calculated from the distribution of job satisfaction, which was assumed to be common knowledge. Therefore, the number of junior workers, who quit after the first period will increase, thus their costs of training are sunk. Adopting a retirement-at-will rule creats a social loss, although the worker deliberately chooses to quit.

However, it cannot be decided a priori, whether a prolongation of the working life is efficient or not: Because under the stated asumptions at T the worker's value of marginal productivity exceeds his alternative wage, but the same is true for the worker, who has just finished his training-period and quits, because of the worsened job prospects. Postponing retirement remains efficient, as long as more older workers retire later than younger quit. Thereby the different expected future tenure should be taken into account, too.

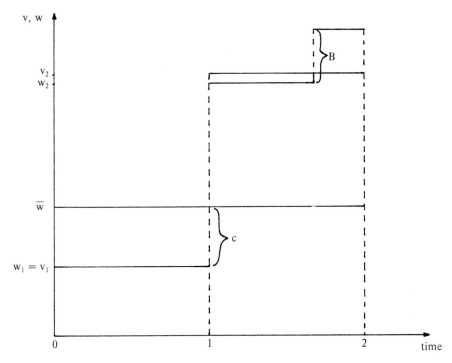

Fig. 5. Wage and productivity profile in Carmichael's Model
Source: Carmichael (1983), p. 255   Figure 1

5. The Empirical Status of Seniority-Based Wage Systems

The three theories considered in the last section share at least two common properties: They predict a long-term employment relationship and rising age-earnings profiles.

Empirical evidence for a long-term employment relationship can be found for the Federal Republic of Germany, the USA and Japan. The statistical analysis is performed in terms of the number of different jobs, completed and expected tenure in the current firm, the fifteen-year and the twenty-year retention rates, which are estimates of the probabilites that workers in a given age-tenure category will be with the same employer a certain time span (e.g. fifteen or twenty years). The completed-tenure data suggest that long contracts are more prevalent in the Federal Republic of Germany compared with the USA: The median of the completed tenure for both genders amounts to 3.6 years for the USA (Hall (1982), p. 717) and 8.7 years for the Federal Republic of Germany (Bellmann (1986), p. 162). The U.S. economy exhibits less long-term employment relationships compared to those of Japan. Among the male workers, 20-24-years old and with tenure of 5 and more years, 65 % in Japan retain the same job fifteen years later, but only 30 % do so in the USA (Hashimoto and Raisian (1985), p. 723). A result which is reinforced by other age-tenure groups and the analysis of the number of different jobs by the authors themselves and by the OECD (1984).

Earnings profiles are estimated by means of so-called earnings functions with logarithmic earnings as the dependent variable. Explanatory variables are usually schooling, experience, experience squared, tenure, tenure squared. Tenure coefficients of earnings functions range between 0.0278 and 0.0692 for Japan and -0.0019 and 0.0196 for the USA, whereas the differences are due to different firm-size groups (Hashimoto and Raisian (1984, p. 730). For the Federal Republic of Germany Bellmann (1986, p. 175 ff.) has estimated a positively sloped tenure-earnings profile. The regression coefficient of the variable tenure squared always exhibits a negative sign. Therefore it seems to be possible to infere from cross sectional data that seniority wages are only prevalent among the younger worker. Since it is impossible to disentangle cohort and age effects, the better earnings prospects of younger cohorts compared to those of the older cohorts are attributed to tenure differences. Therefore it is not adequate to infere seniority wage profiles from cross section instead of longitudinal data sets. The later were used for the Federal Republic of Germany only by Papastefanou (1980), Mayer and Papastefanou (1983), Göbel (1983), Göbel and Schmähl (1983), Schmähl (1986) and Brüderl (1986). But they could account with the exception of Brüderl only for general labor market experience and not for tenure in the current firm.

Quite recently Abraham and Farber (1987) have argued that the statistical procedures used for longitudinal data analysis fail to control for job match quality, thus they conclude that the effect of seniority on earnings is overestimated. Therefore, the authors propose that the econometric model should allow for the possibility that workers earn more *from the start* in long-term employment relationships. Thus it may be concluded that more statistically sophisticated studies are needed to discern, whether seniority causes higher wages or not. And, similarly, the relation between wages and productivity is still under discussion (Bellmann (1986), p. 29 ff.).

6. Conclusions

This paper emphasizes mandatory retirement rules as efficient outcomes of seniority-based wage systems, which are designed to inhibit the worker from shirking and to internalize losses due to seperations in the specific human capital case. Thereby a worker can realize additional gains at the expense of the firm or the jounger workers respectively, when he postpones his retirement date. For the specific human capital case it can be concluded from the standard model that postponing retirement is alway efficient, whereas this need not be true in Carmichael's specific human capital model.

With respect to seniority wages and their microeconomic explanations, it cannot be concluded from the evidence how relevant these theories are. However, if the hypothesis that earnings depend on seniority is correct at least in some firms, senior workers are overpaid there. Then, this problem could and should be solved with the help of the worker's representatives for two reasons: The decreasing productivity of older workers in conjunction with rigid wages encourage the firm to force the older workers to leave their job (Wagner (1987), p. 149 f.). The firms could strategically structure their pension system in such a way that the present value of a pension is the higher the earlier a worker retires. The postponed retirement creates additional gains of some workers at the expense of others, as pointed out in the discussion of Carmichael's specific human capital model, and at the expense of the firm, as argued by Lazear. The deregulation of the retirement age could mean then, that unions and firms bargain about mandatory retirement rules and thus minimize the costs of postponing the retirement age (Wagner (1986), p. 63 f.).

References

Abraham, K.G. and H.S. Farber (1987), Job Duration, Seniority, and Earnings. American Economic Review 77, pp. 278-297

Arai, K. (1982) Theories of the Seniority-Based Wage System. Hitotsubashi Journal of Economics, pp. 53-67

Becker, G.S. (1962) Investment in Human Capital: Effects on Earnings. Journal of Political Economy 70, pp. 9-49

Bellmann, L. (1986) Senioritätsentlohnung, betriebliche Hierarchie und Arbeitsleistung: Eine theoretische und empirische Untersuchung zur Lohnstruktur. Frankfurt a.M., Campus

Bellmann, L. (1988) Supervision of Workers and Wage Structure: A Generalization of Lazear's Shirking Model. Paper presented at the European Meeting of the Econometric Society, Bologna

Brüderl, J. (1987) Effizienzlohntheorie und Senioritätsentlohnung. mimeo., München

Burkhauser, R.V. and J.F. Quinn (1983) Is Mandatory Retirement Overrated? Evidence from the 1970s, Journal of Human Resources 18, pp. 337-358

Carmichael, L. (1983) Firm Specific Human Capital and Promotion Ladders. Bell Journal of Economics 14, pp. 251-258

Dickens, W.T., L.F. Katz and K. Lang (1986) Are efficiency Wages Efficient? National Bureau of Economic Research Working Paper No. 1935

Genosko, J. (1983) Erwerbsbeteiligung und gesetzliche Rentenversicherung: Der Fall der 60- bis 65jährigen Männer. Zeitschrift für die gesamte Staatswissenschaft 139, pp. 625-642

Göbel, D. (1983) Lebenseinkommen und Erwerbsbiographie: Eine Längsschnittuntersuchung mit Daten der gesetzlichen Rentenversicherung. Frankfurt a.M., Campus

Hall, R.E. (1982) The Importance of Lifetime Jobs in the U.S. Economy. American Economic Review 72, pp. 716-724

Hashimoto, M. and J. Raisian (1985) Employment Tenure and Earnings Profiles in Japan and the United States, American. Economic Review 75, pp. 721-735

Hutchens, R. (1986) Delayed Payment Contracts and a Firm's Propensity of Hire Older Workers. Journal of Labor Economics 4, pp. 439-457

Klevmarken, N.A. (1982) On the Stability of Age-Earnings Profiles. Scandinavian Journal of Economics 84, pp. 531-554

Lazear, E.P. (1979) Why is there Mandatory Retirement? Journal of Political Economy 87, pp. 1261-1284

Lazear, E.P. (1981) Agency, Earnings Profiles, Productivity, and Hours Restrictions. American Economic Review 71, pp. 606-620

Mayer, K.U. and G. Papastefanou (1983) Arbeitseinkommen im Lebensverlauf: Probleme der retrospektiven Erfassung und empirische Materialien. In: W. Schmähl (Hrsg.) Ansätze der Lebenseinkommensanalyse. Tübingen, Mohr, pp. 101-122

Organization of Economic Co-operation and Development (1984) The importance of longterm job attachment in OECD countries. Employment Outlook, pp. 55-68

Papastefanou, G. (1980) Arbeitseinkommen im Lebensverlauf: Eine konzeptionelle Anmerkung und exploratorische Ergebnisse. SfB3-Arbeitspapier Nr. 61

Rosen, S. (1984) Commentary. In: Defense of the Contract at Will. University of Chicago Law Review 51, pp. 983-987

Schmähl, W. (1986) Lohnentwicklung im Lebensablauf. Allgemeines Statistisches Archiv 70, pp. 180-203

Schmähl, W. (1987) Demograhpic Change and Social Security. Lecture given at the First Annual Congress of the European Society for Population Economics, Rotterdam

Schmähl, W. and D. Göbel (1983) Lebenseinkommensverläufe und Längsschnittdaten der Rentenversicherungsträger. In: W. Schmähl (Hrsg.) Ansätze der Lebenseinkommensanalyse. Tübingen, Mohr, pp. 126-172

Telser, L. (1981) A Theory of Self-Enforcing Agreements. Journal of Business 53, pp. 27-44

Wagner, G. (1986) Bestimmungsgründe und Konsequenzen des Rentenzugangsalters: Ein ökonomischer Analyserahmen eines wesentlichen Elements der Strukturreform der gesetzlichen Rentenversicherung. SfB3-Arbeitspapier Nr. 226

Wagner, G. (1987) Reform beim Rentenzugang. Wirtschaftsdienst 67, pp. 145-150

Williamson, O.E. (1975) Markets and Hierarchies: Analysis and Antitrust Implicatons. New York, Free Press

Yellen, J. (1984) Efficiency Wage Models of Unemployment. American Economic Review. Papers and Proceedings 74, pp. 200-205

Employment of Older Persons from a Management Point of View

W. H. Staehle[1]

1.

Both in the literature and in management practice it is agreed that a person's age in years is only to a very limited extent a suitable criterion for the definition of what constitutes an older employee (OE). The reason for this is that the age at which a person should start to be considered "older" depends not only on the age of the observer but also on the age-expectations prevailing in given vocational groups (e.g. airline stewardesses, professional sportsmen).

In practice, there has been an emergence of certain age limits in trade and industry above which – except in the case of management staff – there is little or no recruitment, any possibility of personnel development and further training is barely considered and career opportunities rapidly deteriorate. These informal limits now lie between ages 35 and 50, although besides depending on the industry or the vocational group concerned the limits are also very strongly influenced by the level of training, the professional and hierarchical level, the labour market situation and, not least, by existing pension arrangements (cf. for example Benda and Staufer (1987), pp. 7-9).

Statistical surveys conducted among managers have shown that on average the critical threshold above which a person is regarded as an OE in the Federal Republic of Germany is reached at around the age of 50 (cf. Naegele (1983), pp. 90 ff, or Lehr (1987)).

Employment among this group of employees aged over 50 has dropped very substantially in the Federal Republic during the past 10 years. While for men and women aged 60-65 the employment rates were still 73.5 % and 21.8 % respectively in 1966, by 1985 the figures had fallen to as low as 35.2 % and 11.8 %.

Employers, trade unions and *the State* have been extremely inventive in the recent past in devising means of facilitating and encouraging the departure of OEs from working life. What is the explanation for this phenomenon?

Assumption: The three actors in the German industrial relations system take the view that OEs are poorer learners and achievers than other groups of employees and hinder technological and organisational change in firms.

---

[1]   The author gratefully acknowledges critical comments of J. Deters aud U. Stirn to an earlier draft of this paper.

W. Schmähl (Ed.)
Redifining the Process of Retirement
© Springer-Verlag Berlin Heidelberg 1989

What do the three actors in the industrial relations system have to say about OEs? Do they share the above assumption and hence agree with the so-called deficit model of OE capability (the "maximum youth" hypothesis)?

2.

The three actors in the industrial relations system adopt the following positions with regard to OEs:

Employers: Since 1973 the Federal Union of German Employers' Associations (BDA 1980) has regarded it as an important task for social policy that the prejudice that OEs have limited vocational capability (deficit model of ageing) should be overcome. In the BDA's view (1980, p. 11) employers, on the basis of operational considerations and experience, cannot afford to cease employing OEs, whatever labour market factors and developments may indicate. The BDA feels that OEs are not in principle poorer achievers than their younger colleagues, but are in many cases only qualitatively different and indeed in most cases actually qualitatively superior. For the success of an undertaking the abilities of OEs are just as important as those of younger workers; for human cooperation at the workplace they are increasingly becoming indispensable.

Furthermore, OEs will gain in importance because in the 1990s at the latest the size of the working population will start to decrease for demographic reasons.

Trade unions: In 1975, in other words at about the same time as the BDA, the German Trade Union Federation came out against the prejudice that there was an age-related performance deficit by publishing a list of assumptions which it considered were not correct. These were that OEs

- are less able to cope with the physical strain of working life,
- are more often ill,
- are more accident-prone,
- have inferior mental and intellectual capacities,
- are neither willing nor able to adapt to technical and economic change, or
- show less willingness to work.

(Frieling and Sonntag (1987), p. 175).

The State: The amended Works Constitution Act (BetrVG) of 1972 increases the importance attached to OEs. Under its provisions employers and works councils are obliged to take care that employees are not put at a disadvantage on account of having passed certain age thresholds (section 75 (1) BetrVG).

The legislation makes this general duty specific when it comes to vocational training: here the act stipulates that, with regard to the support given to vocational training in an organisation, due consideration must also be given to the interests of OEs (section 96 (2) BetrVG). The statutory provisions further make it one of the general duties of works councils to promote the employment of older employees in the organisation (section 80 (1) no 6 BetrVG).

One of the conclusions of the study entitled "Employees in the later phase of life" commissioned by the Federal Ministry for Labour and Social Affairs was: "The evidence is that age in years is not per se a good criterion for defining a problem group in an organisation. Only in combination with other factors – principally to do with health, the activity itself and qualifications – and with specific part-time labour market conditions can chronological age cause problems and make them more acute" (Naegele (1983), p. 37).

To sum up, I would state that all actors in the industrial relations system involved in the employment of OEs are aware that there is no direct or even causal connection between chronological age and intellectual ability.

There must therefore be other reasons why companies nevertheless prefer to remove OEs from their labour force and in so doing receive support from legislation and from employees' representatives.

3.

To help us identify these reasons, we carried out – with financial support from the German Research Society (DFG) – a written survey on both sides of industry employers' associations and trade unions and held interviews at selected firms (in this case with personnel managers and works councils). The latter, in particular, were a very fruitful source of information about the above problem.

Personnel cutbacks among OEs are mainly relevant in connection with the following measures:

1) *Reduction of the size of the workforce*
Rationalisation investments and/or a decline in the level of activity lead to a surplus of labour (eg. cigarette industry, petroleum industry, automotive industry).

Example: At Opel about four per cent of the total complement of some 55,000 jobs will probably be shed over the next few years under a rationalisation plan. This is the likely outcome of an analysis of overheads carried out at Opel by the management consultancy firm McKinsey. Yet no redundancies are planned, only internal redeployment. The necessary job vacancies will be created by, among other things, setting up a new retirement scheme for Opel workers born in 1928/29.

2) *Restructuring of the workforce*
To enable firms to handle technological change or innovations better, the age or skills structure is improved, i.e. parts of the workforce (older, insuffi-

ciently qualified employees) are exchanged for younger, better qualified personnel (e.g. the electrical engineering industry, EDP).

3) *Making the workforce more flexible*
To adapt the length of the agreed working week to a firm's operational needs as regards working hours (capacity utilisation), the link between the agreed working week and the firm's working hours is broken.

Example: In a company agreement (1984) converting the collectively agreed 38.5-hour week so that it can be applied in a plant in the metal industry in Lower Saxony we read: "If no employee wishes to work a shorter week voluntarily, the OEs' working week shall be reduced in order to achieve the mathematical average of 38.5 hours".

All three measures are usually linked with an *intensification of work,* that is to say the work formerly done by OEs must now be added to the workload of the remaining (younger) workers.

Now why does management, when it has to make cuts in the workforce, think first of the OEs? Contrary to official statements by the two sides of industry, the real reason is still that OEs are thought to give rise to higher personnel costs (longer absences, sickness) and incidental personnel costs (as a result of the seniority principle, more years of service with the firm). In addition, shedding older workers is seen as a *bloodless* solution, i.e. a voluntary reduction in the workforce which respects the firm's obligations to its employees, is socially acceptable and does not damage the firm's good reputation in personnel matters.

Example:

"We have all of us, many of us as people involved in social policy, as trade unionists, as employers, contributed by our schemes and measures to the present image of the "older" employee. Such a person is – it is said – basically "worn out" in career terms. Early retirement spells "deliverance" for him, we are freeing him from the "drudgery" of work!

Gradually we all – more or less consciously – absorb this image of older people. Yet we know from our experience at work that in our firm there are young and old "old people" just as there are young and old "young people". And we know that attitudes to early retirement can vary from individual to individual." (Gerhard Grabner, personnel director, Hamburgische Electricitäts-Werke AG, Analytic Symposium 1987).

It is evident that firms have a great interest in introducing greater flexibility into their retirement policies. On the one hand they want to get rid of their lower-performing and less healthy OEs as early and cheaply as possible. On the other hand they are interested in selective continued employment of skilled employees beyond the existing (early) retirement limits.

In the Federal Republic this trend to greater flexibility is mainly reflected in new forms of working-hours management (cf. Marr (1987), Offe, Hinrichs and Wiesenthal (1983)). Following Atkinson (1985) I distinguish three types of development as far as greater flexibility is concerned.

First, there is *numerical flexibility,* that is to say employers will increasingly seek to tailor the number of their employees or, more precisely, the number of hours worked, to fluctuations in demand (breaking the link between the agreed working week and the firm's working hours). Understandably, this meets with fierce resistance from the trade unions. But in many sections of trade and industry it is a development which has already occurred: I am thinking for example of retailing and variable working hours based on capacity considerations.

The second trend which I note is a movement towards *functional flexibility.* By this term I mean mainly multiple qualifications. Nowadays employees must have several skills if they are to be able to adapt smoothly to changes in their tasks; hence specialists, although still heavily in demand, are losing ground. Without multiple qualifications, particularly in the field of management, there are no great opportunities for further career development. This need for versatility also applies to the skilled manual worker; if he lacks the necessary range of aptitudes, he must be given an opportunity to obtain appropriate additional skills.

The third trend which I see is towards *financial flexibility.* In my opinion we are witnessing an increasing individualisation of wage costs and incidental wage costs and a reversal of the levelling trend seen in the past. Although pay by results in the narrow sense (piecework) is inevitably on the decline, time-based remuneration is being linked in one way or another to performance and this is reflected in the individual wage packet or salary cheque.

Such trends towards greater flexibility have serious consequences, in that they lead to increased "segmentation" of the labour force (Fig. 1). The segmentation takes the form of what may be called a core group surrounded by several peripheral groups. Employees in the first group carry out core activities essential for the survival of the firm. The core group will be made up of skilled workers and managers, highly paid people with great job security – reminiscent of the situation in Japan – while around them there will be gathered one or more peripheral groups, the composition of which may fluctuate very sharply. Employees on low pay, on part-time contracts, with insecure conditions of employment – these people constitute the flexible labour pool now being slowly built up by the corporate sector. Recent recruits to this labour pool are the OEs.

There is no question but that this segmentation strategy is meeting and will continue to meet fierce resistance from the trade unions. But one has to remember where the power lies: so long as mass unemployment persists, the trade unions' position will be far from strong; increasingly far-reaching demands for greater flexibility will be made by the employers, particularly if the unions continue with their campaign for further reductions in the length of the working week. Thus a cut in working hours can now only be obtained in return for greater flexibility. The trade unions must wonder whether they have not made a mistake here, with their demand for a 35-hour week unleashing an avalanche which they can no longer control, breaking up standard and full-time jobs into a multiplicity of flexible, fluctuating employment arrangements. I can well imagine that employers are quite prepared to agree to a week of 35 hours or less, provided only that corresponding flexibility gains are achieved. So this will mean more shift work, Saturday and Sunday working, part-time work by old people, a change from weekly to yearly working time (yearly working time packages being purchased and then spread over the year in line with seasonal activity).

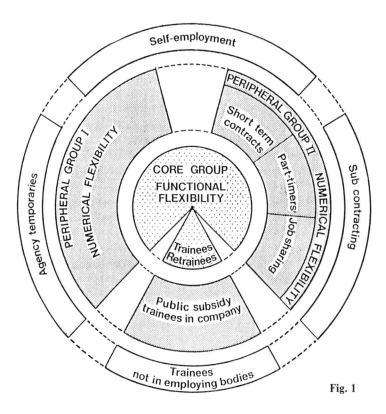

Fig. 1

4.

The view of the OE revealed in this description of the situation can be characterised as the classic business management view. The employee is regarded primarily as a cost factor (input), which is included in the profit and loss account; personnel costs, like all other types of cost, are minimised by suitable action; and output, in terms of performance per unit of time, is to be maximised.

A review of the latest literatur on personnel matters, personnel management and labour relations, however, indicates that there has been a definite change in perspective. Whereas up until the beginning of the 1980s the functional department "personnel" was treated as just one area of responsibility within the organisation among others such as procurement, production and marketing, there has since been a shift in the direction of an integrative, proactive and strategic view of the factor "labour" in an undertaking. Personnel work is no longer merely a matter of applying personnel techniques such as personnel planning, utilisation, development or dismissal, techniques the competent handling of which is entrusted to highly specialised staff in the personnel department, but is now a genuine management task. All actions/decisions connected with the factor "labour" are now planned integratively as "human resources" (HR) activities and harmonised with the corporate strategy.

The following factors are mentioned as reasons for the necessity for a comprehensive human resources management (HRM) system:

- intensified competition (especially the challenge from Japan)
- new technologies (with new requirement profiles)
- problems with productivity and quality
- demographic changes (age structure, women at work, minorities)
- changed values, new lifestyles, altered expectations from working life.

These and other frequently mentioned causes such as, for instance, the person-oriented characteristics of successful firms pointed out by Peters and Waterman (1982) or McKinsey's three S's (staff, style, skills) are plausible at first sight, but they ignore the historical dimension and give no insight into background factors. Also plausible is the explanation that the situation following the oil crisis of 1973 drastically brought home to management in western industrialised nations just what it meant to be dependent on external resources. Certainly the oil crisis made management more aware of the importance of material, financial and also – and increasingly – human resources. It is precisely in human resources that countries poorly endowed with raw materials have a competitive advantage over countries rich in such materials. A firm's success, therefore, depends in large measure on the correct selection, development and remuneration of human resources, including OEs, and their correct utilisation and training.

However, the human resources management idea has its roots in a much earlier period, the end of the 1950s, when work by humanistic management researchers such as Argyris, Maslow and McGregor (cf. Staehle (1988)) was published. With this work the foundations for the transition from a control model to a commitment model of personnel were laid.

Rensis Likert (1967) sought to put such measures, which lead to worse use of human resources, on to an arithmetical basis by using methods similar to those of accountancy. In collaboration with some colleagues from the field of accountancy he developed the first Human Resources Accounting System in 1968. Since then an extensive literature on the subject has come into being, but no convincing solutions have as yeat been put forward to the serious valuation problems involved. An employee's value is difficult to quantify in monetary terms. Moreover, workers, unlike the assets that are capitalised in the balance sheet, are not owned by the firm; investment in them therefor carries a greater risk. Despite these shortcomings, the debate on human resources accounting has had a beneficial effect in one respect: management now gives at least as much thought to the value of a skilled permanent workforce (including OEs) as it does to other resources.

At the end of the 1950s, in response to the Sputnik shock, Gary Becker (1964) and the later (1979) Nobel Prize winner Theodore Schultz (1978) laid the foundations of a "human capital" theory from the point of view of society or the economy as a whole. According to this theory every employee is a part of a firm's net worth, an asset that can be valued like other assets; accordingly expenditure on basic and further training represent investments in human capital. Labour is conventionally regarded as a cost factor, which appears in the profit and loss account and must be kept as low as possible by personnel management techniques. Under the human capital theory labour is treated as an asset, which appears in the balance sheet and the value of which must be maintained or increased by HRM. From the macroeconomic point of view this implies that if a nation regards human resources as the most important source of its wealth, it must be the goal of every economic and social policy to develop and maintain its HR and to ensure its optimum utilisation. Parnes (1984, pp. 16 ff.) distinguishes the following policy spheres for national HRM:

- HR development (e.g. academic and vocational basic and further training)
- HR allocation (e.g. bringing together job-seekers and employers)
- HR conservation (e.g. assistance to the unemployed, job creation measures)
- HR utilisation (e.g. productive use of labour, minimisation of absenteeism, sickness, accidents).

The human capital theory provides an explanation of, among other things, why there is a significantly lower unemployment rate among highly qualified employees than among their less qualified colleagues – for the employer the former represent a higher investment in HR, which he will not so readily dispose of – or why highly qualified people can expect a significantly faster growth in earnings during their career than less qualified people – in this case higher capital investment is amortised in vocational training.

Both micro- and macroeconomic findings of the human capital theory have been (implicitly) taken up by the HRM literature. To sum up, then, at least two strands to the present HRM debate can be identified: (1) a behavioural strand (in which employees are regarded as a pool of many different potential skills, and it is management's task and responsibility to discover how best these talents may be kept up to date, fostered and further developed) and (2) an economic strand (labour is no longer regarded solely as a cost factor but – mainly – as an asset which, for both micro- and macroeconomic reasons, should be preserved and increased). What is specifically new about the present-day HR debate is, to my mind, (3) the systematic combination (integration) of personnel recruitment and development measures which have hitherto been handled separately, (4) their incorporation into the strategic and structural decision-making process and (5) the fact that HR is seen in a general management context rather than from a functional point of view (such as personnel affairs) and that line management is made responsible for HR.

5.

This next section will examine whether the shift of emphasis which is discernible in the literature can also be shown to exist in corporate practice in the form of a reassessment of OEs as HR.

In our investigations we have been able to establish that a few far-sighted firms have remembered or become aware of the value of labour, and especially OEs, as a resource. Only when OEs as a group had almost completely ceased to exist in firms which had carried out drastic cutbacks in their older staff was it realised what resources had thereby been lost.

The knowledge, skill and above all the years of experience, the comprehensive grasp of circumstances within the firm, which OEs have are resources which no firm can afford to dispense with. Consequently many firms have had to organise expensive campaigns to (temporarily) re-recruit employees who had retired.

The OEs' know-how is also urgently required in connection with the switch from individual to group working.

In this way the OEs' social competence, their familiarity with the organisation's "culture" and their long years of vocational experience came to be appreciated.

Obviously, this re-evaluation of a section of the older workforce will necessarily have repercussions for the further training of its members. If employees are again to stay on at work after age 58, there will have to be heavier investment in their further training.

In view of demographic developments, which point to increased scarcity of highly skilled specialists, more and more firms are emphasising that for employment contract and pension insurance purposes retirement basically does not begin until completion of the 65th year of life. However, owing to the generosity of the early retirement schemes organised in the past – for example, people retiring at 55 and younger were placed in the same financial position as if they had retired at 63 – expectations have been created in the minds of employees which now have to be removed by costly measures. Whereas only yesterday it was regarded as a humanitarian imperative that OEs should take their "well-earned" retirement as early as possible, the exact opposite is now being advocated in many firms.

Example:

"Early retirement schemes have made it easier for us to put through many rationalisation measures in the plants; such schemes have an important function today, in these times of high unemployment, in that they create vacancies for the unemployed, particularly the young. Yet it should not be our goal in personnel matters to continuously reduce the age of retirement. It is not humane to keep reminding workers, as soon as they have reached middle age, that the economy really doesn't need them any more. That is an image we must combat." (G. Grabner at the Analytic Symposium 1987).

The philosophy behind a relevant company agreement (1987) concerning the introduction of a flexible retirement scheme was stated by management as follows:

"The population decline in the Federal Republic, combined with an appreciable increase in the shortage of skilled labour, makes it necessary to remind ourselves that the normal retirement age as laid down by law, by the company's old age and surviving dependants' pension scheme and by the contract of employment, is 65. The entitlement to retire at 60 or 63 under the flexible scheme constitutes an exception to the norm and is only possible in special circumstances (due regard being given to the sex of the person concerned, any serious handicaps suffered, the completion of waiting periods and payment of a certain number of compulsory contributions).

Another, extremely important argument against retirement at 58 lies in the high costs thereby incurred on behalf of a section of the workforce which is small in relation to total employee numbers. The fact that the average costs for an employee who is no longer working are twice as high as for one who is working is a clear indication that the limits of what is acceptable have been greatly exceeded."

The reasons behind management decisions to raise the age of retirement from firms and thereby to give an upward push to the pensionable age are to be found mainly in the cost calculations of personnel management. On the one hand the early pension possibilities (scheme for 59-year-olds, social plans, early retirement) have proved to be very expensive on account of their high take-up rate by the OEs entitled; on the other hand, with the departure of the OEs an important store of urgently needed know-how, especially experience, integrative power and specialised knowledge, has been lost to the firms. With the drastic trimming of whole groups of OEs (in many firms there are hardly any employees over 58 left), many firms have also given up a cushion of labour, a pool from which employees could be shed fairly easily and in a socially acceptable way when the firm was going through a crisis.

In anticipation of demographic developments management further stresses that by introducing flexible retirement models as possible means of temporary part-time work by older people for limited periods and a consequent expected extension of the average length of the working life, bottlenecks on the labour market and rising personnel recruitment costs can be combated at an early stage.

In addition, models of part-time work for older people serve as pilot schemes for part-time working arrangements in general. A basis for flexible and inexpensive utilisation of labour is thereby created.

6.

It has recently become apparent that personnel managers are taking a significantly different view of OEs. This explains why it is so important to management that all working time arrangements should largely satisfy the criteria of *controllability by the firm* (early retirement arrangements are organised individually and require approval by the firm) and *reversibility* (possibility of reverting to the original situation).

Across-the-board cuts in working hours and generalised pension plans which apply to all OE groups without distinction and to which all of them are entitled are, however, to be regarded as relatively irreversible and circumscribe a firm's freedom of manoeuvre.

Overall, it can be said that OEs – for reasons of present and anticipated costs – have undergone a substantial upward revaluation in the minds of management in the most recent period. Not only are they urgently needed – albeit selectively – as sources of know-how, but they also serve as a flexible labour pool enabling the firm to cope with fluctuations in the level of activity that are difficult or impossible to foresee.

References

Atkinson, J. (1985) Flexibility, Uncertainty and Manpower Management. Institut of Manpower Studies. Report No. 89, Brighton

Benda, H.v. and M. Staufer (1987) Alter und neue Informationstechniken. Institut für Psychologie. Memorandum Nr. 44, Erlangen

BDA (1980) Bundesvereinigung der Deutschen Arbeitgeberverbände (Hrsg.) Ältere Mitarbeiter, 2. Aufl. Köln

Becker, G. S. (1964) Human Capital. New York

Frieling, E. and K. Sonntag (1987) Lehrbuch Arbeitspsychologie. Bern, Stuttgart, Toronto

Lehr, U. (1987) Ältere Mitarbeiter, Führung von, Handwörterbuch der Führung. Stuttgart, Sp. 1-12

Likert, R. (1967) The Human Organization. New York etc.

Marr, R. (Ed.) (1987) Arbeitszeitmanagement. Berlin

Naegele, G. (1983) Arbeitnehmer in der Spätphase ihrer Erwerbstätigkeit, Bonn

Offe, C., K. Hinrichs and H. Wiesenthal (Hrsg.) (1983) Arbeitszeitpolitik. Frankfurt/New York, 2. Aufl.

Parnes, H.S. (1984) People Power: Elements of Human Resource Policy. Beverly Hills, London, New Delhi

Peters, Th. J. and R.H. Waterman (1982) In Search of Excellence. New York

Schultz, Th. W. (1978) Economic Analysis of Investment in Education. Washington, D.C.

Staehle, W.H. (1988) Human Resource Management. Zeitschrift für Betriebswirtschaft 58. Jg., Heft 5/6, S. 26-37

Subject Index

Welfare – Efficiency – Resources

D. Bös, University of Bonn;
M. Rose, University of Heidelberg;
C. Seidl, University of Kiel, FRG
(Eds.)

Welfare and Efficiency in Public Economics

1988. 28 figures. XVI, 424 pages. Hard cover DM 140,–.
ISBN 3-540-18824-X

Contents: Introduction. – Welfare and Efficiency Measures – General Aspects. – Computing Welfare Effects of Fiscal Policy Programmes in an Applied General Equilibrium Setting. – Welfare and Efficiency of Selected Fiscal Policy Measures. – Addresses of Authors.

M. Faber, University of Heidelberg;
H. Niemes, Mannheim;
G. Stephan, University of Heidelberg, FRG

Entropy, Environment and Resources

An Essay in Physico-Economics

With the cooperation of L. Freytag

Translated from the German by I. Pellengahr

1987. 33 figures. XII, 205 pages. Hard cover DM 78,–.
ISBN 3-540-18248-9

The special features of the book are that the authors utilize a natural scientific variable, entropy, to relate the economic system and the environment, that environmental protection and resource use are analyzed in combination, and that a replacement of techniques over time is analyzed. A novel aspect is that resource extraction is interpreted as a reversed diffusion process. Thus a relationship between entropy, energy and resource concentration is established. The authors investigate the use of the environment both as a supplier of resources and as a recipient of pollutants with the help of thermodynamic relationships. The book therefore provides a new set of tools for workers in the field.

R. Pethig, University of Oldenburg;
U. Schlieper, University of Mannheim, FRG (Eds.)

Efficiency, Institutions, and Economic Policy

Proceedings of a Workshop held by the Sonderforschungsbereich 5 at the University of Mannheim, June 1986

1987. 21 figures. IX, 225 pages. Hard cover DM 75,–.
ISBN 3-540-18450-3

This volume addresses the issue of efficiency and institutions from different angles. First, the efficiency of modern welfare states is analyzed on a general level where topics like social justice, redistribution and rent seeking are studied in an environment of pressure groups and self-interested politicians (papers by Streit, Schlieper, Wickström). Second, several papers deal with more specific issues like intergenerational transfers in a social insurance system, the efficiency of law, and contractual arrangements in the labor market (Witt, Rowley and Brough, Monissen and Wenger). Third, allocation procedures for nonexclusive public goods are analyzed (Güth and Hellwig, Pethig).

Springer-Verlag Berlin
Heidelberg New York London
Paris Tokyo Hong Kong

Springer